SHUT OUT

SHUT OUT

THE GAME THAT DID NOT LOVE ME BLACK

Bernie Saunders and Barry Meisel

Patrick Crean Editions
An imprint of HarperCollins*Publishers*Ltd

Published by Patrick Crean Editions,
an imprint of HarperCollins Publishers Ltd

First edition

HarperCollins Publishers Ltd
Bay Adelaide Centre, East Tower
22 Adelaide Street West, 41st Floor
Toronto, Ontario, Canada
M5H 4E3

www.harpercollins.ca

Pages 337–338 constitute a continuation of this copyright page.

Library and Archives Canada Cataloguing in Publication

Title: Shut out : the game that did not love me black / Bernie Saunders and Barry Meisel.
Names: Saunders, Bernie, author. | Meisel, Barry, author.
Description: First edition. | Includes bibliographical references.
Identifiers: Canadiana (print) 20210272872 | Canadiana (ebook) 20210272945
ISBN 9781443465243 (hardcover) | ISBN 9781443465250 (ebook)
Subjects: LCSH: Saunders, Bernie. | LCSH: Hockey players—Canada—Biography.
CSH: Black Canadian hockey players—Biography. | LCGFT: Autobiographies.
Classification: LCC GV848.5.S28 A3 2021 | DDC 796.962092—dc23

Printed and bound in the United States of America
LSC/H 10 9 8 7 6 5 4 3 2 1

Contents

For my family—especially John and Gail, and my three amazing sons, Jonathan, Shawn and Andrew. And for all my brothers in the Bad Boys Club who fell in love with hockey the same way that John and I did.

—BRS

Thank you, Neil, for blessing me with the opportunity to know and love Viktor. And thanks, Vik, for the gift of a lifetime: introducing me to the grace, friendship and beauty of Bernie.

—BPM

After the game I met Bernie in the locker room. He took off his new uniform among some of the players we'd grown up watching on TV, guys like Marc Tardif and Andre Dupont and new stars like the Stastny brothers, Peter and Anton.

"You were fantastic out there," I said. "I'm so proud."

"I wish you were out there with me," Bernie said.

"You know I was."

—FROM *PLAYING HURT* BY JOHN SAUNDERS, SPORTS BROAD-CASTER WITH ESPN/ABC AND CITYTV (TORONTO)

Author's Note

Much of this work comes from memory. I attempted to support subjective statements and many of the anecdotes with documentary evidence from press clippings or other sources. As an example, when I provide a subjective review of my play in an NHL game, I confirm that account with a press clipping from that game. I use that convention throughout the book. When press clippings were not available, I attempted to verify stories whenever practical by confirming them with the people who were involved or who were in the know. Where dialogue appears and scenes are recreated, my intention was to represent the essence of the conversation and the mood of the scene as closely as possible, but these are not intended to be construed as verbatim quotes.

SHUT OUT

CHAPTER 1

Stoppage in Play

Go back to the plantation, you fucking [N-word]!"

It was a third-period faceoff in the Rochester War Memorial . . . April 6, 1980. Another day at the office, except the crowd was relentless that night because this was the regular-season finale and playoff positioning was at stake. The vitriol flowed like cheap beer. The shit started early and just did not stop.

"Hey, [N-word], where's your basketball?"

The Rochester Americans and Syracuse Firebirds were a point apart for third place in the American Hockey League's Southern Division.

A man pounded on the glass, scratched his armpits and made monkey sounds. "*Ook, ook, ook*, a monkey escaped from the zoo."

I had just been sent back to Syracuse after a successful four-game stint with the Quebec Nordiques, my first games in the NHL. We were one point ahead of the Amerks, so they needed to win, while we only needed to tie, to avoid finishing

1

fourth and having to face the heavily favoured New Haven Nighthawks in the first round of the Calder Cup playoffs.

"Hey, [N-word]. Why aren't you picking cotton?"

Sweat dripping from my forehead inside my helmet, I bent over with the shaft of my stick resting on the tops of my shin pads, anxiously waiting for play to resume. I hated stoppages in play. They were the worst parts of every game because the lone voices pierced the silence. Different rinks had different acoustics, and in many games I only heard the crowd's buzz during play. But stoppages were different, like those dreaded walks onto the ice to and from the dressing room. Oh, how I hated those walks. People yelling obscenities, spitting at me, pouring beer on me, throwing things . . . all because of the colour of my skin.

Once in a while, I was able to chuckle to myself if I heard a clever insult or an inventive phrase. Most of the time, though, I just felt like a snake needing to shed that skin. I felt embarrassed because I knew my teammates heard the comments, and they knew I heard them, too. I always pretended not to hear, because acknowledging the verbal filth would be a sign of weakness. I would never let them know they were getting to me. But they were. The vitriol burned through to my soul. My skin, the subject of the cruelty, felt on fire.

The Amerks were up, 2–1, with less than a minute to go and the faceoff in the neutral zone. As the linesman approached the centremen, the 5,603 rabid fans pierced the silence and started to roar, anticipating the win. With the season at stake, Duane Rupp, our head coach, had pulled goalie Gary Carr for an extra skater and tapped our top line. Once I saw the puck drop, my mind returned to what I was born to do.

As I'd done so many times, in so many games, over so many years I'd spent mastering the move I copied from Guy Lafleur,

I used my breakaway speed to elude my checker and accept the puck from teammate Steve West at the blue line. It took me three strides to reach the top of the right circle and unleash my patented slapshot towards the far corner of the net. The clock said there were 20 seconds to go when the puck blistered over the outstretched pad and under the helpless blocker of goalie Ed Walsh for the game-tying goal. Jubilation on our bench. Complete silence in the War Memorial.

My goal sent the game into overtime. Still tied in the final minute of OT, and again Coach Rupp put me on the ice when the Amerks pulled their goalie, desperate to score and avoid fourth place. All we needed to do was defend the tie, making this the key defensive shift of the game.

We worked the puck out of our zone and counterattacked against the six Amerks skaters. Blair Stewart fired a shot that was blocked by a defenceman, Roland Cloutier had a rebound stopped, and I freed myself in front and backhanded the second rebound into the empty net.

Winning goal. Mobbed by my teammates. Joy.

We carried the jubilation back into the dressing room, but I never enjoyed the postgame scene. I was always the sideshow, and tonight I wanted no part of a circus. I just wanted to bask in the glory of my performance and board the bus for home.

After the beat writers surrounded me and I respectfully answered their questions, two TV stations lined up for on-camera interviews. I didn't want the attention and hated fielding the inevitable questions about being Black and why I would want to play hockey. I just wanted to celebrate with my team.

But on this big night for the Firebirds, the focus remained on me. Newspaper guys, TV reporters, spotlights. It would not stop.

It even got to John DenHamer, our general manager.

"Black is beautiful!" he shouted to anyone listening.

DenHamer was one of my biggest advocates, and of course he only meant the best for me. But the comment stung, coming from my sanctuary, my own dressing room. I didn't want to be the Black hockey player. I just wanted to play the game that I loved.

I couldn't ignore, outwork or evade this thing. I was exhausted from another night of abuse. It was satisfying to beat the other team on the scoreboard, for sure, but I could never escape a certain sadness. Good, bad or indifferent, my Blackness was all people were seeing. I once naively believed that it would all stop when I reached the NHL, but I had just encountered a couple of stinging incidents the week before during my four-game call-up.

My mind was in a daze. An Amerks fan so repulsed by the treatment I had endured that evening wrote a letter to the editor of the *Rochester Democrat and Chronicle* that was published a few days after the game:

> *Maybe I am naive, but I had hoped that we white people had come a long way in overcoming our prejudices in the past few years. Well, I guess not. As if watching the Rochester Amerks lose a decisive hockey game to the Syracuse Firebirds on Easter Sunday wasn't bad enough, I was subjected to some of the most ignorant dribble from the mouths of fans that I've ever heard.*
>
> *Bernie Saunders is a fine hockey player for Syracuse. In fact, it was this talented center who scored the tying goal with just 20 seconds left in regulation and the winning goal in over-*

time. While I don't expect Rochester fans to exactly embrace Saunders as their hero—after all, it was he who defeated the Amerks—I never expected to hear what I heard that night in the stands at the War Memorial.

Saunders is a black man—one of the few playing professional hockey—and was the target of many catcalls from all corners of the arena whenever he entered the game. What kind of person talks this way? I'd love to hear their explanations, but I'm afraid those explanations would be as articulate and intelligent as the jeers that prompted this letter.

This kind of talk shouldn't be allowed. War Memorial rules prohibit abusive language. Is this not abusive? I had hoped things had changed. Those bigots in the stands have shown me how wrong I was.

As difficult as it was playing in those Roman lions' dens, I grew to understand that it was my fate. Trailblazers navigate uncharted trails. Most people had never seen a Black hockey player before. Not the fans, not my coaches, not my teammates.

Willie O'Ree broke the NHL colour barrier with the Boston Bruins in 1958, but that historic accomplishment was virtually lost for 16 years before Mike Marson, Bill Riley, Tony McKegney and I appeared on the scene.

I was the fifth Black to ever play in the NHL, and for most fans I was the first they had ever seen. Most people just didn't know how to act. Don't get me wrong, I knew I had to take all that crap if I wanted to play the game I loved. I took it from fans, I took it from opponents, but I was most repulsed when it happened in my own dressing room.

Taking it from my own team was the hardest.

I didn't deserve the filth from racists. I didn't want the attention from the curious. I just wanted to be a part of the whole. Belonging is a basic need among Maslow's hierarchy, and I stopped feeling like I belonged after I turned pro.

That's why I left the game I loved, but didn't love me Black.

I'm a guy who accepts responsibility for his own actions. It was my decision to leave after three seasons as a pro, and it was the right path.

But this crap just won't stop. It rears its ugly head every year. In April 2020, the New York Rangers set up a Zoom call to introduce newly signed defenceman K'Andre Miller to their fans. A racist infiltrated the comments section with repeated N-words. I cringed. The Rangers and the NHL quickly condemned the Zoombombing incident, but the damage was done. It took me back. I don't know the kid, but I felt his pain as if he were my child.

All he wants to do is to realize his dream of playing in the NHL. Why does he need to deal with that? Progress has been made, but if we're honest we have to admit there is a long way to go. Covert racism still lurks beneath the surface. Hockey is a game that is resistant to change.

It's been almost 40 years since I left the game. I often worry that, by my silence, I am complicit. Coming out isn't going to be easy.

But I felt it was time for me to speak up.

CHAPTER 2

The Fifth Wheel

That game in the Rochester War Memorial took place more than 40 years ago. As a Black trying to break into the NHL, I was on the front lines, like in the middle of that famous beach scene in *Saving Private Ryan*: knee deep in the surf as I struggled to reach the proverbial shores of Normandy, intense artillery fire raining down upon me from all directions.

As far as my NHL hockey career was concerned, I never made it ashore. Although I only played in 10 NHL games, I was the fifth Black ever to make it. I left the game at a point where I believed much more of the battle lay ahead, but I had lost my passion to fight or offer resistance.

I made the right choice for me. I course-corrected and enjoyed a fruitful career in the pharmaceutical industry. When I left the game, I never looked back. I am 65 now, a man who still truly enjoys his anonymity.

But I am also a man who has grown increasingly impatient with the plight of people of colour in the world. Leaving hockey was no panacea. I faced overt and covert racism throughout my entire business career. Almost every time it was my turn for

7

a promotion or a raise, something mysterious happened. The rules changed, or the goalposts were moved. It was frustrating, but all I could do was work harder and fight within the system.

That was how I dealt with it, and I managed to retire early, at 62.

I learned how to navigate the system as a Black man and I thrived. But I always regretted not having helped others. In a way, it felt selfish. My brother is John Saunders. Most know him as the gregarious sportscaster with telegenic charm. John was one of the early broadcasters who helped build the sports behemoth ESPN. Torontonians also know him for the years he worked with Gord Martineau and the crew at Citytv.

John suffered from depression, a dark disease. Mental illness is stigmatized and often fought off in the shadows. John's instinct was to brave the criticism and write a book about the subject in order to help others. To bring depression out of the shadows. When he passed away in 2016, his book, *Playing Hurt*, was not completed, so I collaborated with his co-author, John Bacon, so that my brother could successfully tell his story.

John was the public face of the Saunders crew, not me. Aside from the beautiful family he left behind, his book will be his lasting legacy. I wonder about my own legacy. Social injustice has been on my mind in the wake of Eric Garner, Trayvon Martin, George Floyd and on and on. As a former hockey player, I also view social injustice through a player's lens. I am heartbroken every time one of today's Black players suffers through the latest racial attack. Every time a new incident surfaces, I wonder: Am I complicit in my silence? My heart bleeds for these athletes, and it pains me to think that my career was in vain.

In 2018, Devante Smith-Pelly was accosted by a fan in the penalty box at Chicago's United Center. A verbal racial assault. He was so upset, he grabbed his stick and addressed the assailant. You could sense how mortified he was. I watched the video with tears in my eyes, because I had been in virtually the exact same place on Madison Street, although I played in the old Chicago Stadium, when I suffered a similar dose of racial abuse.

I read stories of Akim Aliu and the vitriol he faced from his own teammates while playing junior hockey. Aliu speaks of the horrible hazing incidents he had to endure while he was a member of the Windsor Spitfires. Losing seven teeth when a teammate took a hockey stick to his mouth. Or the time he was called the N-word by his coach, Bill Peters, for playing rap music in his own dressing room. Peters was coaching the Calgary Flames when this story broke and resigned after admitting he used racial slurs while coaching the AHL's Rockford IceHogs. Aliu, at one time a highly regarded draft choice, is now out of the NHL.

The internet racist who ruined K'Andre Miller's videoconference introduction burned through to my soul. Because of COVID-19 restrictions, the New York Rangers were introducing Miller to their fans on a Zoom call, when a person used the chat function to repeatedly type the N-word. Two of my own sons played hockey, and I thought of K'Andre as my own when I heard of his experience. I felt his pain as mine.

And it's not just the overt racism that pains my heart. I look at P.K. Subban, who burst into the NHL full of youthful exuberance and had the potential to become a megastar, not to mention a marketing bonanza for the league. But he gained a reputation for craving attention and being overly animated in his scoring celebrations. He was forced to tone it down by the conformists. In my mind, all he was guilty of was acting

Black. Although he shrugs off the criticism, I don't see the same player I watched in Montreal.

One book is not going to change the world, but before I undertook this project, I often wondered if my speaking out would move the conversation forward. Hockey is eager to attract more minorities. The NHL's head office is working hard on the issue, but I believe that the keys to the castle rest with the players. To a large degree, this is a book about empathy. I want you to understand the game from a Black player's perspective.

This is also a love story. Unrequited love, but love nevertheless. Hockey made me and my brother. Although I am happily estranged from the game, I identify to my core as a hockey player.

There is a second impetus for writing this book. Natalie Goldberg said it eloquently in the audio version of her timeless book *Writing Down the Bones*: "We all have a dream of telling our story and we also have a dream of connecting with ourselves. Writing is a great way to connect with ourselves."

Man, did that resonate with me.

When my brother passed away, I just felt lost. I needed to connect with myself. We lost John way too early at 61. He and I had a strange relationship because, although he was the older brother, in many instances I performed that role. I suffered through his depression alongside him, trying my best to be supportive, and to listen and talk openly about his feelings. Hockey was my identity, and I lost that. But I had another identity to which to gravitate: I also identified to the world as John Saunders's brother. But now I had lost that, too.

Another inspiration for taking on this project is to familiarize the world with Black hockey history. To pay respects to the brothers who first landed on the beaches of hockey's Normandy. I have a strange relationship with history. I am either not remembered or when I am mentioned, it is often in the context of being John's little brother. I have always embraced that status as one of life's blessings, but even the moon craves its own identity.

The NHL Network broadcast a story of hockey's pioneers called *Soul on Ice: Past, Present and Future*. I remember hearing about the program and being excited to see how the producers depicted Black hockey history. I didn't expect a major mention, but I grabbed a beer and nestled in to enjoy the documentary. I wasn't expecting to be featured, but I was hoping to at least hear my name. But the credits rolled and there had been nothing, even though most of the players featured in the biography were my contemporaries and one particular story involved me.

On February 19, 2007, a blog called *Greatest Hockey Legends* published an entry titled "A History of Black Hockey." Part of it lists, in chronological order, the Black players who had played in the NHL up to that date and includes a quick bio for each of us. Here's what the author wrote about me:

5. Bernie Saunders, 1979—He only played in 10 games. His brother is John Saunders, studio host and play-by-play commentator for ESPN.

The writer at least gets my place among the first 10 Blacks to play in the NHL correct. As for me, he suggests that my career highlight is having a famous older brother. Plus, the main topic of the paragraph is me, but it hyperlinks the reader to John's Wikipedia page, not mine. It's kind of comical.

In 2003, a veteran sports reporter from New York named

Cecil Harris wrote *Breaking the Ice*, a historic book that chronicled the Black experience in professional hockey. It is a great book, and probably the definitive read to date on Black hockey history. One of my pet peeves is that I read many articles that get it wrong when they discuss the history of Blacks in hockey. Many of my fellow brothers are lost to the vagaries of time. Mr. Harris's book corrects the record on a variety of issues. He talked to seven of the first eight Blacks to play in the NHL. Instead of me, he called my brother. The book also includes an anecdote about John's hockey experiences, not mine. John never played professional hockey.

Don't get me wrong, I appreciate all these important works on the Black hockey experience. I'm not asking for a feature segment or chapter, but it strikes me as odd that nobody ever cared to ask about my experience.

But I have nobody to blame but myself. When I left the game, I never looked back. For years, I refused to discuss my career with anyone, including my brother. Eventually, even John stopped asking.

So, here goes; I am jumping into the deep end. And I want to point out from the start of this journey through my life that I am neither out to expose people from my past, nor to castigate villains who have "done me wrong."

If anything, I thank all those who touched me in some way. It was all of you who helped shape me into the man I am today.

All I ask of you is to keep an open mind—don't question every anecdote. In a lot of ways, this is a book about empathy. Put yourself in my shoes, spending your early years preparing for something that you love, and then discovering a very different environment from those depicted in your childhood dreams.

CHAPTER 3

An Eye for an Eye

Willie O'Ree was the Jackie Robinson of hockey. Why it took decades for history to lift him from obscurity confounds me to this day. Although hockey has finally introduced this pioneer to the world, I believe his monumental achievement is vastly underappreciated. Not only did he break hockey's version of the colour barrier, not only was he Jackie Robinson on skates, but he reached the NHL when it was only a six-team league!

That's the most impressive thing about his feat, and his story was lost to all but a few hockey historians until the NHL rescued him from his security job in San Diego and decided to showcase his achievements. Jackie Robinson is one of the world's widely known names, one of the most influential figures of the 20th century. Willie O'Ree? He is now recognized mainly because, in 2018, he was inducted into the Hockey Hall of Fame—in the Builder category.

Builder? Not as a player? As a Black man, that just doesn't satisfy me.

I relate to Mr. O'Ree, but not for reasons you might automatically think. I was only 18 months old when he played his first NHL game, and John was three. We were living in Montreal, where I was born. John and I were too young for this historic moment to have a direct impact on us. The United States was as close to Canada as Yugoslavia, at least in our young minds. Willie's NHL career had come and gone long before I graduated from diapers. I knew little about the man.

After Jackie Robinson broke baseball's colour barrier on April 15, 1947, two other Blacks wore major-league uniforms the same season: Larry Doby, on July 5, and Hank Thompson, 12 days later. Mr. Robinson pushed open the doors. I'm not calling it a Black Friday rush, but several other talented Black players quickly reached the major leagues.

Hockey didn't get the memo. It took 16 years before Mike Marson followed O'Ree. I had never heard of Marson, either, until he showed up in my living room on a black-and-white TV, playing in October 1974 for an NHL expansion team I had never heard of, the Washington Capitals. Until then, John and I thought we were the only Black players on the planet. I assume Mike and his younger brother Larry felt the same way.

The hockey world acted like everything was hunky dory after Mr. O'Ree quietly penetrated the invisible barrier. But that 16-year gap was when I was developing, and for much of my youth, I never knew there was another Black hockey player on Earth not named Saunders.

I didn't know that Bill Riley and Tony McKegney, Ray Neufeld and Alton White (who had broken into the fledgling World Hockey Association in 1972–73 and was actually the second Black to play major professional hockey) were also starting their journeys.

Nobody properly recognizes that 16-year gap. We were all Willie O'Ree all over again, all pioneers reaching for an NHL as white as fresh snow. And I didn't know about Marson or Riley, White or McKegney. I didn't know there was a small but significant group of young Blacks about to change the game.

For most of my career, I felt like I was the first Black of my generation, needing to shatter the barrier that Willie had barely breached. As much as I admire O'Ree, I was disappointed when I saw the updated edition of his autobiography, *Willie*. It's the subtitle that bothers me: *The Game-Changing Story of the NHL's First Black Player*. I disagree. Hockey is a game stubbornly resistant to change.

O'Ree became a significant figure in my life for one other noteworthy reason. I had heard all kinds of excuses for why people of colour could not compete in the NHL. Among the crackpot theories we were told was that Blacks had weak ankles, that the Black athlete's anatomy was more suitable for running than skating.

John and I were led to believe that was why Blacks excelled in football, baseball and basketball: that our ankles were too fragile to support the instability of thin blades skidding across glassy ice. This seemed absurd to me, even as a young kid, because I skated as well as the next kid from the time I first laced on a pair of skates as a four-year-old.

But the Saunderses *are* infamous for our scrawny legs. John and I as teenagers had already developed massive thigh muscles and plenty of gluteus maximus, but our trunks were supported by Nigerian calves. We both heard the term *chicken legs* more than once during gym class.

So, could it be true? Could we not be cut out for hockey? The human mind can play tricks. In 1954, two years before I was born, the four-minute mile seemed impossible until Roger Bannister broke the barrier. His trail-blazing run shattered this brain-limiting myth and opened the door that several other runners soon ran through.

Willie O'Ree was my Roger Bannister. Growing up, we would hear inklings about his existence. Somebody would see us play and mention something in passing. Over time, it became apparent that a Black had indeed skated in the NHL for the Boston Bruins. He became a mystical figure. People had heard of him but couldn't recall his name. His story, the little of it I understood, convinced me that if one man had broken the colour barrier, then I could surely follow; it was a faint voice in the snow urging me to "go the distance."

John and I never faced another Black player in all our years of youth hockey. Everywhere we played, we were treated as a novelty act. I didn't meet Tony McKegney until a Major Junior A training camp. I next ran into a Black player named Peter Blair when I was recruited by St. Lawrence University.

Willie is almost 86 years old and still looks like he would command respect in the corners. He is the NHL's director of youth development and an ambassador for the NHL's diversity program. He is a kind gentleman, and his identifying mark is his glass right eye. It's the indelible memory of the slapshot that blinded him, the impediment he was able to hide (unlike the skin colour) so that he could better pursue his NHL dream.

To me, Willie O'Ree is a Hall of Fame player. *Player.*

I get the argument that O'Ree only played parts of two seasons, and only scored a few goals. But he did it while confronted with so much resistance in a six-team league, and he was such an inspiration to future generations. Can someone alert the ostrich committee? Vladislav Tretiak, a white Russian who never played a game in the NHL, was inducted as a player. There are now women in the HHOF as players, as there should be. They didn't play a game in the NHL.

Racism is the reason Mr. O'Ree didn't play more than he did. However, he merits induction based on his playing career outside the NHL. He scored nearly 500 goals and 500 assists in a brilliant minor-league career of more than 20 years. And he accumulated all those points while overcoming two physical impairments: blindness in his right eye and being Black. And off the ice, it is hard to find a better example of a Hall of Fame résumé. His impact multiplies every day.

Hats off to the NHL, as it seems that every Black History Month, they find a new way to honour Mr. O'Ree. In January 2021, the Boston Bruins announced his number 22 jersey would be retired and hung in the TD Garden rafters on February 18. (Because of the COVID-19 pandemic, the ceremony was rescheduled for January 2022.)

In July 2021, the U.S. Senate passed legislation to award him the Congressional Gold Medal, Congress's highest honour, for being the first Black to "play" in the NHL. But he can't get into the HHOF as a player!

Only a Black man could pull off such a feat.

His acceptance is so important to me because I battled the forces of systemic racism my entire life. After my hockey career ended, I became a high-ranking pharmaceutical executive and experienced resistance at every stop. When it became time to penetrate the company's smallest inner circle, I hit an impenetrable barrier, and yet I was good enough to be honoured with the company's highest award. The world never seems to get it: the rules are always just a little different when you are Black. The NHL has worked hard to improve its image. If the rest of the hockey world wants to signal that they get it, I believe this is an obvious place to start: Mr. O'Ree merits acceptance into the players' smallest inner circle—the Hockey Hall of Fame.

And as long as we are cleaning out the closet, I would love to see the NHL follow suit by ditching the racially insensitive jerseys worn by the Chicago Blackhawks.

I know everybody loves that jersey for its artistic appeal, but it's just time.

CHAPTER 4

Skateless Herbert Carnegie

ere is the second part of a two-part quiz. Have you ever heard of Herbert "Herb" Carnegie? I didn't think so. As legend has it, Herb is one of the greatest players to lace them up, certainly among the best Black players in history. However, history also took its eraser to his work.

Many argue that there weren't more Blacks in the NHL because they simply weren't good enough. Not enough players of colour were playing the game. I don't disagree with that sentiment, but it doesn't cover the whole truth. Blacks played in the Coloured Hockey League in the Maritime provinces and were responsible for many innovations, including the slapshot and goalies going down to their knees to stop shots. You will never convince me that some of those players couldn't have played in the NHL. The Herb Carnegie story is another case to consider— not to mention his brother Ossie and linemate Manny McIntyre.

If you follow the narrative, Herb not only should have played in the National Hockey League, but he probably would have been a star. Instead, he is the sport's ultimate black ace. It is widely believed that Herb was denied a shot at plying his craft in the NHL because of the colour of his skin.

Sports folklore suggests that, in 1938, Conn Smythe, who owned the Toronto Maple Leafs, scouted Carnegie when he was playing for the Toronto Young Rangers, a Junior A team. After witnessing Carnegie whiz around in practice, it is alleged that Smythe declared he would pay $10,000 to anyone who could turn Carnegie white.

It's a matter of debate as to whether Smythe uttered that remark, but this much is certain: Herb was so talented, he deserved a shot to play at hockey's highest level.

Because Herb never skated a single game in the NHL, you have to triangulate history to understand his talent. He was a star in the Quebec Senior League, where he competed against eventual NHL superstars Jean Béliveau and Doug Harvey.

Now do the math. Béliveau was a star in the minors, and Herb was his contemporary. Béliveau became an NHL superstar, a Hall of Famer and one of the game's all-time greats. It stands to reason that Carnegie likely would have been a star, as well.

Sports historians are loath to compare those who make it with those who don't. It makes a certain amount of sense, because every frustrated jock on the planet could apply this thinking to his or her career and create a legend in his or her own mind.

But there have to be exceptions to this rule. Carnegie is one of them. He was held back because of his race, and that is why we should be allowed to compare him to his contemporaries who went on to the NHL.

Carnegie was selected the most valuable player in the Quebec Provincial League for three straight years: 1946, 1947 and 1948. And he skated on an all-Black line called the Black Aces (among other things) with his brother Ossie and Manny McIntyre. You know them, right? In the 1947–48 season, Herb amassed 127 points on 48 goals and 79 assists in 56 games. Wayne Gretzky numbers.

You want to insist Carnegie would not have been an NHL star? Fine. But don't tell me the man could not have played in the league. That is simply asinine.

The plain truth is Mr. Carnegie was deprived of his dream of playing hockey at the highest level.

Why do I blame it on the colour of his skin? Paint yourself black for a month and you'll answer the question yourself. Herbert Carnegie should have preceded Willie O'Ree. He should have been hockey's Jackie Robinson, perhaps even before 1947, the year Jackie changed America when he broke in with the Brooklyn Dodgers.

To be fair and accurate, there are accounts of the Carnegie story that blame Herb for turning down opportunities for financial reasons. In fact, this is the other twist to the mystery I find even more fascinating. In 1948, late in his career, Carnegie was offered a contract by the New York Rangers. He attended the Rangers' training camp, performed well and scored at his normal clip.

As the story goes, Rangers GM Frank Boucher told him, "You're an excellent hockey player, but I'd like to make sure by sending you to New Haven first." According to David Lengel's *Guardian* article, "The Forgotten Story of Herbert Carnegie's Attempt to Break Ice Hockey's Color Barrier," those words were said to have devastated Carnegie. As a 29-year-old with a family and proven talent, he wasn't interested in anything less than an NHL salary. Carnegie rejected the offer to play with the Rangers' minor-league affiliate.

"The most devastating thing to me," he was quoted as saying, "was knowing that players on my team were getting the opportunity whose record wasn't as good as mine, which clearly showed discrimination and racism of the highest order. I was losing faith in humanity, you might say."

Who knows what really happened, but can you offer up an example remotely comparable? I would like to see any white counterpart work his entire life for something that he loved, only to be excluded because of the silly reason that he is white. You would be mind-blown.

My buddy Neil Smith, years after he led the 1993–94 Rangers to their first and only Stanley Cup since 1940, relocated the historic Johnstown Chiefs of the ECHL to Greenville, South Carolina. While visiting Neil in this idyllic city, I stumbled across a statue of Shoeless Joe Jackson, who is honoured with a museum there.

Jackson was a major-league baseball player, a superstar mired in the infamous Black Sox scandal. In 1919, eight Chicago White Sox players were accused of intentionally losing the World Series to the Cincinnati Reds. Jackson, an outfielder and the Sox' best hitter, was implicated. His participation in the scandal is disputed to this day. Nonetheless, he received a lifetime ban from the sport he loved.

We will never know the truth about Shoeless Joe, but think of the crime of which he is accused: throwing games and betting on his sport. Pete Rose can attest that betting on your game is the ultimate sin.

History occasionally lies and sometimes distorts, and who knows what really happened? But juxtapose Jackson's fate with Herb Carnegie's. Carnegie was banished from a career in the NHL because of the colour of his skin. Yet there are no statues erected in his honour, no museums in his name.

According to Cecil Harris in *Breaking the Ice*, the late Jim Gregory, who was chairman of the Hockey Hall of Fame's selection committee before he died, was once quoted as saying, "I did some investigation when I was younger and what I found out was that it [racism] didn't exist."

Right, Jim. Hallelujah. Racism is dead.

I hope Gregory regretted that unfortunate quote and better understood the real world of hockey in the 1940s and 1950s before he died. I'm not going to compare myself to Carnegie, but after reading *A Fly in a Pail of Milk: The Herb Carnegie Story*, I felt there were many similarities. Racism is alive and well. Yes, Herb needed to shoulder some of the blame for his life's path, but there is no question in my mind that he would have played in the NHL if he were white.

Sometimes, life can be downright cruel. The most valuable player in the Stanley Cup playoffs receives the Conn Smythe Trophy, an award created and named for Smythe in 1965. The same Conn Smythe who is said to have wanted to turn Herb Carnegie white before he would play him. The same Conn Smythe whom Willie O'Ree called a bigot in his autobiography.

Conn Smythe sounds like hockey's version of Robert E. Lee, but I am all about common sense. I'm not going to suggest the name of the award should be changed the way people are indiscriminately tearing down statues, although I recognize some statues need to be torn down. It is unfair to ascribe today's values to events that happened decades ago. But it would be wonderful if the hockey world started recognizing Herb Carnegie in some meaningful way.

CHAPTER 5

The Saunders Rule

We were your normal, everyday dysfunctional family.
A family of five—sort of: Mom, Dad, older brother
John, me, younger sister Gail.

Bernie Saunders Sr. was seldom home. He was a good-looking, muscular man, a former athlete. His smile could light up a room. Dad played football in the development leagues for the Canadian Football League's Hamilton Tiger-Cats. I remember idolizing old pictures of him, bulging out of his black and yellow Hamilton Panthers uniform.

He had a charm that was both an asset and a curse. Dad came from a large family of Jamaican descent. His father and mother both spoke with thick, heavy Jamaican accents. As kids, Gail, John and I could never understand what the hell they were saying. Dad had two older sisters, followed by a steady stream of brothers, four in total.

Dad was the baby. His sisters were solid, church-devoted individuals, but his brothers weren't the best role models. One made a name for himself at the local horse track, while the others did their best to survive life in Hamilton. We were never close with the Saunders side of the family. Dad had high ambitions and was drawn to the brighter lights of Montreal and Toronto. After failing in a musical career, he adopted a more traditional lifestyle. He held a few quasi-normal jobs throughout his working career, and thus fared better than his brothers. However, he was deeply flawed and inept as a family man.

Dad always found a reason to avoid being home. When we lived in Montreal, he spent most of his time in Toronto. When we lived in Toronto, he was in Montreal. When we reached our teens, Dad migrated to the United States while we remained in the Montreal suburbs, a few miles off the island.

Dad worked in Lorain, Ohio. He came home for cameo appearances, but over time, they became less and less frequent. We visited him in Ohio a few times, during summer break—a week at the Lorain Holiday Inn. But for the most part, he was an absentee father.

Jacqueline Phyllis Courtney Saunders was always there, with and for us, but she adhered to the gender roles of the '60s and early '70s. Working was not one of her survival instincts. Her intent was good, but her impulses occasionally led her down a wayward path. To her credit, it had to be difficult to be charged with the task of controlling two testosterone-popping boys and a shy little girl. Gail, more than John and me, truly missed having a traditional family structure and gender roles.

Mom became my chief disciplinarian. I nicknamed her Hurricane Molly because she not only beat us when we were bad, but her methods were often brutal. She would order us to strip down to our underwear and would delay her appearance while our stress and fear levels rose. Following the agonizing time lag, Hurricane Molly would appear at the bedroom door with leather belt in hand. More than a few times, John and I showed up in gym class with welts on our legs. Whenever we travelled in the car, Molly draped the strap across the window mirror as a gentle reminder for John and me in the back seat.

She was a gunslinger. She could draw that strap, whip us in a snap, and never drift from her lane. It was like a frog snapping up a fly. In today's world, Family and Children's Services would be called to investigate an alleged case of child abuse. But back in the day, this was casually referred to as parental discipline.

John suffered worse abuse from our father: physical violence with bare knuckles, stuff you just don't do to a child. I was too young to be on the receiving end of Dad's physical wrath, but I also never baited him the way John did. Discipline has to come from a place of love, and John never felt it did. John suffered from depression and often associated it with the way Dad treated him.

I won't dwell on this phase of our lives, but I'm comfortable describing ours as a troubled upbringing. Still, I know we weren't the first to have Mommy and Daddy issues.

John was everything to me: big brother, best friend, father figure and much, much more, including a pain in my ass. I pestered him the way any younger brother should. As a kid, I felt woefully inferior. And who am I trying to fool: I felt the same way as an adult. Mom wanted to name my brother Bernie. Having been stuck with the unfortunate name his entire life, Dad rejected the idea. The first son required a much more dignified name than Bernie. Plus, they could kill two birds with one stone as both their fathers were named John.

So they named the golden child John.

When I arrived a year and a half later, it wasn't as important. So, naming me Bernie was fine.

To understand my life, all you have to do is read *The Birth Order Book* by Kevin Leman. I am the stereotypical middle child. It is a burden and a blessing. Middle children are Wednesday; they're George Hincapie. Middle children are often forgotten, or identified relative to our other siblings. We are born too late and too early.

First-borns, on the other hand, are overrepresented in leadership roles. It's a fact that many American presidents have been first-born sons. So, it follows that John was the star. He was our family's promise. In high school, he was elected vice-president of the student council.

Gail Yve Saunders was not only the baby of the family, but the lone daughter. She was the most beautiful thing your eyes could set sight on, and her looks were parlayed into beauty pageantry. As the lone girl, she commanded the adoration of the entire family. People were drawn to her whenever she strode into a room.

There I was, sandwiched between Prince John and Princess Gail. What did I have to offer, other than tightly matted hair and a perpetually runny nose? I had no shot.

In many other ways, my birth order provided a distinct advantage. I spent over 35 years in the business world; I was a pharmaceutical executive when I retired. Early on in business, you learn you are expected to set goals or object-ives. Management training dictates that you state what you wish to achieve within a given chunk of time, and then try to accomplish or surpass that goal. When the year is done, you are judged and compensated based on your progress relative to that goal. Management by objectives, or MBO, is studied ad nauseam. As a middle child, I didn't need Peter Drucker's management theory; I learned his lessons innately. In fact, you could alter the meaning of the abbreviation to "middle brother obsession."

With John hovering above me, I aspired to surpass him in selected activities—especially sports. He was a talented athlete and I was 16 months younger, so this was a tall order. His dominating presence created a measuring stick I constantly used to evaluate myself.

To my credit, I was realistic. I knew there were certain characteristics where I literally had no shot. John, almost from birth, had a natural gift for communication. For me, talking was more than a shortcoming, it was a pathological impairment. Our mother often tells the story of John asking for a cookie. When she complied, John followed with "Can my brother have a cookie, too?" I often remained silent, even after my mom, in an attempt to get me to speak, would respond, "Your brother is going to have to ask for his own cookie."

Early in life, John did much of the talking for me. However, I quickly learned that with sports, I not only could catch him, but I felt driven to surpass him. I had patience and was more than willing to put in the hard work to attain my objective. Parts of my life became defined by the goal of overcoming my brother. To this day, I identify with the world as John Saunders's little brother, living in his shadow. He was born, appropriately, on February 2, 1955—Groundhog Day.

Mom was the one who took us to our hockey practices and games. Not only was Dad seldom around, but during the years he slept in the same house, he was preoccupied with his work. When I was just four years old, my parents put double runners on my feet. John began his hockey career at six years old, as a goalie with State Farm Insurance—a house league team in the Metropolitan Toronto area. I can still remember the old wooden barn on the outskirts of the city where the team played, John out there on the glistening ice in the blazing crimson and white State Farm Insurance uniform, with its tri-oval logo representing auto, life and fire insurance. Mom made John wear a blue knitted hoody underneath his clear goalie mask to keep his ears warm. The atmosphere tickled my senses.

Watching John's practices and games, I wailed from beginning to end. I could create quite a ruckus in the warm lobby area overlooking the ice surface. Mom always watched practice through the glass in that heated area, because the old barn was frigid. One day, the coach passed by as he left after practice. When he heard this loud commotion, he stopped and asked if he could help. Mom sheepishly explained the problem: Bernie wanted to play hockey, too.

Somehow, although I was only five, the coach managed to arrange for me to play. A year early, I joined my first hockey team. I was finally in one of those crimson jerseys.

Better still, I was out there with my big brother.

Soon after being introduced to the game, I was smitten. Here I was, playing this fun and exciting sport . . . and doing it with my big brother. We played every chance we could. Back in those days, we didn't need an artificial ice surface in a controlled environment that charged by the hour. Whether in Toronto or Châteauguay, where we moved when I was 11, I found that kids just hiked to the nearest neighbourhood park and joined the current game of shinny. Outdoor rinks were scattered all around. When the ice became slow or if it snowed, which happened frequently, there wasn't a lumbering Zamboni trudging out to manicure the ice. No, we all grabbed shovels and refreshed the surface the old-fashioned way. In fact, I believe ice scraping with a shovel was a precursor to modern-day resistance training, an idea before its time. The activity was no different from the present-day devices like parachutes designed to enhance skating stride and technique. This rather unsophisticated activity forced us to skate while trudging a shovel blade against the challenge of the heavy snow, and then heaving the load high over the boards. As the winter grew longer, the pile grew taller. We didn't mind; we just wanted to get on with the game.

Most house league games were played outdoors. Rain, snow or sunshine, we were out there. Parents didn't have heated bleachers to watch the games; they stood on the snow piles we had created. You haven't skated on real ice unless you have skated on outdoor ice. Pond ice is the best, but the skating was still pretty tasty on those outdoor neighbourhood rinks.

Shinny is how we learned to play. It is hockey in its rawest form. One puck, two teams, a sheet of ice. No body contact. No raising the puck off the surface. We often played in our winter clothes, without equipment, rendering a misplaced shot hazardous to the shins. And if 10 players per team showed up, we'd skate 10 players per team. It was a swarm out there. In this environment, the law of the jungle prevailed: only the strongest—or in this case, the most talented—survived. With so many players crowded onto the ice surface and only one puck, you learned skills no coach could teach during a one-hour time slot in a heated arena.

John and I skated for hours, day after day. Our toes often froze, forcing us into the heated shack adjacent to the rink for a break and a nickel cup of hot chocolate. I can still smell the stench of that wooden building, the aroma of the sweet, hot drinks battling a thick mixture of body odour and the unmistakable fragrance of sweaty leather skates and gloves.

After soothing relief from our hot cocoa, we were back on the ice. Most rinks were strung with lights like Christmas, so we played long into the night, literally until the lights went dim. If there were any homework assignments, they would have to wait. Much is still waiting.

John and I played organized hockey from the time he was six and I was five, and we landed on separate house league teams. Immediately, John became a leader on his team and I became a top performer on mine. With only a few teams in the league, John and I battled often. And even as young boys, our games developed into all-out Saunders-vs.-Saunders wars.

We were brutal: flying elbows, face washes, flailing high sticks, violent bodychecks. We each tried to beat the other's brains out. John was a big, bruising defenceman with promising offensive skills. I was a fleet forward. Our collisions were inevitable.

It got worse when John turned seven and I turned six. As much as I wanted to score goals, John wanted to punish me for the thought of even trying. By the time John was nine and I was nearly eight, our battles were vicious, the fights violent.

As a matter of fact, those clashes were so epic that, at the end of that season, the house league in Châteauguay, Quebec, made an important rule change: from then on, brothers would have to play on the same team.

The Saunders Rule.

CHAPTER 6
Raging Bull

That wasn't the only Saunders Rule. Let me share another. As a bit of background, John believed it was perfectly acceptable for him to beat, brutalize and maim me.

And he did.

However, no one else was permitted to even look at me the wrong way. As the typical younger brother, I constantly tested this unwritten tenet. One summer day, we were casually eating lunch. Our kitchen had this little alcove into which the kids' table fit snugly, framed by two benches against the walls where John, Gail and I sat. We usually ate our meals here, rather than at the formal dining room table.

I was sitting and eating my sandwich when John, at the opposite side of the table, flicked Kool-Aid at me. Accidentally or deliberately, the intent didn't matter. After inspecting my wet T-shirt, I peered back at him and hesitated while clutching my full glass of grape Kool-Aid.

At stake was an important hierarchical decision for me to make, and no one, not even Hurricane Molly, could control the inevitable outcome. John stared at me—saying nothing, but snorting those menacing, flaring nostrils in a way that resembled an angry bull. No movement of the cheeks, just a stare and a snort that communicated, "Don't even think about it, dummy." Think of bodybuilders flexing their pecs.

I gave it careful thought. And in the spirit of younger brothers everywhere, I couldn't resist. I doused John, turning him purple, and immediately bolted for the front door. Mom shrieked but was helpless. This was between John and me.

I sprinted across the street and into a vast farmer's field where lazy cows grazed. The hay had been freshly cut, leaving hard, dry stubble. I was much faster than John in a sprint, and I giggled as I ran away from him through the straw, beginning to enjoy my momentary victory. Unfortunately, I failed to factor in John's bullheadedness and determination. He would never give up that chase, and gradually my prodigious lead dwindled. As I realized John was refusing to concede, my giggling turned to whimpering as the Raging Bull drew closer. It might have taken a mile and a half, maybe two, who knows? John's resolve always prevailed.

He flagged me down on the far side of the pasture where the Châteauguay River flowed, wrestled me to the stubble and proceeded to teach me a lesson I have never forgotten. John beat me to a pulp and left me lying there, hearing my mother's futile calls for civility echoing hopelessly in the distance. As hard as she tried, this was out of her jurisdiction. It was older brother vs. younger brother. I had no chance.

Now, before you judge John for this abusive behaviour, remember he had another side . . . an incredibly protective side.

I owned a hardcover book by Gordie Howe appropriately titled *Hockey . . . Here's Howe!* This prize was tough to get. It was available only through an exclusive promotion with the Campbell Soup company. You had to mail in the front panels from three cartons of Campbell's Red Kettle Soup mix, and the supply of books was limited.

When it finally arrived, I treasured it. I was the only kid in the neighbourhood to land a copy. I can still picture the white front cover featuring an action painting of Gordie, in his Detroit Red Wings uniform, dropping the puck for a face-off between his young boys, Mark and Marty, who were also wearing Red Wings uniforms. Who would have imagined then what a harbinger of the future the cover would become: years later, the three played together in the WHA and then in the NHL—in Hartford in 1979–80, Gordie's final professional season.

I hated school and despised reading anything other than *Superman* and *Batman* comic books. But I wore this book out. I felt like Gordie was my personal teacher, and I could not take my eyes off the pictures of Mr. Hockey demonstrating his deft skills.

One day, the book vanished. John and I were certain something sinister had occurred, as there was absolutely no way I could have misplaced this sacred tablet. Somehow, John figured out a neighbourhood kid had pilfered it. We lived in a cul-de-sac and the suspect lived a few doors away. The Raging Bull marched right into the neighbours' home while the family was saying grace at the dinner table. He just barged in, stomped up the stairs to my friend's bedroom and found the book on the nightstand.

My friend's father didn't say a word. Nobody, not even a father protecting his home, messed with John when his nostrils flared. John walked out with my prized possession, strode defiantly across the driveways and handed my treasure back to me.

Case closed.

This second example is a little more violent.

Our version of the corner store in Châteauguay was a place called Lecuyer's, a home with a garage that had been converted into a store. The family lived upstairs. Lecuyer's was a short mile from our house, but we probably trekked there 10 to 15 times per week, fetching a variety of items for our mother or ourselves. I can still hear Mom yelling, "B, can you go to Lecuyer's for cigarettes?" And off I went, eager to satisfy my pack-a-day parents.

Châteauguay is a short distance from Montreal. Cross the Mercier Bridge, pass through the Mohawk reserve known as Kahnawake and you reach Châteauguay.

The town had a French and English side of the tracks, except in our town the Châteauguay River was the divide. We lived in Châteauguay-Centre, on the English-speaking side. Even though this was where most of the English-speaking inhabitants settled, francophones still dominated the area.

One day, I was heading to Lecuyer's when I ran into the French bully of our neighbourhood. For some reason, he brutally attacked me. He was taunting me in French, and I couldn't tell whether it was because I was an anglophone or because I was Black. All I knew for certain was that he wanted a piece of my ass. I remember wearing a plain white T-shirt that day, all white with nothing on it . . . until the bully got finished with me and my T-shirt turned blood red. From my blood. When I got home, my mother shrieked and called the police.

My first time in a police cruiser, and I remember peering out the window as it circled the neighbourhood as we searched for my assailant.

We didn't find him during the police cruise, but we knew who he was. The bully lived a few blocks from us, and he had to pass our house to get to his, unless he travelled far out of his way. When John got home and found out what had happened, predictably, he became incensed. Our house was located on a corner lot. Our street, Rue Wilbrod, ended two houses down from ours—it would later be extended and new homes added. Clad in white brick and split-level in design, the house featured a small, unsightly cement porch and staircase on the exposed side. The porch overlooked Rue Brébeuf, which provided the only access to the main neighbourhood behind us.

That small landing, barely large enough for a barbecue grill, overlooked the intersection. John knew the bully needed to trek past this crossroad, so he sat and waited. He camped out on that cement porch and refused to move. It seemed like hours.

The Raging Bull wasn't budging.

Eventually, it grew dark. Finally, my assailant appeared, sauntering innocently towards his home. John spotted him, rocketed off the landing and confronted him in the middle of Rue Brébeuf. It wasn't even a fight; it was a beatdown. John punished this kid so badly that eventually his father got word and raced to the scene, panicking. When he arrived, John glared. Nostrils flared. The bully's father didn't speak a word of English, but he understood. He backed off. John finished the job and walked away, and nobody called the police. I guess they had realized what their son had done.

It was part two of the Saunders Rule. No one messed with John's little brother.

CHAPTER 7

Burned

My next stop on the hockey ladder was a midget travel team, as a 15-year-old playing for Loisirs (Hobbies) St-Jean-Baptiste. Roger St. Onge, the coach, was closely connected to Jacques Demers, who, before he earned fame as a successful WHA and NHL head coach, directed a highly visible Junior B team, les Ailes de Châteauguay—the Châteauguay Wings. Jacques drove a Coca-Cola truck during the day and coached at night. Every kid in the area dreamed of playing for the Wings.

Playing midget, which was a de facto feeder to Junior B, guaranteed you would be watched closely by Demers or a member of his staff. John and I starred on the midget team and drew significant local attention, including our first feature newspaper article. John was the stronger player, a solid, hard-hitting offensive defenceman.

Midget hockey was when the racial abuse really heated up. Hockey is a rough-and-tumble game, not for the faint of heart. Intimidation was standard protocol, and any anomaly was going to get picked on . . . making us easy targets. People try to separate intimidation from racism, but for me, on the receiving end, it was a distinction without a difference. It's like saying, "I didn't kick you in the balls, I only *punched* you in the balls." Even as a kid, losing one's dignity seemed a high price to pay for playing a sport. I always felt that race should be off-limits. When I discussed the dilemma with Mom, she reminded me that there were plenty of other sports that I could play.

We first met Demers at the Phil Myre Pro Sports Hockey School in 1972. Myre was an NHL goalie with the Atlanta Flames who had grown up just outside of Montreal. He held his hockey school in Châteauguay each summer, and his instructors included Demers and future WHA superstar Marc Tardif, who at the time was a left wing with the Montreal Canadiens. My brother was the star of the camp, and Jacques had an eye on him from the drop of the puck. John had some promising offensive skills and also was a big kid who liked to throw his elbows around. As a matter of fact, Jacques called John up to play a junior game at the end of the year.

That was a proud moment for us both. I can still remember John on the ice in the red and white Wings jersey. It was a really big deal having your number stitched not only on your back, but also in smaller versions on the sleeves. My big brother! I remember the game to this day. It even produced a moment of levity as John became so nervous, he lined up on the wrong side of the faceoff circle—with the opposing team. Fortunately, a polite opponent redirected him to the proper spot.

No matter. John was skating with the Junior B team.

I didn't do badly that summer, either. I've kept my report card from the hockey school—I was graded as Very Good (the highest score) in all 11 categories they measured. And after a successful year with the midget team under St. Onge, I earned a full promotion to Junior B.

My career began to blossom, while John's began to wilt.

John's rough-and-tumble style, even at this young age, often left him injured. First, it was a nagging shoulder problem that started in midget and grew so bad, he needed surgery during the season. Then, just when the shoulder was getting better, an unfortunate incident with gunpowder and a short fuse (not John's) resulted in third-degree burns to the inside of his legs.

John and I got chemistry sets for Christmas that year. John was so smart, he figured out how to concoct homemade gunpowder. Excited to test his creation, he filled a plastic lemon squeezer with the substance and coaxed me across the street into the farmer's field.

We thought we'd throw the imitation hand grenade harmlessly into the field. John held the short wick he made, I lit it, and before John could toss the container, it exploded. Between his legs. *Bam!!!* The ambulance rushed my dazed brother to the hospital as he writhed in pain from the huge blast. It took six weeks before he was released, the third-degree burns were so severe.

That incident delivered a fatal blow to his career. The pain from that wound kept John off the ice, and with his idle time he found a different form of chemistry. At age 17, he turned to weed.

I stayed focused during my first year playing without my big brother. My Junior B team was loaded with rookies and my buddies from the Kahnawake reserve: Bobby "Smo" Simpson, Floyd Lahache and Kerry Kane joined me as first-year players. The Kahnawake boys were tough. At Howard S. Billings High

School, disputes were settled off the school grounds, across the street on the front lawn of a church, one on one through bare-knuckle fights. Word spread throughout the school when a particular bout had been organized. As a result, a large student gallery formed a circle on the church lawn before class, allowing the day's combatants to square off inside the makeshift ring.

I remember Kerry and Floyd destroying their opponents on that church lawn. They were fearless. Indigenous people tend to be darker-skinned than whites, and I believe that's the reason I related to them and felt more comfortable in those days.

I did not understand it at the time, but it's an obvious observation today. With few people of colour in the community, I was an anomaly, wondering where I belonged.

Demers was a great coach, teacher and mentor. That is how we knew him: a down-to-earth, blue-collar type. Jacques lived around the corner from our last apartment. When the WHA was formed in 1972, the Chicago Cougars named Pat "Whitey" Stapleton, a former Chicago Blackhawk, as their player/head coach. Stapleton needed someone behind the bench to assist him in changing lines while he was playing, so he offered Jacques the job. When Demers was named the Cougars' director of player personnel, he came to us, knowing that my father had worked in the States. He wanted to get an idea about life in this foreign land. Dad represented one of the few resources at his disposal.

JOHN WAS VERY popular in school. He had an army of friends, and he started spending less and less time at home. I started to grow extremely resentful of these people who were stealing my brother from me. Years later, before John died, I would see some of his old friends at reunions and still feel a dose of jealousy. They are now grown men with successful careers, but to me they remain thieves from a lifetime ago.

I did not know for sure back then, because John kept it a secret from me, but he had veered down a bad path. Not only was he using weed, but eventually he and some of his buddies began dealing it. I suspected it, but I never dared broach the subject. They all wore their hair defiantly long. John sprouted a puffy four-inch Afro, à la Jimi Hendrix. He worshipped Hendrix and even copied the headband, which cut a groove into his Afro and left a channel around his crown.

There was a headband for every occasion, even one made of a golden glittery fabric for formal occasions. John was not subtle with his new hobby, either. He was bold enough to grow a marijuana plant right in his bedroom. Mom eventually grew suspicious, but John pawned it off as a houseplant. My brother could even talk his way out of a bag of marijuana.

John's burns and bad shoulders kept him from pursuing sports, and it was the worst thing for him because he filled his free time with other, uncomplimentary activities. As I developed my game in the Junior B ranks, John developed a drug clientele. He never really played a full season of organized hockey again until he attended college, a full three years of lost development.

He bounced from team to team at Indiana University, the University of Michigan and Western Michigan, barely playing a game. When he finally landed at Ryerson Polytechnic Institute in Toronto four years later, it was amazing he could compete at that level, given the time he had wasted.

John spent most of those early years off in the distance. We were never exactly sure what he was up to, just that he was seldom home.

He spent a great deal of his life resenting and blaming our parents for our unstable upbringing. I never really did. I just saw two incredibly flawed individuals who happened to be our parents. I felt equally slighted by John's absence, but I don't blame him, either. John had to follow his own path and journey, and I get it. However, I chased him all over the continent. We are all flawed in our own particular way.

The way I dealt with our tyrannical father was to remind myself where he came from. Dad came from a big family and a father who was distant and quick to use corporal punishment. If Dad had followed his older brothers' lead, then he could have sat in Hamilton with no ambition or drive. It could have been an entirely different picture for us. Although not perfect, Dad advanced the cause a few strides, and this incremental improvement helped John and me get off to a better start. It was Dad's passion for more that showed John and me that there was a world out there that we could access should we put in the work.

Plus, I always felt that I was master of my own destiny. I believe that, no matter what happens in the past, it should have little bearing on one's future. That is how I've lived my life.

CHAPTER 8

A Canary in a Coal Mine

Playing Junior B during the 1972–73 season placed me on the proper track to the pros. The Châteauguay Wings competed in the Richelieu Junior B Hockey League, which comprised teams on the outskirts of Montreal. It was also the first year I began collecting press clippings. The three Kahnawake boys, Simpson, Lahache and Kane, and I were all thinking about the big leagues ahead.

Kane was a strong, tough defenceman who could handle the puck—and himself. He racked up quite a few penalty minutes with his pugilistic style. Lahache was younger than the three of us; he had raw talent and was tough as nails. We actually had another Indigenous player on the team: Danny White. Danny was older, with a physique that resembled a sumo wrestler on blades. His body was so rotund, his jersey looked like a shrunken novelty T-shirt with his number, 2, popping out of its stitches. Nobody messed with Danny.

Simpson was a flashy winger who had one of the quickest slapshots I've ever seen. Slappers come in a variety of types. Some are hard and heavy, like a brick hurtling towards its target at full force. Some are fleet and light, reaching their destination in a flash. Bobby's howitzer was the second kind. Our crowd jumped to its feet in anticipation every time he wound up. Bobby became one of our star scorers that year, and eventually played in the NHL for the Atlanta Flames. Lahache made a different name for himself in junior. He would later set the Quebec Major Junior Hockey League's single-season record for penalty minutes, with 296. He eventually made it to the WHA, playing with the Cincinnati Stingers when they were coached by Demers. Again, Jacques proved to be a loyal guy who always preferred players he knew and could trust.

As for me, I was referred to as *le petit noir*, or "the little Black," in the local newspaper. This unimaginative epithet referenced my two main deficiencies as a blossoming young player. One was my size, which I worked hard to change by hanging out in the weight room. The other? Let's just say it was something that I couldn't hide or outwork.

Here's a piece from a French newspaper article I recently had translated. The undercurrent of racism was evident in French. However, as the article from *Le Soleil de Châteauguay* states, I was already showing signs of being a pro prospect.

The little black Bernie Saunders gave an exciting performance last Sunday in a hard-fought 7–6 win for the Châteauguay Wings. Indeed, the rookie scored three goals amidst a strong offensive display and showed that he'll become an excellent hockey player. Bernie has a remarkable intuition around the net and has proven it by converting nice passes from his teammates Yves Laberge (who has had a good start to the season) and Serge Leblanc (who performed well) and scored when the opportunity arose. Saunders, who last year played with the Midget des Loisirs St-Jean-Baptiste, is the only Black player in the Richelieu-Montreal Junior League. There's also a half-caste player, Mike Lynch, who is part of the St-Michel squad. If only Saunders could demonstrate more power, he'll certainly play at the pro level in the future.

Demers had taken a risk on this scrawny Black kid, but it was an informed one. He had followed me during my midget year and knew me from Phil Myre's hockey school. I showed great promise as a scorer, with a clear need to beef up in the next few years if I had any hopes of continuing up the amateur hockey ladder.

I have always been a hockey purist and opposed premeditated fighting. If you want to read gruesome hockey stories about bench-clearing brawls and epic fights, I recommend Val James's book, *Black Ice*. It is a good hockey read. Val is the eighth Black to play in the NHL, and the first born in the United States. He and I were born in the same year and played with many of the same players, but our hockey paths never crossed. Our careers were very different.

I believe fighting degrades the game and demotes it to something akin to *All-Star Wrestling*. This is especially true for the much-coveted United States audience that fails to understand hockey's intricacy. In stark contrast to me, Val made his career as a pugilist.

Our hockey philosophies are diametrically opposite, but we have a lot in common. And we ran into a lot of the same characters over the years, since we both reached the professional ranks and broke into the minor leagues in the late 1970s. He had on-ice battles with a number of my ex-teammates, notably Lahache, Terry Johnson and Paul Stewart, just to name a few of the tough guys from that era.

Val discussed these players in his book, based on their mutual roles as combatants, and so did Stewart in his book, *Ya Wanna Go?* Both are interesting reads if you fancy bench-clearing brawls.

Whether I liked it or not, I knew fighting was going to be part of the deal if I wanted to make it to the NHL. It was nearly impossible to survive as a player if you couldn't handle yourself. And being Black, the target was painted on my back. It meant I was going to be challenged constantly—and I mean by the opposing team, their fans, their coach, the guy selling popcorn in the stands, everyone. The heat really ratcheted up during the previous year in midget, but it rose to a new level during my first Junior B season. "Several players were the target of sticks to the face, like Bernie Saunders, who had to visit the clinic at the hospital in Ville LaSalle to close a wound resulting from a blow from a stick," said the *St. Lawrence Sun.*

A trip to Thetford Mines that season became a defining moment. This rough-and-tumble mining town in central Quebec was the type of place where the only thing to do on a Friday night was chug several beers and jam into the tiny rink to root for the local team. I already knew I needed to get tougher, and always had the instinct to attack my own weaknesses. I was determined to get bigger and tougher so I could assert myself more physically, and in this season, and at this rink, I was put to a test.

Nearly every road game, I was subjected to racial catcalls from the stands and verbal and physical abuse from my opponents. The N-bomb was hurled at me routinely, sometimes with the French equivalent: *maudit nègre*, or "damned Negro."

I believe I became a man that day in the Mines. It was a

weekend game, and the barn was packed with animals. The fans started in on me from the first drop of the puck. Early in the game, a verbal attack escalated into a fight. We dropped our gloves. The benches eventually emptied. Even the goalies started going at it, with the fans heaving beer and throwing pennies at us.

It was one of those nights when you feared your world might end. Eventually, it took the police to stop the brawl and restore peace. Our team was ushered back to our locker room. They had to lock the room down to prevent the angry crowd from mobbing us right there in the arena. Our bus driver even pulled the team bus adjacent to the door to protect us.

I remember little of the fight. What I do remember is sitting in the dressing room, recovering, my whole body trembling like a child. Whoever sat beside me laughed and said, "Holy shit, Bernie! Did you ever beat the crap out of that guy. I didn't know you had it in you."

Apparently, I had gone crazy in self-defence and annihilated the guy who challenged me. But I had no idea. I had zero memory of the fight minutes after it ended. To this day, I cannot remember anything specific about who I fought and how I beat him.

But like the canary in the coal mine, it forewarned me of what lay ahead. Thetford Mines was where I gained my "sea legs" as a fighter. I hated that part of the game as much back then as I do today. But one thing became crystal clear: if Bernie Saunders planned on excelling in the sport he loved, and if Bernie Saunders planned to remain Black, he was going to have to fight.

In hockey, as in life, you have to learn how to give a punch and take a punch. And this was my coming-out party. The police escorted our team bus out of town, and that was a smooth ride for me.

I was a new man. I worked hard at that part of the game, grew strong and became a good scrapper. I deleted *petit* from the media's description of me.

But there was nothing I could do about *noir*.

CHAPTER 9

A Raisin in the Sun

Following a successful Junior B season, I went undrafted by the QMJHL but ended up at the Montreal Bleu Blanc Rouge training camp—the team's name translates as "red, white, blue," in reference to the colours of the venerable Montreal Canadiens. As the Canadiens' Major Junior A affiliate, they played their home games in the legendary Montreal Forum and wore a similar uniform. Big-time stuff!

I don't remember whether Coach Demers got me the tryout or they recruited me, but I found myself skating in their preseason training camp. As a scorer, I had confidence I could produce a point per game, no matter how tough the competition. During camp, I played free of nervous tension and turned several heads from an audience probably not expecting much.

At a certain point, I was challenged by Pierre Bédard, the son of head coach Roger Bédard, who was also in camp, vying for a position. It appeared obvious the brass was putting me to the test.

I assumed the objective was to see whether this young Black kid could hold his own. Since major junior hockey is considered the primary training ground for the NHL, I guess Bédard figured fighting was part of the curriculum.

Well, I flunked the test.

I was fast with my fists, and had improved as a fighter since I began to handle myself the season before, but I was no match for a heavyweight bout with a Major Junior A tough guy. This was a whole new echelon.

I don't think I landed a punch, and I was a bloody mess by the time Pierre Bédard was done with me. After receiving several stitches, I marched out of the trainer's room and returned to the scrimmage. When I got back to the bench, Mario Tremblay, the star of the team at the time, leaned over to me and said in his strong French accent, "I will take care of dat for you."

Sure enough, the next shift, Mario hopped over the boards and kicked the living crap out of Pierre Bédard. Remember, this was the head coach's son. Mario didn't care.

This was the same Mario Tremblay who went on to win several Stanley Cups with the Montreal Canadiens. The same Mario Tremblay who became the Habs' head coach in 1995 and who, in his first season behind the bench, instigated the infamous exchange with defiant goalie Patrick Roy. You'll recall that Roy got lit up by the Detroit Red Wings one night in Montreal, and Tremblay refused to pull him. Roy allowed nine goals in an 11–1 drubbing. Roy fumed, vowed never to play for the Canadiens again, and got his wish when the team sent him to Denver to play for the Colorado Avalanche.

I saw the incident live on TV, watched Roy on the ice, disgusted because he felt he was being embarrassed by Tremblay, and thought to myself, *There is no way Mario is giving in.*

Tremblay was adhering to the Canadiens' long-standing tradition of putting the team ahead of any player. It was part of NHL lore. No player was ever bigger than le Club de Hockey Canadien.

It didn't matter that Roy was an icon in the city and a Stanley Cup champion—the team came first. Mario wasn't about to budge. I knew that about Mario from the moment he kicked Bédard's ass after Bédard kicked mine.

I doubt Mario will remember the incident with the Bleu Blanc Rouge, but I was always grateful for the way he stuck up for this little Black kid from Châteauguay on that Saturday afternoon.

THE EARLY 1970S saw the Quebec separatist movement gain widespread support among francophones. Surviving in the province became increasingly uncomfortable for any anglophone as intraprovincial tensions mounted. Among other things, the movement pushed for a shift from bilingualism towards emphasis on French. The street signs that read Arrêt/ Stop were altered by city crews travelling the streets with buckets of red paint and brushes, covering the word *Stop*.

The book *So They Want You to Learn French* outlined the Consumer Packaging and Labelling Act, a federal law that extended requirements for bilingual packaging to many goods, including food. Some suggested this is what forced Kellogg's to add *Flocons de Maïs* to the iconic Corn Flakes box. History confirms that the cereal company, based in Battle Creek, Michigan, introduced bilingual boxes in 1907, but you get the point. Most threatening to us was the fear that French would be made mandatory in high school, which raised the possibility of not graduating. I struggled in all classes but had no shot at learning a new language, or so I believed.

Much more important than fearing I would fail French class in high school was the fact that in 1973 our parents' marriage was deteriorating. And our family was running out of money. By now, Dad was living in the States full time. Our only means to survive was off his weekend wire transfers of money.

On most Fridays, Mom, Gail and I drove into Montreal to the money order office to collect the week's funds. Sometimes my father sent the money, but more often than not, he didn't. All too often, we made the 40-minute drive back to Châteauguay wondering how we would get through the next week.

The next morning usually greeted us with some big excuse or mishap that was never his fault. Meanwhile, I became far too familiar with the bill collectors who repeatedly knocked on our door. It got to where I was on a first-name basis with them. Mom usually had me greet them, armed with the latest fib. John knew to lie, too, but he eventually flew the coop in disgust.

It's funny how certain elements of strife become intrinsic to your life. To this day, I love potato pancakes. Potatoes were about all we could afford to feed ourselves when Dad stopped sending money each week. The three of us subsisted on this inexpensive treat. To this day, the recipe is simple to me: a fresh sack of potatoes from Lecuyer's, and grease to fry them in. That's it. When shredded and fried to a crisp, a spoonful of sour cream and a sprinkle of black pepper produced one of the tastiest, cheapest meals imaginable. Thinking about it now, my mouth waters.

The house at 76 Rue Wilbrod offered the most stability in our childhood. It originally had a sunken two-car garage that tunnelled under the living room. But the harsh northern winters made it nearly impossible to keep the recessed driveway clear. It was a bottomless pit. We'd shovel it out, only to have the snow fill the ditch moments later.

One slippery evening, Mom locked her brakes and managed to park her station wagon in the garage—sideways. It was packed in there so tightly, we needed a wrecker to tug it out with a hook. That was enough to convince my father to fill in the hole where the driveway once sank and convert the under-house area into a family room. The renovation produced a ground-level driveway that was much easier to maintain, fair trade for the lost garage.

Dad lived with us on Wilbrod for about three years while he worked in Montreal. Those were the days when he coached us in baseball and football and was around the most. We played catch with him in the backyard and invented a running-the-bases game that simulated a batter getting caught between bases. The object was to steal the base while the infielders tossed the ball back and forth trying to get the runner out. I was quick, and I loved it. Those were the years when a semblance of normalcy existed—whatever that means, since that home was also the scene of abuse and infidelity.

Although inept as a family man, Dad was a man with high ambition. At first, he attempted a pro football career, which morphed into thoughts of becoming a musician. Dad played upright bass and became good friends with Oscar Peterson, the legendary jazz pianist, and Ray Brown, the bass fiddler in the Oscar Peterson Trio. Dad accompanied them on a few road trips, and the group adopted him into their inner circle.

I was born in Montreal and we spent a lot of time with the Petersons. Montreal was a hotbed for jazz mainly due to prohibition when Montreal was one of the few cities in North

America where you could buy alcohol legally. As kids we were so close to the Petersons that we called them Uncle Oscar and Aunt Lil. As a matter of fact, John's full name is John Peterson Saunders, after Uncle Oscar, and mine is Bernard Raymond Saunders. The middle name *Raymond* is a tribute to Ray Brown, or Uncle Ray as we called him. Uncle Ray was married to Ella Fitzgerald, the great jazz singer.

My mother also sang beautiful jazz. Both my parents had presence. It was as though they were both born for the stage. It is something that the three of us inherited and an attribute that later served John in his career.

After my father's musical aspirations ended he kept digging for gold, planning to get rich quick, looking for the next big thing with the zeal of a gambler. And he had some near misses. When automatic car washes were invented, Dad had a hand in the original design. In what resembled a scene out of *A Raisin in the Sun*, he received a financial windfall for his role in the car wash innovation, and he rewarded himself with a boat.

But the gold rush was short-lived, as he tried to parlay the original idea into a scheme he thought was better . . . but which ended in disaster.

He thought, "Instead of bringing cars to the car wash, why not bring the soap and water to the object that needed to be cleaned?" So, Dad helped design a mobile washing unit, basically in the back of a truck. This meant you could bring the washing station to whatever article you wished to clean—ideal for airplanes, billboards and things of that sort.

The idea flopped. Dad lost all the bonus money he made from the car wash invention. I don't think he owned that boat for even a year.

Dad soon leaped into another strike-it-rich scheme. A

Canadian-built model home company named Salaberry Park Development needed a representative in the States. Prefab homes were going to be the next big thing. Dad ventured to Cleveland to market prefabricated homes with unique promotional strategies, including erecting homes inside local shopping malls.

The idea was that, in the future, every new home would be made in a factory instead of being built on site, shrinking the cost and construction time. The result: better homes at a lower cost—1,500 square feet of living space for $30,000. Dad chased the dream and was off to Cleveland. He erected a house in the Home and Flower Show at the Midway Mall. The idea flopped, he never saw the money, and he never returned. Later in life, he became a sucker for lottery tickets.

His departure left me, my mother and Gail to fend for ourselves. We ended up making a couple of moves within Châteauguay, the Wilbrod house becoming ancient history. By 1973, we had relocated to a tiny apartment, and we hit a tipping point that summer with the French-English strife. Dad wasn't around day to day, but he still wanted to sign off on every big decision.

Mom and I kept my tryout with the Bleu Blanc Rouge quiet for as long as we could, but we eventually had to tell my father. When it seemed the brass was considering keeping this mystery kid on the team for the 1973–74 campaign, my mother told Dad my chances looked promising. That's all Dad needed to hear. He knew that if I played major junior hockey, I would be ineligible for a college scholarship in the States, so he forced me to leave. The next day's paper reported, "A player has left the camp: Bernie Saunders of the Châteauguay Wings, a player of colour . . ."

That summer, Mom, Gail and I packed our belongings and moved to Ajax, Ontario, a suburb east of Toronto, on the banks of Lake Ontario. As much as I wanted to learn French, we knew I would struggle learning a new language on top of my other course obligations and we didn't want to risk my ability to graduate. I will always consider myself a Quebecois and truly regret never mastering the language. The move also put us closer to Dad in Cleveland, and for a brief period we thought we'd see more of him. That was a stupid fantasy. We barely saw him there, either. I had just finished my third year in high school, and Gail was just getting started.

It was a critical point in both of our lives. Like drifters, we simply packed our belongings and moved.

Au revoir . . .

CHAPTER 10

Three Strikes, You're Out

Being the middle child offered me an advantage I believe belongs on the unofficial list of life's little secrets. When you are in the middle, you feel rejection because of your status as a kind of fifth wheel. Your siblings get all the privilege and spoiling. The anthem of the middle child are the words "Life is not fair."

Almost every article on middle children mentions that four-word phrase. It may seem like a pessimistic take, but in reality it is amazingly realistic, and one of the best lessons you can learn in life. With this understanding, middle children are better suited to cope with life's vagaries and setbacks, because of the lens through which we view the world.

My middle-child resilience was about to face its biggest challenge as we made the transition to Ajax, Ontario. It was predictably difficult for an introverted teen. I have three sons, and I can't imagine how their lives would have been disrupted had I, as their father, made a similar move.

Actually, I recognize that some can handle it. My oldest son, Jonathan, moved around a lot to pursue a hockey career. Growing up in the United States, where the hockey talent pool pales in comparison to the rich Canadian crop of promising young players, Jonathan had to travel to find the toughest competition.

He begged me to let him venture out, even though it meant billeting with hockey families away from home. We eventually succumbed to his wishes, and as a result, he attended five different high schools in four years and played for a variety of teams across the United States. But, being such a gregarious kid, he made friends at the drop of a hat.

Jonathan was appropriately named, because he is my brother's silhouette. My brother, John, coasted through high school. He was always one of the most popular students on campus, all the teachers loved him, and he had tremendous social dexterity.

I was often assigned many of the same teachers John had had a year or two before me, and at some point, they all arrived at the same conclusion. They would approach me and give me this quizzical look that suggested, "Jeez, John is so perfect. What happened to *you*?"

I was a social misfit. My few friends in Châteauguay were outcasts and fringe types. I was the kid who suffered at the back of the classroom, praying the teacher wouldn't call on me for an answer. The one who never raised his hand in class. The guy who avoided any social activity, who never had a girlfriend because he was usually too shy and nervous to attempt a conversation with a girl.

The rare times I did? I often broke into a stutter that was embarrassing in any stressful encounter. In front of a pretty girl? Horrifying.

Relocation, at this critical juncture, was a prescription for disaster. But we had no choice. Mom, Gail and I had to forge a new life in Ajax because we needed a fresh start. The move placed us miles away from the bill collectors in Montreal that we always managed to outpace by a half step. Computers did not exist in those days, which made it easy for insolvents like us to walk away from debts and start anew.

We must have lived in 15 different houses, condos or apartments between Montreal and Toronto during my childhood. It was always the same, hauling boxes after losing one place, dropping them off in another.

I enrolled at Ajax High School and learned that transferring from a Quebec high school to one in Ontario provided an unintended benefit: in one fell swoop, the move from Châteauguay to Ajax allowed me to leap to the 12th grade, with extra credits to spare. It was like travelling to a foreign country and learning that your dollar is now worth $1.25. The timing could not have been better, and the boost took a lot of pressure off of my school work.

Socializing was a different story. Being as introverted as I was, I grew anxious that it would be nearly impossible for me to make new friends. I crept around the school building, praying no one would notice this new Black kid slinking around a nearly all-white school. My situation was not completely hopeless. For me, sports provided salvation from loneliness. Hockey doubled as my fraternity, because my teammates always became my closest friends. Back in Montreal, my best friends were guys from the Billings High School team, and later the Junior B Wings.

As far as hockey was concerned, my number one mission was to join a Junior B team in the Toronto area. After a successful rookie season with the Châteauguay Wings, I needed to have a solid second season if I was going to stand any chance of continuing my hockey ascent. My former Indigenous team-mates, Bobby Simpson and Floyd Lahache, went the major junior route, playing for the Sherbrooke Castors. Since Dad was insistent that I get a collegiate scholarship, and major junior players received nominal salaries that violated NCAA regulations, playing Junior B hockey was my only realistic option. And since I had already played Junior B in Quebec, I presumed it would be easy to land a roster spot in the Toronto area.

Wrong.

I tried out for three teams: the Toronto Nationals, the Wexford Warriors and the Toronto Red Wings. Hockey try-out camps are full of eager players, and I quickly learned that unknown kids have only a slim chance of making the grade because there are so many players and so little ice time with which to impress.

I worked hard, did what I could. I certainly didn't blend in, but I still failed to draw the attention I needed. One by one, camp by camp, I was cut. It was so frustrating to me because I knew I was better and had more experience than most of the others. Do I believe these were racist incidents? Not at the time, but I do now. But not in the way that you probably think.

With me parachuting into their camps out of nowhere, I doubt those coaches could ever conceive of a Black hockey player. That's one of the many difficulties of racism: it can be a matter of degree. There is a form of implicit bias called implied incompetence. I doubt there was any malice intended, but nobody had ever seen a Black hockey player before. So, even though I already had a year of Junior B under my belt, those coaches likely could not see me as a qualified player.

To make matters worse, the coaches were ruthless in the way they announced the cuts. There was no human interaction.

Instead, a list was taped to the wall outside the dressing room. If your name failed to appear, it meant your services were no longer required. Gazing up at those lists and failing to see my name left a deep scar. Hockey was my identity; it was a part of my soul. After the third cut, I was nearly suicidal. I remember crying inconsolably that night inside our Ajax apartment.

My world was turning upside down. I didn't know how to survive without being on a hockey team.

Mom and Gail tried every which way to console me, but I was so distraught, I ran away. Well, sort of. I fled our high-rise apartment in tears, running off into the night. Hours later, when they finally realized I might not be coming home, they went looking for me.

They found me in the first place they searched: the Ajax Community Centre. At my lowest point in life, I retreated to the only place where I felt safe—the hockey arena.

Mom and Gail found me sulking in the bleachers, watching a recreational game. The two put their arms around me. No words were needed. We slowly walked home.

I remembered this personal pain my entire life—especially decades later, when I took up coaching, first in house leagues and later with high-level youth. I refused to forget how those Junior B coaches' inhumane method of communicating made my experience so excruciating. I vowed never to take the coward's route as a coach, and I didn't. I always communicated my roster cuts in person, or over the phone if a face-to-face moment wasn't possible.

And in those conversations that meant so much to every young man trying to make it a step higher in his hockey life, I provided constructive feedback on what that individual needed to do to improve. It was a difficult duty, and I cried inside every time. I saw my own sad eyes in theirs, as they learned the horrible news.

People often assume that because I reached hockey's highest level, I never experienced the ignominy of the chopping block. The opposite is true. The road to most success includes much failure, but failure can be handled humanely.

CHAPTER 11

Benevolence

There are people who do amazingly kind things for others, for no apparent reason other than the goodness in their heart.

Here I was: a quiet, shy, socially awkward, academically challenged Black kid plunged into a new teenage ecosystem. Among other things, I was in the 12th grade, my senior year. I was lonely and depressed after losing one of the things that mattered most: hockey. Making my miserable young life worse, my upper central incisor, the focal point of my smile, was grey and dying from a lack of dental care.

For the past few years, our family could barely afford food, so a toothache was not something that got anyone's attention, and a precautionary trip to the dentist was a fantasy. Consequently, I developed a hole in the back of my front tooth, which I could feel every time I nervously flicked my tongue.

Concealing my smile became a coping mechanism. To this day, I carry an emotionless face and have never developed a sincere laugh or been one to flash a demonstrative grin.

Gary Murphy is one of those rare people on this Earth. He was one of the most popular guys at Ajax High School. He dated the prettiest girls. If you consulted central casting, you couldn't find a better candidate to play the prom king. He was one of those big men on campus, and he had no reason to notice me. Heck, if he wasn't such a decent human being, he could have made me feel even more unwelcome than I already felt. But not Murph. As I was trying to slink around this nearly all-white school unnoticed, Murph sensed my reticence and took it upon himself to make me feel welcome.

"So, where do you live?" he asked me out of the blue one day. "Where did you come from?"

At first, I avoided eye contact and mumbled one-word answers. Gary persisted. Eventually, he included me in his activities and took it upon himself to pull me into his circle. He never stopped asking me questions about myself, never stopped caring. Through his inquisitive probing, he eventually discovered my hockey past, and I learned that he happened to be a star for the Pickering Panthers Junior B team, one of the top programs in the Metro Junior B Hockey League, coached by a budding young hockey mind, Sherry Bassin.

You can believe what you want about the universe; I don't believe in coincidences. These are not just random events. Upon discovering my hockey background, Murph arranged for me to attend a midseason tryout with his team. It was a one-day arrangement. I was invited to skate at a team practice with no guarantees, since roster spots were already secure. I don't know if I was more excited about the tryout or grateful for Gary's kindness and consideration.

Nonetheless, I had another kick at the can.

My mother dropped me off at Don Beer Arena in Pickering.

My body trembled. This tryout meant everything to me. I expected to meet Gary outside the locker room so that he could make the requisite introductions, so I waited for him in the lobby.

I got nervous as the time ticked closer and closer to practice hour. It finally dawned on me that Gary must have arrived ahead of me and was already inside. My shyness engulfed me. I couldn't muster up the courage to walk into that dressing room unannounced. I knew this was my big chance at something so important to me, but I was still this lost, shy kid just trying to survive in unfamiliar terrain.

I couldn't do it. I could not bring myself to walk into that dressing room without Gary escorting me. I stared at the ice surface in silence.

When the Panthers skated out to begin practice, the players did their routine loop around the ice surface to stretch and loosen up. Once Gary skated by, he saw me through the Plexiglas and his face expressed complete disbelief. I could barely look him in the eye. I found a pay phone and asked my mother to come back and get me. It was a quiet ride home.

I can't remember how I explained the mishap to Murph the next day, but it didn't matter. I had blown this big opportunity. Coach Bassin, who became a huge success in the Canadian major junior leagues, considered behaviour like this to be sacrilege. Who wouldn't show up for a gift tryout for the team?

But the embarrassing experience stirred something inside. Seeing the Panthers on the ice at practice lit a flame, and I knew I had to get back into a hockey uniform. I couldn't stay "retired."

In the Canadian hockey strata, juvenile hockey was best suited for teenaged players who were not good enough for

Junior B and probably should have already decided to get on with their lives, but who kept hanging on for that one last chance at the dream.

It wasn't going to put me back on track to the NHL, but it was what I needed for my soul. I decided to join the Ajax juvenile team.

It became clear from the start that I was too advanced for this level. I scored at a high clip and instantly became the team's star. Playing juvenile wasn't going to help my career, but it did wonders for my confidence, and gained me some street cred around the schoolyard.

Weeks later, walking down one of the longer halls in the high school, I stumbled upon Murph, wearing his patented grin that could make anyone melt. "What are you doing tonight?" he asked.

Now, my dance card was never full, so I told him I was free and asked what was up. "You're going to be getting a call to play for the Panthers tonight. Three guys broke curfew."

Coach Bassin, a strict disciplinarian, needed emergency replacements so he could make examples of the trio who broke one of his rules. Murph admitted later it took some convincing, because Coach was still angry about my no-show a few weeks earlier, but I was in the lineup. Murph suggested I show up early for the 7 p.m. tilt.

Hours later, I was in uniform for my first Junior B game in Ontario. To complete the fairy tale, I played on a line with Murph and we jelled instantly. Flying up and down my wing, I scored a goal and Murph added a pair in a 10–5 drubbing of the Oshawa Legionnaires. Out there on the ice, in those situations, is the only time I ever felt free. All the pressures of life were lifted for a couple of hours.

Following his postgame talk, Coach Bassin walked directly over to me in the dressing room and declared, in his inimitable hoarse voice, "No way you're going back to juvenile." Shy, afraid to make eye contact, I grinned while I looked down at my skate laces, holding back the tears of joy. The next morning, the Ajax paper reported, "Bernie was brought up from the Ajax juvenile team along with Marty Streeter. Both played excellent hockey and didn't look out of place with the Panthers."

Streeter was sent back down after the game, but I remained. Unfortunately, a fellow high school student, Glen "Birdhead" Ross, got cut when Bassin opted to keep me. I always felt bad about replacing Glen, as I always try to consider the other side. But I knew from experience that disappointment was part of the game.

The Panthers made it official by adding me to the roster the next day as I joined the team along with Bruce West (who later followed me to Western Michigan University). The next game was a critical showdown against St. Mike's, led by future NHLer Paul Gardner. I scored again in another big victory, and before long, Murph, left wing Jim Snetsinger and I were lighting up the Metro Junior B League as one of its most potent lines.

The Murphy home was the Ajax version of the TV family *The Waltons*. Arnold and Mary Murphy had two sons and four daughters before they "adopted" me as their third son. Murph didn't know what to do with me as we grew closer, as I became increasingly "cool," learning to be comfortable in my Black skin.

Having lived close to Montreal and Toronto, I've always craved big-city life. It's paradoxical to my fanatically anti-social nature, but I was most comfortable in urban environments. Murph, on the other hand, was a small-town guy. He was happiest hanging out at a local pub for the evening, so I often had to "drag" him into Toronto for a night on the town.

I remember one evening when we were preparing to go into the city, but he was dressed like a country bumpkin, so I told him he was not going out with me looking like that. Mr. Murphy had just returned home from the General Motors plant in Oshawa, where he worked in management. He was sitting comfortably on the living room couch, leisurely reading the newspaper after a hard day's work.

Murph, knowing I was serious, asked his dad if he could wear the shirt he was wearing. Mr. Murphy looked up over his black-rimmed glasses, quietly removed his top, handed it to his son and went back to his paper.

I looked at Murph, shook my head, and declared the pants wouldn't work, either. So, Murph asked his dad again, and this time Mr. Murphy peeled off his trousers.

Murph tugged them on and I finally gave him the thumbs-up. As we left, we glanced back at Mr. Murphy, in his boxers and tank-top undershirt, still reading the paper as if nothing odd had happened. I guess when you have six kids, you learn to go with the flow.

I still laugh when I think of that scene, and then smile when I remember how Mr. and Mrs. Murphy helped bring stability to my new life.

And Murph did so many other things to help me adjust. I wanted to get my driver's licence, but with my father out of the picture, I had nobody to teach me to drive or provide a car to practise in. Murph worked it out.

We seldom took a team bus to road games, since most of

our games were played in the Greater Toronto Area. Four of us lived in Ajax: Murph, Cam Smail, Chuck Durocher and me. The three of them took turns driving to away games, until Murph learned that I needed to practise for my road test.

On a cold and snowy day, Murph, Cam and Chuck drove to my apartment on Falby Court and parked their cars. I was going to drive Mom's car, with my teammates as my "instructors."

I was both nervous and excited. It was my first trip behind the wheel and I wanted everything to go perfectly. Preparing for my teammates to arrive, I pulled Mom's car from our building's garage into the circle in front of the building. I made sure the car was nicely heated. I parked in front, opened the trunk, ran upstairs to retrieve my equipment and raced back as the guys arrived. One by one, we threw our bags into the open trunk. We were all set.

Except there was one problem: I had locked the keys inside the toasty-warm car. "Someone get a hanger!" Murph screamed.

We struggled for a while but eventually got the car door open. Now running late, Murph had to race us to the game across town. We didn't get there in time for puck drop, so in true Sherry Bassin fashion, he benched all four of us.

Our shorthanded teammates played two periods with only two lines, and inevitably we fell behind, 3–1. Coach finally inserted us for the third period. I scored two goals, Murph and Chuck netted one each, and we won, 5–3. Murph allowed me to drive home.

To this day, Murph and I still laugh about that funny fiasco.

The lessons I learned from Murph still live inside me. If we could only care for one another, the world would be a much better planet. Murph didn't have to befriend me. He could have been a typical big-shot senior and ignored me, or subjected me to high school cruelty.

I was a quiet, fatherless, Black kid with a decaying front tooth, invading Murph's domain. I was weak prey, and he could have furthered my miseries. Instead, this wonderful human being took me under his wing and was instrumental in turning my life around. That's the kind of person I want to be. That's the kind of world I want to live in.

Benevolence.

And did I say Murph is white? Did I have to? Sure, he saw colour, everyone does. But he saw past colour. He just saw someone in need.

CHAPTER 12
D.A.

Murph wasn't my only friend at Ajax High during my senior year. Dave "D.A." Thomas was the bright, good-looking son of a successful Jamaican lawyer. And he struck up a relationship with me as well. His mother happened to be white, making Dave biracial.

But as the saying goes, half Black is Black.

As I look back on what was happening to me during this critical year of my life, I believe that what drew the two of us together was a desire to explore our Blackness. There were few Black Canadians in our community, or in my high school. Dave was a track star who, ironically, detested hockey. He tried to be the coolest bird on campus, always communicating in Ebonics and Black slang. It seemed forced to me, but I'm certain he seemed cool to others.

The Thomas family lived up the street from the Murphys, and that produced a mental puzzle for me. Whenever I rode my bike past Murph's house on the way to D.A.'s home, I felt like I was cheating on my surrogate family. But there was another side to me I felt thirsty to explore.

Murphy and D.A. were acquaintances, but they were not friends. I had separate relationships with each. And in both cases, although I spent a great deal of time in both, their worlds were foreign to me. Both households had the stability I craved: loving parents and upper-middle-class incomes. The Thomas house had a swimming pool and a sauna. It seemed like living in Beverly Hills whenever we splashed around the backyard pool. I didn't realize it at the time, but I was experimenting with my own Blackness being with Dave, learning to be Black (or, at least, hip) in a white community.

Through Dave, I learned my Blackness didn't have to be a disadvantage. In fact, there existed a natural "coolness" to people of colour that I learned others envied. Dave was also into education and he made school fun. He used his rich vocabulary to never communicate a bland sentence.

He would never say the ordinary. As an example, "I have to go to the bathroom" became "I have to rid myself of some foreign matter."

Unknowingly, D.A. also introduced me to dating. In yet another benefit to my fresh start in Ajax, nobody knew about my introverted past. So, whenever the subject of the opposite sex arose, I explained that I had had to break up with my girlfriend Thea when we moved. Thea was actually my first love. I silently adored this pretty Kahnawake girl, admiring her from afar. The miserable truth was that I was morbidly shy and too timid to ever approach her. I didn't date anybody in Châteauguay, but nobody had to know that.

So, I did the only thing I could do: I lied. I told my new friends in Ontario I had dated Thea for years, and I fabricated a dramatic story about having to break up when we moved. I had a story for every occasion. At one point, D.A. wanted to go to his girlfriend's prom, and for some reason, he wanted me to attend. The problem was, I didn't have a date. Dave solved the glitch by asking his former girlfriend, Sandy, to go with me. We attended the prom and had a nice evening, and I was covertly thrilled to be on my first date.

Sandy seemed to like me, so we kept seeing each other. D.A. not only had no problem with the arrangement, but endorsed and promoted it. Sandy, unofficially, became my first girlfriend. She was the daughter of a General Motors executive and starred on the Whitby High School swimming team.

One time, I picked her up at the pool and she was still wearing her swimsuit. I looked at her and thought to myself, "Oh my God, that is my girlfriend!" She looked so beautiful in her drenched red one-piece. And I will never forget our first kiss. My knees buckled when I touched her soft lips, though I struggled to slough it off as no big deal.

The relationship didn't last long, but I now had the confidence to date. I met my second girlfriend through a more traditional route—I asked her out. We dated for several months, and I liked her, but our relationship introduced me to the reality of race in my important associations. One day, I picked her up and she was unusually upset. She wanted to talk. We retreated to a quiet park, where she explained that her father was struggling with her dating a Black person. Sure, it surprised me, but I wasn't blown away at the time. I was stoic and told her that we should just break up, that I didn't wish her to betray her father. So we did.

The incident didn't hit me hard at all in real time. Such incidents sank in much harder later, when I first lived in the States and found myself engulfed in the racial divide. Sure, I felt racism in Canada, but I never felt that constant pounding until I migrated to the United States. But let me be clear: racism hurts, no matter the volume.

The Sandy affair helped me gain confidence with the opposite sex. I will always remember her for that. But the exhilaration of dating was offset by the reality of life. I was a Black man living in a white world. As a typical young man in my teens, I was attracted to the prettiest girls. Since there weren't many Black girls my age, that meant my only option was dating white girls. This meant there would be complications.

My relationships with D.A. and starting to date helped prepare me for the reality of race. The timing could not have been more perfect. I had dipped my toe into the water, but would soon become fully submerged when I moved to the U.S.A.

CHAPTER 13
Sherry Baby

Every time the Panthers took the ice at Don Beer Arena for another packed home game, the sound system blared the timeless hit "Sherry Baby" by Frankie Valli and the Four Seasons. In a scene pilfered from college basketball, the fans came to see our coach, Sherry Bassin, as much as they did the players.

Sherry had an incredibly demanding style and was notorious for his attention to detail, sarcastic wit and punishing practices. He was the type of coach for whom you would skate through the sideboards. A great moulder of talent, his teams mimicked his personality in much the same way the legendary college basketball coach Bobby Knight's teams at Indiana University mirrored his.

But don't picture Robert Redford playing the lead role in the movie. Sherry was a skinny version of Danny DeVito, with a full head of curly hair.

This much was guaranteed: when a player graduated from a Sherry Bassin–coached team, he was fully groomed for the next level. Bassin's storied career would ultimately take him to the major junior Ontario Hockey League, including eight trips to the Memorial Cup tournament. He also eventually coached the Canadian national junior team. Sherry coached so many future NHL players over the years, I wasn't sure he would even remember me . . . until I heard from him in 2016 when my brother died. Sherry expressed his condolences, complimented me on my hockey career all those years later, and reminded me that one of the most important things a great coach does is care about his players.

Even all those years later.

Coach Bassin was one of the most influential people in my life, a paternal authority for a young man coping with an absentee father. His hockey lessons became life lessons to me. He taught me the value of hard work, discipline, dedication and attention to detail. I learned that what you are today is only a reflection of what you have done in the past.

He incessantly drilled into our heads at practice a critical nuance that so many of today's players still fail to grasp: never skate by the goalmouth on a rush. I see so many NHL games where a three-on-two ends with a loose puck in the crease that is easily corralled by a defenceman because the speedy forwards without the puck failed to stop in front of the net.

It's not easy. It takes discipline, effort on your skates and a willingness to take a pounding from the defence. But I can't tell you how many times in my career I tapped in some loose change because Sherry taught me early on not to take the easy way out.

Coach Bassin had a way to get into a player's head. One time, we helped him move his family into a new home. Or, more accurately, Sherry unilaterally decided that four of us would become his manual labour. It was a brutally hot August day and we baked in the heat, working our tails off so that Sherry could save a few bucks. We happened to have a training camp practice that evening, so we assumed Sherry would go easy on us.

Wrong.

He drilled us harder that night than ever. That was Sherry. He didn't want to be predictable, and he never wanted any player to get too comfortable. There were times when I expected a practice to be gruelling, but he took his foot off the gas. He was a hard-nosed guy with a purpose. He taught players lessons we took onto the ice, but they were lessons that directly applied to the real world.

Sherry used what I still consider to be the best drill in hockey, a developmental exercise unlike most standard coaching tools. While many coaches at all levels often conclude a practice by spreading players across the goal line and having them skate end to end, Sherry introduced "sideboards."

It is simple, yet it's a stroke of genius. Instead of repeated 200-foot sprints that eventually exhausted players and created bad skating habits due to fatigue, Sherry drilled us in 85-foot, width-of-the-rink blasts: skate across the ice at top speed, stop abruptly, reverse pivot and accelerate back to the original side. Even today, I think about them and want to vomit.

The first set was over and back, over and back, over and back. Starting with a quick-footed stride, rapid acceleration to longer strokes, brisk achievement of maximum velocity, a reverse lean and abrupt hockey stop, a reverse shift of body weight with a quick crossover stride, a quick-footed burst and acceleration.

You could feel the lactic acid seeping into your thighs.

And Sherry timed us, which seems obvious today but was ahead of its time in the 1970s. Timing allows the coach to chart improvement. Only after each player had satisfactorily completed the first set of three sideboards would we be rewarded with the thrill of dropping to two sets, then one.

And as a team, we were not finished until everyone had finished within the allotted time, everyone stopped fully and didn't cheat by making a quick circle turn, everyone touched the boards with his stick on every turn and everyone kept his head up.

Most days, we wound up doing multiple sets because some unfocused idiot turned the wrong way or failed to touch the boards. But even this detail was strategic because it built team accountability. Nobody wanted to be the reason why we had to do more sideboards than absolutely necessary.

At practice the day after one disappointing game, the entire session consisted of sideboards. Sherry yelled at us while we were skating, and he yelled even more between sets. We thought we were lucky to be catching a breather while he screamed at us between sets, but years later, when I was coaching, it dawned on me that even *that* was part of the strategy. Sherry knew that, for maximum effectiveness, gruelling skating drills required rest periods. When Sherry was barking at us while we spit, coughed and caught our breath, he was actually allowing our bodies to recover—critical to peak performance on the ice. Then the whistle would blare again.

To me, the greatest benefit of any valuable drill is that it forces you out of yourself. Thinking is critical to any game, but at a certain point, you must stop thinking. Mimicking Zen philosophy, the best moments I had on the ice were accomplished in a near trance-like state: a place above mind. It is a difficult threshold to understand if you have never visited it. However, I believe all superior performers—athletes, artists, musicians, scientists—frequent this place.

Have you ever considered how guitar aficionados ply their craft? Eric Clapton is my favourite. The speed at which he plays select lead pieces is incredible. When guitarists train, they often use a metronome and practise scales and scale sequences. You can do the same thing on the piano. When you first do these sequences, it gets clumsy. Your mind is directing your fingers where to go while your digits struggle to keep pace. There is a state of conscious incompetence. However, as you develop as a musician, you can eventually gain tremendous speed and sync up with the metronome.

To gain maximum speed and play at a pace of the masters, one must travel outside of mind. The sequence must just happen where the fingers are moving to the proper spot on the fretboard; the fingers must know where to go. That is where true genius exists.

Sideboards are scales on ice. In the beginning, there is visible conscious incompetence, but towards the end of the season, many players will have reached a level of unconscious competence. Perfect execution is drilled into muscle memory. The ebb and flow elevated to a state beyond thinking. You could almost hear music as the players raced back and forth. Practising in that state allowed us to perform that way more often during real competition. We knew we were way better prepared than our competitors. Games were won before they began.

I played three seasons of Junior B hockey: one under Jacques Demers and two under Sherry Bassin. I don't believe I could have been more thoroughly trained. Years ago, I was travelling through an airport with a couple of my hockey buddies when two flight attendants approached us from behind and observed, "You guys must be hockey players." How did they know? Our butts were still chiselled from the years of physical training.

One of the travesties of my pro career is that when I reached the NHL, too many people ignorantly assumed I didn't know what I was doing. The truth was, I was one of the best prepared prospects imaginable, based on the tutelage I received under Jacques and Sherry.

Sherry didn't coach us to win games. He trained us to improve as athletes. Winning was the outcome of the training. That is the most important role of a youth coach: take whatever natural raw ability a young athlete has and nurture it. I always tried to train that way as a player and teach that way as a coach. It is a philosophy gleaned from playing the game under great mentors. When I retired, I coached elite young teens and helped several gain college scholarships. Two made it to the Los Angeles Kings. I haven't watched much hockey over the years, but my favourite Black player is Wayne Simmonds, who I watched grow up with Matt Greene and Scott Parse on the L.A. "Baby" Kings, as they were known. Both Matt and Scott did their share of sideboards for me.

Not everybody is as lucky as I was to train under such gifted coaches as Demers and Bassin. However, I believe a player should never wait for a coach to develop his game. That is the player's responsibility. There are innumerable things players can do to improve themselves during the season, and during the off-season.

I GREW UP watching the Montreal Canadiens. The Flying Frenchmen were an exciting team, and right wing Guy Lafleur was their most mesmerizing star. Watching "the Flower" play on *Hockey Night in Canada* each Saturday night was must-see TV. And the more I watched, the more I wanted to mimic his marquee move that generated probably 30 percent of his goals. Guy would race down the right-wing boards, typically accepting a pass in full flight while striding just inside the offensive blue line.

Since helmets were not yet mandatory, Guy's blond hair flowing behind him in the wind as he motored down the ice was poetry. When Guy hit the top of the faceoff circle in full stride, he unleashed a booming slapshot, aiming for just inside the far goalpost. When he elevated the puck inches above the opposing goaltender's extended right toe and below the blocker, you could visualize the goal seconds before it happened. The red light shone, the horn blared and the Flower and his teammates gathered for another goal celebration.

It was Guy's patented play. A few years later, Mike Bossy perfected the same exciting play when he joined the upstart New York Islanders.

Soccer has been called the beautiful game, but there is nothing that rivals the fast-paced fluidity of a well-played hockey game. From the stands, it can sometimes resemble organized chaos. In reality, it is choreographed improvisation.

The choreography comes from the coach, who dictates strategy and style. The improvisation comes from the licence each player possesses because certain situations arise repeatedly throughout each game. And so, the player who masters specific moves in these predictable conditions gains tremendous advantage.

I modelled myself on Lafleur. Before Guy, Henri Richard made a similar move, so I always wondered if Guy borrowed the idea from Henri.

I worked on the play for years. Bernie Saunders was the Black Flower racing down the right-wing boards, minus the flowing golden locks. Before practice, after practice. On the way home from practice in my mind.

In the off-season, I found a spot to shoot against a wall. Sometimes, I found an outdoor rink and used a heavy puck while shooting off the dry pavement. And I never cut corners. The shot had to be precise: high enough to sail over the goalie's right foot, yet low enough to whiz under his blocker, angled wide enough to hit the inside of the far goalpost and ricochet into the back of the net. Misses had to be on goal, because missing wide of the far post caused the puck to career around the boards and out of the zone.

Remember the "10,000-hour rule" in Malcolm Gladwell's book *Outliers*? I know I took more than 10,000 shots by the time I left junior and matriculated to college. I still remember a Blueline Club gathering after one of my college games, when a boy asked me about the goal I had scored that night. Before I could answer, the father interjected, "Son, it just comes naturally to Bernie." And I smiled inside and out, knowing the father had no idea how much rubber I had slapped to be able to execute that shot so flawlessly in a game situation. Hard work has a way of making things look easy.

Just as Guy Lafleur did, I scored approximately 30 percent of my goals off my choreographed play. After I perfected that play, I added a couple of others to my arsenal to make sure my game wasn't predictable or one-dimensional.

In one of my attempts to be innovative when I coached, I allotted time at the end of practice for each of my players to work on their own patented play. I had to approve each player's move, but once I did, I assigned time at every practice for them to perfect their move.

Given my success, I wanted my players to achieve their own.

CHAPTER 14

Black Panther

If there was any such thing as a sports nerd, that was me. I had no interest in reading a book or going to the movies. All I wanted to do was work on my game. Being a social misfit allowed me the extra time to do that.

In addition to playing hard at all times, I instituted a personal workout program. I wove weight training into my office workouts at a time when weight training was mainly a football concept. I wanted to beef up, so I lifted weights religiously and did 500 push-ups every day.

It seems obvious today. But 45 years ago, you were as likely to run into a hockey player at the library as at the gym.

When I joined the Panthers, you trained for hockey by playing hockey. And when you weren't playing, you weren't training. Many players were pack-a-day smokers. In the pros, many smoked as a part of their lifestyle, and the more dependent ones . . . smoked between periods. Even Lafleur was a notorious chain-smoker!

My workouts and training regimen were somewhat revolutionary, and even drew attention in the press.

Taking personal responsibility for my career was important,

but Coach Bassin's lessons would have a long-lasting effect extending far beyond the rink. Sideboards are a metaphor for life. When I studied memoir writing in preparation for this project, I stumbled across Natalie Goldberg, who recommends that writers should write. Keep moving the pen across the page, back and forth, over and over, until you become proficient. Fill notebooks with words. I mentioned the guitarist's training exercises earlier. I applied this ethic to my entire business career and was astounded at how I outworked my competition.

There was another lesson that I learned from Coach Bassin that served me equally well. Coach was a huge proponent of the notion that no individual was bigger than the team. I doubt that philosophy would carry water in today's professional sports culture, but we all bought into that unselfish concept.

The idea was critical for me. Although the Metro Junior B League was a true development league, with an emphasis on hockey skills rather than on fighting, I still faced racial taunts from my opponents and from the spectators. Operating within the team concept enabled me to better discipline myself when I sensed the urge to react selfishly.

When I was doing research for this project, I recognized several commonalities with most of my brothers in hockey. This one ranked high. Many concluded that self-sacrifice was the best approach: rather than responding to all the abuse and being goaded into the penalty box, most of us tried to beat the competition on the scoreboard. When I was younger, every time someone dropped the N-bomb, my gloves were on the ice and my fists were in his face before the *-rrr* faded. It became Pavlovian.

But here's the kicker: my teammates had my back that season more than at any other time in my career. I didn't have to react to racial obscenity on the ice as often because my team-mates jumped in for me. Although it was greatly appreciated, the team's protective nature embarrassed me.

Belleville's Memorial Arena was a hostile place for any visiting team, and the Belleville Bobcats were our archrival. During one intense battle, the racial obscenities poured from the bleachers. Late in the game, Coach Bassin had had enough, and he literally stopped the game by refusing to put our players on the ice. I sat on the bench, staring at my skate laces, horrified to be the centre of all the attention.

The referees skated over to the bench and threatened to penalize our team or require us to forfeit the game, but Coach did not budge. And he prevailed. It took an exhausting seven minutes or so, but security eventually threw one drunken bigot out of the arena and the game resumed.

We finished the regular season in first place with a record of 34–6–4 and prepared for the playoffs. Bassin had us playing like a philharmonic orchestra. Under his tutelage, we were one of the strongest teams in the Metro Junior B League, and I performed on one of its top lines. We thought we had a chance at the title, but we lost a hard-fought semifinal series to the Belleville Bobcats.

We had given our all, but Belleville was stacked, and the bounces failed to go our way. We were all exhausted from the series and dejected as we peeled off our uniforms for the final time that season.

As we undressed, I looked over and noticed Murph lacing his skates back up. After he had undressed, I could see that he had nothing on but his CCMs as he returned to the ice surface and skated a few extra laps. It broke the sombre mood after our defeat . . . leadership in action. Murph's antics helped put the season in perspective. We had a great team, a great season, we fell a fraction short, but there was nothing to be ashamed about.

Murph streaked, the press loved it, and we all couldn't help but end the season with smiles on our faces.

At the end of the season, the St. Louis University Billikens recruited three of our players. The Billikens ran an impressive program, led by head coach Bill Selman, in the Central Collegiate Hockey Association. They were a nationally recognized program, and they shared the St. Louis Arena, later known as the Checkerdome, with the NHL's St. Louis Blues.

To have three players matriculate from one Junior B team to the U.S. college ranks is an impressive feat. And having Murphy, Jimmy Wells and Brian Roll all going to the same school is more impressive. But this was no coincidence. Coach Bassin had a great working relationship with Bill Selman, and Selman knew that players from the Pickering Panthers system had the pedigree any top NCAA team could appreciate.

I WILL ALWAYS feel indebted to hockey. There are so many off-ice contributions that the game has made to my life. My first season with Pickering was a pivotal one for me as a teen. I shudder to think how things could have fallen off the rails if hockey hadn't saved me. When I sat in the Ajax Community Centre that day after getting cut three times, I said a little prayer.

As it turned out, I adjusted to my new environment in Ontario, grew closer to manhood, learned a little about my Blackness and even experienced my first kiss. However, there was a pitfall to the year. With my late arrival on the Panthers,

I played only 20 of 44 games. If you projected my scoring over a full season, I would have ranked in the league's top 10. I scored 15 goals with 20 assists for 35 points in only 20 games. That's 1.75 points per game, which should have filled my mailbox with recruitment letters.

But I arrived on the scene too late. I made a blip on the radar of several college scouts, but not until all the scholarship money had already been doled out. Although I was the team's playoff MVP and had performed on one of the league's most potent lines, I was on the outside, looking in.

CHAPTER 15
Tony the Tuna

Remember the kids' game Where's Waldo? The Saunders family had a version called "Where's John?"

In classic John fashion, my older brother navigated a circuitous route to begin his collegiate career. It was the fall of 1973. While I was getting accustomed to my new life in Ajax, John was a wide-eyed freshman enrolled at Indiana University.

But he stormed out of there after about a week. He had chosen IU because the Hoosiers' club hockey program was promising to enter Division I. Dad had a connection there, so John was enrolled sight unseen. This would turn out to be his first civil rights lesson south of the border. When he checked into his dorm room, his roommate showed up with his parents. And right in front of John, the roommate turned to his parents and exclaimed, "I'm not staying with no fuckin' [N-word]."

That was that for Indiana.

John transferred to the University of Michigan, but the Wolverines were stacked and John found himself stuck on the practice squad. Having missed several years of hockey development, there was no way he was going to be able to climb the depth chart. Coach Dan Farrell was building a program that would eventually become a team perpetually ranked in the nation's top 10. After playing well in an exhibition game against Western Michigan, John negotiated a transfer 100 miles west along I-94 to Kalamazoo, where Western Michigan University is located.

And immediately upon arriving, John tried to get the Broncos to recruit me. The Broncos' coach was Bill Neal, but Neal, like everyone else, hadn't had a chance to see me play during my abbreviated Junior B season in Pickering.

He wrote me this note on May 5, 1974:

Dear Bernie,

Mr. Bassin gave you a fine recommendation and thinks very highly of you as a person and a hockey player. We arrived at the mutual decision that another year of junior hockey would be in your best interest. I would have an opportunity to see you play (as would other College coaches) and would feel better about an offer of financial aid in my own mind. At this point, I would have very little to offer in terms of financial aid.

Of course, I'd still be very interested in having you attend on your own with the promise of aid the following year if you made a significant contribution to the team. This is obviously not a desirable alternative from your standpoint, but I mention it only because I do have the interest in you.

Best of luck and please contact me if I can be of assistance. Say hello to John and your father for me.

Bill Neal

Neal's note confirmed the sad truth. College coaches and scouts hadn't seen me play when scholarship money was still available. And by the end of the season, when I had started to get some attention, the well of financial aid had gone dry.

Bottom line? The move from Montreal to Toronto cost me half a year of junior and a full year of college, because our family couldn't afford tuition, especially with two of us attending. I was going to have to play another year of Junior B in Canada in order to qualify for academic aid.

My half season with Pickering did draw attention from a familiar source: I was selected in the 14th round of the Ontario Major Junior Hockey League draft by the Kingston Canadians. Tony McKegney, who had played Junior B for the Sarnia Bees and would become a top NHL prospect, was Kingston's first-round pick in the same draft. And since the Sault Ste. Marie Greyhounds drafted Val James, the 1974 OMJHL draft actually included three young Blacks, all of whom made it to the NHL.

Like many Canadian youngsters, I still had an infatuation with Major Junior A. I attended Kingston's camp against my father's wishes again, as he still insisted that I follow John into college. But Dad lived in the States; so, just like when I attended the Bleu Blanc Rouge camp, out of sight, out of mind. Once I got to camp, I busted my ass to earn a spot with the Canadians, and coach Jack Bownass liked what he saw. When he said there was a spot for me on the roster, Punch Scherer, the Canadians' colourful general manager, attempted to sign me.

At that point, we had to tell my father. And that went badly. Very badly.

He was livid. He did not care that major junior was my

preferred path to a shot at the NHL. He threatened to march to Kingston from his residence in Cleveland and physically remove me. He didn't care that in 1974, few players with their sights set on an NHL career took the college route.

Dad didn't want me to bet my life on a major junior season and the hope of an NHL contract. In his mind, college hockey meant a college degree, and a college degree meant I would have choices if I didn't make it to the NHL.

He was adamant. And in the end, I returned to Ajax so I could audition for a college scholarship one more time with the Panthers.

Back to Sherry Baby for one more season.

I've sometimes wondered what would have happened if I had played for Kingston. McKegney, who enjoyed a successful NHL career, was the first Black hockey player to whom I was exposed, and we became acquaintances. Tony became the first Black star in the NHL. Although our only time together was on the ice at Kingston's training camp in 1974, we socialized occasionally over the decades. A few years ago, he told me a story about that training camp.

He was a day late in reporting to Kingston, and when he showed up as the highly touted (and Black) first-round pick, the camp was up in arms. It seems the Canadians brass had mistaken me for him that first day! He told me the organization was in a panic "because they thought their prized pick [meaning McKegney] was flopping around the ice like a fish, gasping for air."

According to McKegney, they thought "he" (meaning me) had no business being on the ice and they were worried they had wasted their number one draft choice on Tony the Tuna. Only when McKegney actually reported on day two of camp did they realize they had selected two Black players in one draft.

OK, it was a funny story. But all those years later, those words stung like a slapshot to the groin. I know McKegney didn't mean any harm. He didn't know much about my career and probably felt I was honoured just to be drafted by a Major Junior A team.

But, after we hung up, I pulled out my press clippings from those days. Mike Crombeen, who made it to the NHL with the St. Louis Blues, had nine goals in training camp. Gord Bottin had five. Tony McKegney and Bernie Saunders followed, with four each. If I was flopping around the ice that camp, I must have been flopping in the high slot! Tony and I were tied for third in camp scoring.

CHAPTER 16

Pickering Panthers: The Sequel

P laying another year of Junior B introduced an interesting twist. Because I had fulfilled my Grade 12 requirements after one year at Ajax High School, the United States educational system considered me a high school graduate. That meant I was academically eligible to attend an American university.

That provided me with a choice while I played for Pickering again. I could enrol in a community college and take a few courses to start pecking away at my freshman year . . . or I could take the academic year off and work.

It was an easy decision. Dad was as unreliable as ever, so money wasn't arriving regularly from Cleveland. As bad as my blackened front tooth was, Mom's entire set of teeth was in miserable shape, to the point where it affected her overall health. Mom's teeth were literally rotting out of her head and causing other health issues.

I found a job on an assembly line at Berkeley Pumps, working nine to five in a cold, grey factory earning $3.75 per hour. I stood to make $150 per week, plus overtime, building pumps all day long. It was monotonous and boring, and my co-workers were primarily high school dropouts. Most were already married, and each had their own story.

Before long, the manager saw potential in me, as I didn't fit the mould. He pulled me off the assembly line and had me assist him with more creative special projects.

The promotion made the time pass faster and I enjoyed the challenge. We designed a way to automate their lengthy pump-testing process. I learned a lot. But the greatest lesson I learned at Berkeley Pumps was that this was not how I wanted to live my life. It was a dead end. Prior to that experience, I had never focused much on education. I was happy to scrape by with passing grades and then go work on my hockey skills. But standing on an assembly line, or learning how to better test a pump pneumatically, woke me up to the fact that I couldn't punch a time clock every day for the rest of my life.

The other unintentional consequence was stability at home. Mom had entered the workforce as well, and with me contributing my paycheque from Berkeley Pumps, we were no longer reliant on money from Ohio. It was nothing less than liberating.

I don't know what made me happier: Mom's smile from the new dentures I got her, or the joy in Gail's eyes when I took her to the mall so she could race from store to store, shopping for the clothes a girl her age deserved. It was one of the happier years of my youth.

The three of us fending for ourselves presented an awkward challenge as roles changed with every situation. I was Gail's brother, but a surrogate father. Mom was her mother, but often acted as her best friend. I was a son, but I was also a breadwinner.

One day, I came home from practice and Mom was alone.

"Where's Gail?" I asked. "Out on a date," Mom replied sheepishly.

It was Gail's first date, and I was furious because I felt I deserved a say. Instead, it was Mom, acting as Gail's best friend, conspiring with her to keep the news from me that she had gone to the movies.

Mom told me they had agreed Gail was to be home by 9 p.m. I marched down the stairs to my workout room and grabbed my weights. My bedroom window sat adjacent to the driveway and was positioned exactly at eye level. Pumping the dumbbells like a jackhammer on my weight bench, I was able to keep one eye on the driveway and another on the clock.

When the clock struck nine, I was jacked . . . in more ways than one. And then the phone rang, precisely on the hour. I could hear Mom upstairs, negotiating a 45-minute extension. *You must be kidding me*, I fumed to myself. An extension? Gail needed to get her ass home!

I confronted Mom, but she insisted we give Gail some space. Furious, I returned to the weight room. By the time the headlights flashed in the driveway, I was loaded for bear. I charged up the half flight of stairs and darted out the front door. I headed directly for the driver's-side door.

Just as I reached it, Gail jumped out of the rear passenger-side door. In my fury, I took a look at the driver, my intended red meat: a minister. I saw his collar and the horrified look on his face as he scrambled to lock his door and protect himself . . . from me.

In the meantime, his son, Gail's date, sat innocently beside him in the front passenger's seat. I was inches from accosting a minister. Once Gail was out of the car, they screeched out of the driveway like a bat out of hell.

Poor Gail, blossoming into a young lady and having to deal with me as a surrogate father. Of course, I wouldn't have hit anyone. But heck, poor me, trying to be a parent to my beautiful sister instead of a brother. Gail was strikingly beautiful and I found myself always trying to fend off all the male advances. As difficult as it was for me trying to survive our broken family setting, at least I was a male and had hockey as an escape.

My brother-in-law, Paul, still laughs at the crap I put him through before he proposed to Gail years ago. One time, he showed up at our apartment and I slammed the door in his face, leaving him waiting in the hall. I was pathetic. However, I like to think I scared off all the riff-raff so Gail could find one of the most solid individuals on the planet. My methodology was lacking, but I played a role in helping Gail find someone truly worthy.

Gail died way too early. She never really found peace here on this Earth. But I know that she is one of God's favourite angels in heaven.

Sideboards!

Did I mention I wasn't happy about playing another year of Junior B? I wasn't . . . except that another season under Sherry Bassin would be advantageous for any aspiring player, and I knew that after my abbreviated first season, I was returning as a known commodity.

Anticipating increased ice time, I expected to be used on the power-play and penalty-killing units. It would mean a greater opportunity to showcase my talents, the best way to draw a ton of college offers. And right from the start, Sherry placed me on a new line with Cam Smail and Chuck Durocher, two amazingly talented players. Chuck was an exceptional left wing who had been the rookie of the year the previous season. And Cam was one of those naturals who never understood the breadth of his talent, but was outstanding even if he was an underachiever.

Playing with Murph at centre the previous season, I'd keyed off him. He was such a clever and predictable playmaker who knew how to lead me up the wing so that I could unleash my patented slapper. But because Cam had a much different style and was unpredictable, I developed greater chemistry with Durocher.

Chuck liked to carry the puck wide through the neutral zone, attacking the defenceman in front of him. He had this knack for squeezing along the boards and sliding through the defenceman's attempt to plaster him thanks to his unique combination of slipperiness and strength.

All I had to do was slide around the other defenceman and head towards the net with my stick planted on the ice. When the defenceman checking me was forced to rotate towards Chuck after he beat the first guy, I sprang open at the far side of the goalmouth. Like clockwork, *bang*, Chuck would hit me on the tape with a lateral pass that I deflected into a virtually open net.

My scrapbooks still include crumbling yellow press clippings with pictures of me stopping at the top of the crease, throwing snow, and scoring another key goal on our patented play. We executed that play so often, even the newspaper photographer figured it out and knew exactly when to flash his camera. Thirty percent of my goals came off that marquee play.

We finished atop the league's Eastern Division with a record of 25–6–7. The only hiccup to my solid year was the fact that Coach Bassin brought in an overaged right wing named Steve Falkner to provide depth and stack the team for the Ontario Games, a provincial mini-Olympics. At the age of 20, with a broad body and great hands, Falkner was a grown man amongst the 16-, 17- and 18-year-olds playing Junior B.

Falkner played with Cam and Chuck on our top power-play unit, which reduced my ice time and ability to rack up points. I couldn't blame Coach Bassin, because Steve pumped in 50 goals and a team-leading 76 points.

In 34 games, I still scored 27 goals and 28 assists. It's hard to be disappointed scoring 1.61 points per game, but that's my competitive nature. My stats placed me not only among the leaders on the Panthers, but also in the top 10 in the Metro Junior B League. We probably had the top scoring line in the league.

Sherry's plan worked: the team qualified for the Ontario Games and we flew to Thunder Bay. However, we had a few American-born players on our roster and learned that they were not eligible to play. As a result, we played the games shorthanded.

The flight was one of the most memorable things about the Games. When we went through security, the airport agent asked Cam Smail if he had anything in his pockets.

"I have a gun," Cam joked.

Coach Bassin did some of his best work to coax the agents into allowing Cam on the plane. Can you imagine if that were to happen in today's climate?

During the tournament, there was one opponent who was particularly abusive towards me, but we could not retaliate with so much on the line. The next day, when our team arrived at the arena, and while that same team was playing, my teammates gathered in the stands towards their defensive zone. Every time the discriminatory player skated by, they yelled, "Hey, Whitey." My teammates wanted to let him know what it felt like to be abused becasue of his race. They caused such a commotion that the player stopped appearing on the ice. We didn't know if it was his choice, his coach's, or just a coincidence, but he was benched for the duration of play.

I always felt humiliated whenever these incidents occurred. Having my teammates stand up for me was greatly appreciated, but each incident just left me embarrassed. But Sherry's team concept was a model for dealing with racism.

Racism shouldn't be a "me" problem, it should be a "we" problem.

CHAPTER 17

Free Ride

As promised, Bill Neal came to see me play during the season. So did several other college scouts. I strongly favoured Western Michigan because that's where John finally ended up. He'd had to sit out a year after he transferred from Michigan but would be eligible during my freshman year if I played at WMU.

I craved closeness to my big brother.

The game Neal attended happened to be against the Kingston Voyageurs. One of their star forwards was Kipp Acton, and he had an exceptional game. Ironically, Kipp had attended the Kingston Canadians' camp the previous fall, when I was there with McKegney.

Kipp could fly. Not only did he have the wheels, but he had a flashy style that drew attention from everyone in the rink. Naturally, Coach Neal was smitten with Kipp, but he liked what he saw from me, too.

He recruited both of us.

But what perturbed me is that he offered Kipp a full scholarship and only offered me a partial ride. I never knew for sure, but I believe he hedged his bet, knowing I wanted to be with my big brother. But the level of financial aid I stood to receive from a school topped my priority list; so, WMU's offer made what should have been an easy decision heart-wrenchingly complicated. That's because, although my father had promised years earlier to pay for me to go to college, I had no confidence that he would. Dad was already paying John's tuition, so I was skeptical there'd be money left for me.

When Neal awarded Kipp the full scholarship and scrimped on my offer, I decided to not attend Western. Why go there on a partial ride when I had full offers at several other schools?

And there was interest in me from all over the country: Boston University, the University of Michigan, Brown University, St. Lawrence University and Colby College, to name just a few. Boston U was a powerhouse, and the word was they only recruited the players that they wanted because they "always got their man."

Don Cahoon was the BU assistant coach who talked to me several times. The head coach was the venerable Jack Parker. Years later, Cahoon coached at UMass and recruited my middle son, Shawn, who played there for four years. That's six degrees of separation at its best. He recruited both father and son.

The one team that was conspicuous in its absence, a school where I thought I could end up if it wasn't WMU, was St. Louis. The Panthers' pipeline to the Billikens program now added my linemate Chuck Durocher, and they also wanted our centre, Cam Snail. But somehow, I failed to make their recruitment list. Murph did everything he could to get Coach Selman to recruit me, but Selman wouldn't. There would be no reunion with my buddies.

Coach Selman was one of the coaches who wouldn't recruit me because I was Black—as I understand, not because he was a racist. Friends told me it was more because he was concerned about the lifestyle, given that the university was parked close to a ghetto.

St. Lawrence University really appealed to me. For one, leaving my mom and sister was a chief concern of mine, and the school was only a three-hour drive from home through the majestic Thousand Islands. And they did a great job of recruiting me.

They invited me to campus, where I watched a game in the Appleton Arena. This rink is a gem of a place to play, with old wooden bleachers and an appealing charm. At a postgame party, I was introduced to a cute Black coed. I don't know if it was intentional or not, but man, I had never seen such a beautiful Black woman my age before in my life. My heart raced at the thought of attending and getting to know her better.

The assistant coach at St. Lawrence was a brash young guy named Bill Wilkinson, who also coached their freshman squad. But it wasn't Wilkinson who showed me around campus. My chaperone was Peter Blair, a fellow Canadian from nearby Ottawa who had just graduated from the freshman team.

Peter is Black. Yes, St. Lawrence pushed every button on my decision tree.

I was leaning against the other schools for a variety of reasons. Boston University was an enticing but scary choice. An ECAC powerhouse, the Terriers were led by Vic Stanfield, an offensive-minded defenceman; Rick Meagher, a crafty centre; and a guy named Mike Eruzione, who just a few years later got a lot more famous for scoring a third-period goal against the Russians.

I was just a Canadian with a narrow world view, a little more than intimidated by the bigger cities in the States. We had made a couple of summer trips to see my father in Ohio, and two of our summer vacations were to New York and Washington, DC. Both were quite the experience. Manhattan was, to me, a scary and dangerous place. Times Square was a virtual war zone in those days.

My main drawback in attending college in a big U.S. city was fear. I was aware of the race riots and tension in places like Boston and Detroit. I adopted an air of confidence throughout the recruiting process, but the fact is, I didn't want to be the first Black player at BU. Truthfully, it scared the crap out of me.

Michigan registered high on my radar. It was actually my top choice until John left for Kalamazoo. The recruiting visit happened to be during a two-game series against the Wisconsin Badgers. Both teams ranked highly in the national polls. The two games in their converted basketball barn, Yost Ice Arena, were amazing. The place was packed, the fans were raucous, the atmosphere electric.

Who wouldn't want to play there?

And for dessert on this recruiting weekend, there was a football game, Michigan hosting Ohio State—only one of the most intense rivalries in all of sports. The Wolverines versus the Buckeyes. The Maize and Blue vs. the Red and White. Bo Schembechler vs. Woody Hayes. They held a big rally the night before the game and burned a dummy of Hayes in effigy.

I was sold, as any impressionable teenager would be. Although the Wolverines roster was loaded with talent and I worried about the amount of playing time I would draw, the school had so much to offer that my decision came down to St. Lawrence or Michigan.

Although I never seriously considered myself an Ivy League guy, I even attracted attention there, from Harvard and Brown.

I visited the schools and loved them both, but the academic requirements were intimidating.

Sometimes, I wonder what would have happened had I picked one of those prestigious schools. I wasn't the greatest student at the time, but I knew I wouldn't flunk out because I never backed down from a challenge. I believe I would have applied myself enough and figured out how to get by the same way I did athletically, and the way I would later in the business world.

Bernie Saunders, Harvard grad, has a nice ring to it. Barack Obama did OK there.

AFTER COMPLETING ALL the campus visits and factoring in the most important criteria—family, social implications, size of the school, hockey program, ability to play right away, and academic program—I decided on St. Lawrence. The proximity to Gail and Mom at home made it the safe and pragmatic choice.

My plan was to tell the other coaches that I had decided to go elsewhere before calling Bernie McKinnon to accept St. Lawrence's offer. And then the damnedest thing happened.

While I was on the phone with Bill Neal at WMU, I had a split-second change of heart. *To hell with all the other factors*, I told myself. I wanted to be with my big brother. Instead of saying, "Coach Neal, I am not attending WMU," I changed my mind and stammered, "Coach, I am attending WMU."

That was it. I committed to a Michigan team, but not the fabled Wolverines of Ann Arbor. I was headed to Kalamazoo to be reunited with John.

Even the name of the city is weird. "Yes, there really is a Kalamazoo" is a slogan on T-shirts sold around town. And I committed to a *partial* scholarship. I got three-quarters of my tuition paid, instead of all of it, so my father (who had promised to pay for our full educations) kicked in the rest. I was ready for the next step. Most important, John and I would finally be united after all those years apart.

Or so I thought.

CHAPTER 18

What's Happening, Dude?

The next stage of my journey was upon me, and the drive to Kalamazoo from Ajax was unforgettable. It was a lonely eight-hour trek, just shy of 400 miles, on a cold, rainy, gloomy day. It was one of those days where you want to crawl back under the warm blankets and call the whole thing off.

I sported a bad hangover from the party my friends had thrown the night before, but I climbed into the mustard-yellow Mercury Cougar my dad had bought me months before.

As I sped west across the flat Ontario terrain on Highway 401, I passed through Major Junior A towns where I had dreamed of playing: Toronto . . . Kitchener . . . London. To me, Toronto meant Brad Park. Kitchener meant Larry Robinson. London meant Darryl Sittler.

After 250 miles, I hit Windsor. I thought of the Spitfires as I recognized that my Canadian leg of the trip was over. As I approached the Ambassador Bridge, I couldn't help but marvel at the city of Detroit. When the auto industry was booming, Detroit was the pride of the nation. Now it was the heart of the rust belt, a sorry sight.

As I crossed the bridge and the Canada–U.S. border, I had this palpable feeling I was crossing into a new frontier . . . but I had no idea at the time how prescient that realization was.

One of my favourite advertising campaigns of all time is the Nike challenge to "Just Do It." Three powerful words, a philosophy I have applied to my life many times. This was a prime example. I didn't give my departure from Ajax for Kalamazoo a great deal of thought. Although leaving Mom and Gail for the first time caused me great angst, I didn't stress about the challenges that lay ahead: the cultural shock of living in the United States, the racial tensions of the time, the ascent to college hockey, the idea of living on my own.

Oh, and don't forget the books.

When I arrived at WMU, I drove across the campus's cascading hill into the valley and found my assigned dormitory: Ackley Hall, sixth floor. All male freshmen athletes were assigned to that floor. I would like to meet the genius who came up with that dorm placement strategy.

Exhilarated but exhausted from the drive, I rode the dinged-up elevator to the top floor. As I struggled with my key, the door to my room flung open and a towering 6-foot-2 teddy bear wearing boxer shorts greeted me. His name was Mike Brown, a freshman defenceman from Detroit on full scholarship.

"What's happening, dude?"

Brown's was a high-pitched welcome spiced with Detroit slang. I had no idea what to say. Coming from Canada, this introductory question sounded like a foreign language. And although Mike was white, his Detroit upbringing began my indoctrination into the racially divided world of the United States of America.

Remember the Disney film *The Jungle Book: Mowgli's Story?* That's how I felt moving from Canada to the United States. If you don't know the story, Mowgli lived in the jungle and grew up with the animals. Although he was a boy, he didn't know what it was like to be human. I had never been around many people of colour. Yes, I was Black, and different from my white countrymen in Canada. But in a strange way, I didn't know how to *be* Black.

Mike Brown's welcome was so unfamiliar. And yet, somehow it sounded right. It felt good.

There were four athletes in our two-bedroom quad. I roomed with Matt Dietz, a freshman defenceman from Chicago. Mike roomed with Scott Meyer, a freshman catcher on the baseball team. Between our bedrooms sat one shared bathroom, and I have tried to erase from my mind all memories of that communal space—it was disgusting.

For me, this was the perfect "frat house" to help with my transition into this brave new world. Matt was a quiet type like me. He grew up in Deerfield, a suburb north of Chicago, and he'd played hockey for Deerfield High School. He and I were the perfect pair. Mike, a big city dude, was outgoing and fun. Scott was an outlier. We saw less of him because he was a baseball prospect, but he still fit into our foursome like a glove.

Matt and I became lifelong friends, but to this day we have never discussed how he felt the day he learned he was rooming with a Black person. I am happy I didn't get the same reception that my brother received in Indiana.

I enthusiastically jumped into my studies and quickly settled into a routine that afforded me enough time to study the basic freshman courses I was taking as I contemplated a marketing major, while also giving me time to prepare for the hockey season. I was accustomed to an eight-hour work day from the Berkeley Pump experience, so I merely applied that ethic to my schoolwork. I rapidly felt confident I was on top of the academic aspects of my new life.

As for hockey, we began with a vigorous off-ice program. I was in such good condition from my summertime regimen that I easily finished in the top group of every exercise. In fact, as a freshman I challenged for the top position in the much-coveted bench press test.

On the ice, I felt very comfortable as well. The pace was dramatically faster than in Junior B, but I was already one of the fastest skaters out there. The biggest adjustment I needed to make was with regard to hockey IQ; I found that the collegians with at least a year under their belts were clearly smarter players than those I had played against in Junior B.

My first collegiate hockey decision was what number to wear, but they didn't give much choice. Ever since I was a kid, I wore number 10 because of Guy Lafleur. But Murray Pickel was a sophomore who already had Guy's number, so I picked the closest available, which was 12. Rob Hodge wore number 9, and he graduated after the season. So, for my sophomore year, I ditched 12 and grabbed the number Gordie Howe, Rocket Richard and Wayne Gretzky (doubled) made famous.

The biggest early challenge I faced was navigating the obvious factions on the team. From day one, it was clear the upperclassmen ruled the rink. Hierarchy was obvious everywhere. The team had a modest budget, so while the upperclassmen were issued new equipment, the freshmen and sophomores got used gear. On the ice, the veterans were afforded higher status on the depth chart. The rest of us had to earn our spots.

Most obvious to me, the juniors and seniors on the team hung out together in cliques. Freshmen were neither invited, nor desired. It was nothing out of the ordinary, and we freshmen banded together. It was all fine and understandable to me, until the team partook in a particular hazing tradition I despised.

Indoctrination to the WMU Broncos hockey team began after the final roster was posted. I can't cite the origins, but the hazing ritual was well established when we arrived. The upperclassmen mobbed each freshman, one by one, stripped us and shaved our balls, then painted the newly barbered twins brown and gold, the school colours.

Phil Eve, a senior forward who could have been mistaken for one of the Hanson brothers of *Slap Shot* fame, handled most of the shearing duties. He wasn't a gentle beautician. Because I was shy and introverted, the idea of my teammates merely seeing me naked was horrifying. I was the guy who jumped into the shower and back into my towel before anyone caught site of a hair. So, this entire fiasco petrified me.

One by one, the seniors scalped the freshmen. Before my turn came up, I managed to elude an invasion in which they got to several freshmen at once. In my mind, I was sure I would be able to avoid this ignominious indoctrination. When they plotted a second time to corner me, I caught wind of their covert scheme. They planned on ambushing me in my dorm room after dinner. At the appointed hour, I raced from the dormitory to my car, which I had conveniently parked in a lot atop a hill overlooking Ackley Hall.

I was sitting in my car, hidden, when I saw the mob arrive at the front door of the dorm and pour into the clunky elevator, making their way upstairs towards their prey. I couldn't withhold a chuckle as I witnessed the same gang leave empty-handed, their quarry nowhere to be found.

But I paid dearly at practice the next day. I had planned my after-practice escape, but they didn't bother to wait. Phil and the gang surrounded me in the dressing room before we began the day's drills. They took a skate lace and strung it around my balls so that they didn't have to touch skin. Phil tied the lace around the plastic garbage pail in the middle of the room. Shaving cream was applied. Razors appeared. And away they went.

Obviously, the procedure was hardly executed with a beautician's precision. When I tell the story all these years later, I can feel the cuts still stinging. At one point, Neil Smith entered the room, impersonating Sergeant Schultz from the 1960s sitcom *Hogan's Heroes*, as he always did. He gave a salute and kicked the garbage bucket, not knowing it was affixed to my genitals.

Aaach-*tung!*

Practice was unpleasant that day, but at least this gruesome tradition was over with. Pissed, I vowed never to do this to a rookie.

CHAPTER 19

Revisionist History

Before the Miracle on Ice headlined the 1980 Winter Olympics in Lake Placid, New York, I had three encounters with the U.S. national hockey team. My first game at WMU happened to be against the 1976 team that was preparing to compete in Innsbruck, Austria.

Remember I mentioned the vagaries of history? There's something that history mysteriously overlooks about "Badger" Bob Johnson's 1976 Olympic team. Herb Brooks coached the University of Minnesota and, conspicuously, there were no Minnesota Golden Gophers on the Olympic roster. Brooks wouldn't allow it. He was too competitive to lend his players to the '76 Olympic team.

Minnesota won the national championship in 1974 and would win again in 1976, so it wasn't as though they lacked Olympic-level talent. They boasted stars like Reed Larson (who owned one of the best slapshots ever), Mike Polich and Les Auge.

Badger Bob wasn't happy but remained polite as ever. "I guess it's a throwback to the Wisconsin–Minnesota rivalry," he told the *Kalamazoo Gazette*. "But I do know that there are two Minnesota players we would like very much and Brooks won't let us have them."

Who knows how the pages of history would have been altered had Larson quarterbacked the Olympic team's power play and launched missiles at the Soviets in '76. Do you understand the hypocrisy? Brooks, the architect of the 1980 Miracle on Ice, likely sabotaged the 1976 program, which failed to medal.

And if that isn't enough, one of Herb's best 1980 Olympians was Mark Johnson, Bob's son! The legendary Brooks ultimately profited from the significant contributions of the son of the colleague he shafted four years earlier. It would make the perfect episode for Malcolm Gladwell's podcast of things that are overlooked and misunderstood.

To quote the great Napoléon Bonaparte, "History is a set of lies agreed upon."

We played Team USA '76 at the Lawson Ice Arena. The season had a special buzz because WMU had just been promoted from Division II to Division I, and this was the season opener in front of a raucous, packed house. What a way to start my career.

Lawson had opened only one year ago, and the building still smelled like a new car. It featured a horseshoe design that put the fans right up against the ice. The Zamboni end of the rink had temporary bleachers in a section the school used for other activities, like racquetball. That subtle modification enabled Lawson to qualify as a multi-purpose facility, which helped the school's budget.

That became the student section. Students loved to stand on those metal bleachers, stomp their feet and make the building shake. During the 1975–76 NCAA hockey season,

Lawson ranked as one of the top college arenas. With Team USA in town on opening night, the patrons wanted to put on a show.

So did the school. The lights were dimmed during the introductions, and we were introduced to the fans one by one, under a spotlight. I felt nerves and my juices flowing before every game I played, but this was special. My first college game. Lawson shaking. Against Team USA. Skating out alone to greet our fans for the first time, my body shuddered with excitement.

This must be what the NHL feels like, I thought to myself.

With all due respect to Canada's major junior system, every college game felt like a playoff Game 7.

We played them tough. The score was 1–1 through two periods, before the Olympians broke through in the third with a pair of power-play goals and ended up beating us, 4–1. Although it was our first game against a squad well into its exhibition season, we gave them all they could handle: a high-intensity effort the game of hockey deserves.

"It was the best game we've had since the West Germans," Johnson told the *Kalamazoo Gazette* afterwards in praise.

I had made a strong NCAA debut. Playing on a line with Murray Pickel and Bob Gardiner, I recorded my first college point in the second period, an assist on our lone goal when fellow freshman defenceman Barry Murchie scored off my screen.

THE CHALLENGE FACING any Black hockey player is to try to fit in while it is impossible not to stand out. I was accepted into the team with ease. Having my brother there helped immensely. For the first time, I wasn't the lone Black. Plus, a big part of acceptance is not being uptight about things. Phil Eve had a big nose adorned with bottleneck glasses, so you know he endured his share of flak about that. Mike Brown solved my elephant-in-the-room problem by giving me the nickname "Bro." Quite often in a fraternity, humour is the best remedy, and that is how we always handled the anomaly of my Blackness. Dietz's father, "Big Bob," owned a produce business in Chicago, with the main fruit being watermelon. Don't think I didn't take my share of ribbing about that. But it was all in good fun and was our way of making light of an obvious anomaly.

Off the ice, the situation for my brother, John—and my indoctrination into the United States—didn't go as smoothly. John was walking to class one day, sauntering down the hill below the valley dorms, when he noticed three portly Black coeds approaching. When they passed John, each of them uttered, "What's happening, brother?"

It was the standard Black refrain displaying solidarity towards the cause. John, not accustomed to the protocol or the cause, kept right on walking.

Insulted that a brother had failed to respond, the three sisters stopped, circled back, surrounded my brother and proceeded to cuss him out.

"How dare you blow us off?"

"Who the hell do you think you are?"

John didn't understand what he had done wrong and why these three crazy women were so offended. It scared the crap out of him. John was incredibly conservative. In marketing speak, there are late adopters and then there are laggards. John was a laggard. When bell-bottom jeans were first introduced in the '70s, John held on to his straight-legged Levi's until they disintegrated in the wash. It was going to take a while for him to adapt to Black culture and dapping each other with a verbal salute.

I, on the other hand, felt more at home with this sudden immersion into Blackness. My friendship with D.A. Thomas in high school dipped my toe in the water, but now I was exposed to the real thing. D.A. had already conditioned me to shake hands like a brother, with my thumb as the main uniting force, but now I was learning all kinds of new moves. Two Black freshmen track athletes lived across the hall, and they constantly blasted the Ohio Players and Earth, Wind and Fire from their huge dorm room speakers.

The first time I heard this sound, my ears awoke. Now I was witnessing bodily movements I didn't know existed. I wasn't a dancer, but I couldn't help but absorb the rhythm and that booming bass. The music touched my soul.

Earth, Wind and Fire became my pregame ritual. Mike Brown loved the sound, too, and we cranked up the volume for every drive to Lawson for a home game: "It was Saturday night, the moon was bright, shining down its harvest light."

My comfort level with blending into the scene provoked discomfort in others, and I had to deal with the inevitable social conflict. I began receiving threatening phone calls in our dorm room. I couldn't tell if one particularly angry party on the other end of the line was Black or white, but the caller had an issue with a Black hanging out with whites.

There remained significant racial tension. Kalamazoo was only 120 miles from Detroit, where race riots had been staged only seven years earlier. At most colleges, dormitory cafeterias were still highly segregated, and WMU was no different. Segregated by choice, by the way, not by design. But my Canadian mindset wasn't programmed along the social divide. I sat with the hockey players, who happened to be white. And I roomed with three other freshman athletes, who happened to be white. I was still viewing life through a Canadian prism. I laugh now because it was painfully obvious, but I didn't give it much thought at the time. I just hung out with the people I always did.

The anonymous caller failed to reveal any specific racial bias; he was just unhappy with my behaviour. I wasn't sure if I was being accused of code-switching by a Black or an N-word by a white. Blacks didn't see me as Black. Whites saw me as Black. I saw myself as human. I don't know how this particular troublemaker saw me, but when the calls persisted, they got more threatening.

He warned me not to venture outside in the dark. He started making death threats. At one point, I was offered police protection. Eventually, I got fed up with it. I waited for the next crank call, and when it came, I told the guy I was headed outside immediately.

And I stepped outside, calling his bluff. And that's when the calls stopped. The paradox of the situation is that I was treated as a social pariah because I was Black, and yet I didn't know how to be Black.

Thinking back, I probably should have been more concerned than I was. I didn't take the incident completely seriously. The episode confused me more than it scared me. Having been raised in Canada, I felt the unjust sting of prejudice from whites. But I did not embrace, or even agree with, Black militant behaviour, either. I have always been a Martin Luther King guy over Malcolm X.

However, I must admit after 65 years on this planet, I am getting to the point where I just want to tear some shit up.

A MAGAZINE RATED the top party schools in the nation in 1976, and WMU ranked in the top 10. Kalamazoo was a bar town, with a wide variety of hot spots owning a specific night of the week. Coral Gables, situated on the opposite side of town, hosted Boomba Night on Thursdays, and that was where we needed to be.

My Cougar sported an imitation soft top and was a coed magnet. When four of us drove to Coral Gables one Thursday evening, we pulled up in front of the bar and it felt like somebody tilted the Earth and every coed on campus slid in.

It began as a relatively tame evening. As the driver, I knew I had to be careful. Drinking and driving was known to be stupid, but it wasn't taken as seriously as it is today. The designated driver concept had not been formalized in our culture, but we utilized common sense . . . somewhat.

The night hit a palpable inflection point. I don't remember much, but one of my buddies challenged me to the boomba record. It could have been Kipp Acton; it could have been Dietz.

Boomba, in urban speak, is a term of endearment for one's girlfriend. But at Coral Gables, boomba represented an oversized plastic mug full of draft beer. The aim of the boomba record was to drink a given number of boombas within a ten-minute span. When one of those clowns challenged me to break the record, knowing I seldom turned down a dare, it was on. At this point in my freshman season, I had two main talents: playing hockey and drinking beer.

I don't remember the exact outcome, but I either beat or tied the record. People were chanting my name and we had a fun evening, a typical night at a bar in a college town. When last call rolled around, fun had been had by all. We realized we had one problem.

I was driving.

I can't explain this with any credibility, and I am certainly not proud of it, but I have always had the capacity to sober up when I get behind the wheel. It is a reckless and irresponsible admission, but I opted to drive. I was probably the least drunk person in the vehicle anyway. Campus wasn't that far from the bar, but you had to navigate downtown.

As you might expect after a night like this, the car was packed. I don't remember the exact number, but there were more students than seats. Girls were sitting on guys' laps, and guys were scrunched together to make room.

I navigated back to WMU without incident. But just as I pulled onto campus, one of the guys pinched one of the girls, and she screamed just as I was steering around a sharp turn within sight of the valley dorms. There's a ridge overlooking the valley that is protected by a guardrail, with a large parking lot to the left hidden behind a bank of older dorms. When the girl screamed, I lost my focus and the car struck the curb to the right. The impact broke the right front tie rod, and the tire collapsed.

Two campus police officers were sitting in the adjacent parking lot, observing the entire mess. Seconds after I struck the curb, a cherry light started flashing in the parking lot to the left. The car emptied to the right. My passengers scrambled over the guardrail, sprinted down the hill and crossed the soccer field below, to the safety of the valley dorms.

Everyone escaped except me. The captain remained with the ship. Boomba Bernie was busted.

The officers arrested me for drinking and driving. They took me to the police station and placed my drunken ass in jail. I am a proud person, and the idea of imprisonment demoralized me. Still intoxicated, it felt like my world was ending. School and hockey were an opportunity for me to escape, and now I felt like a total failure. I didn't want to live anymore.

When the officers left me in my cell to sober up, I stripped off the belt from my blue jeans and attempted to hang myself. I had it strapped around my neck but couldn't get the thing tied around the top of the bars. The officers heard the commotion and flung open my cell door to rescue me.

They stripped off my clothes, forcing me to sleep nude in the cold cell. There was no blanket. Dried excrement accompanied me on the cold stone ledge where I slept. My only companion was a stainless steel toilet, which lacked the dignity of a toilet seat.

I lay there alone with my thoughts.

Depression runs in my family. This misunderstood illness contributed to both John's and Gail's deaths. I can sometimes feel it deep within myself, but I am the fortunate one. I see the world differently. Although I maintain a poker face, likely a result of the embarrassment of my teenage dentures, I value life. I live with a pall inside and never get too high or too low.

On this night, however, after way too many boombas, I nearly succumbed to the darkness. It is a night I occasionally reflect upon but rarely discuss. I write it off as teenage binge drinking and try not to overanalyze.

Interestingly, nothing much happened in the aftermath. The judge placed me on probation and required me to take

Alcoholics Anonymous classes, complete 20 hours of community service and see a psychologist. The incident never made it into the newspapers and was kept quiet around campus. If anything, it may have saved my life because I became hypervigilant. "Cars are not bars," I started proclaiming to my teammates after the episode, trying to turn my mistake into a positive to teach others.

Nevertheless, for a while on campus, I had to live with the unfortunate moniker "Boomba Bernie."

CHAPTER 20

"I Am Not a Crook"

One day before a midseason practice, Coach Neal congratulated me on making the dean's list for my first semester. I had no idea what he was talking about and mistook it for some hockey award, rather than a recognition of high academic achievement. As I mentioned earlier, I had taken the lessons gained from the Berkeley Pump experience and applied them to my studies.

I was on an eight-hour-a-day regimen, which to me was a piece of cake:

Classes, 3 hours
Practice, 2 hours
Study, 2 hours

Amazingly, that left me another hour, which allotted me more time to enjoy my college experience. I am no prude; I stepped out as much as anyone. However, my social life never began until my homework assignments were complete. Predictably, I learned to enjoy learning. Unexpectedly, I discovered I wasn't as dumb as I thought. My brother was such a gifted student, he never had to work at it. Comparing myself to him, as I had done throughout my life, I believed something was wrong with me. Until college, it never dawned on me I simply had to apply myself to my studies. I couldn't model John's behaviour and expect to produce the same result.

Most of my teammates stepped out at night, then slept through classes the next morning until it was time for midday practice. They fell woefully behind in their studies. We lost several players to academic ineligibility by our first Christmas break. It was silly. Given my own success, I tried my best to be a leader on our freshman floor.

No matter how late we were out the night before, I dragged myself out of bed in the morning, took a shower and walked the floor, stopping at all the players' rooms to urge them to go to class. I was famous for my morning proclamation, "Man in the night, man in the morning!"

I don't even think the coaches suspected I was the one keeping some of my teammates eligible with my morning wake-up calls. And unfortunately, several still managed to flunk out.

To my horror, one of them was my brother.

While I was working myself onto the dean's list, John was working himself onto the shit list. He played in only two games that season before becoming academically ineligible by the Christmas break. It never dawned on me that I should have been getting him up with my morning routine, too.

Those first few months of the season, it was impossible to fully enjoy my early success because I was witnessing John's game, which was on life support. While I had been honing my skills in Junior B, John had been sitting out, managing his nomadic existence. When he earned a roster spot at WMU, he was woefully behind the other players because he had not played organized hockey since our midget season.

As a sophomore, John spent most of his free time with Neil Smith and Bob Gardiner. The three were inseparable. Neil was captain of the team his sophomore year, a quick-skating defenceman with great hands and great vision. Bob was a big left winger with a booming slapshot. The three loved to laugh, and they were forever playing pranks on each other. They were a clique on a team of cliques. John chose his friends the way I did, from the fraternity of the game.

I saw little of John other than at practice. His dorm was across the campus, and because we didn't take the same courses, our classes were far apart. John saw me as his little brother, whom he loved dearly but did not deem mature enough for his social circle. In addition, the team was fragmented. Seniors hung out with seniors, juniors with juniors, and so on. That was another thing I vowed to change when I became an upperclassman.

Cutdown day brought extra stress. As a top recruit, I had no anxiety about making the team. But when I walked over to Lawson Ice Arena to see the final roster, I was panicked about John's chances. We arrived at the hockey offices at the same time, examined the names and glanced at each other with relief as we spotted John's name listed on the posted roster. I am not sure what I would have done had "John Saunders" not been there.

Now he was headed home anyway. As hard as I worked at my classes, John let his academic opportunity go to waste. He was so smart, all he needed to do was to show up to make good grades. But he slept through too many classes after too many nights of partying.

After flunking out at the Christmas break, John returned to Canada to live with Mom and Gail in Ajax and try to sort out his life. After I had made the life-altering decision to follow my brother to college, he left me once again. It is challenging to articulate my disappointment. I wasn't sure what I would do at the time.

HOCKEY IS FULL of characters, and Neil Smith was one of the most colourful there was. He was a gifted skater who could dish out a load of clever assists, which eventually propelled him to the WMU Athletic Hall of Fame. Selected as a Division II All-American as a freshman the year before I arrived, Neil became the first WMU Bronco to be selected in the NHL draft. The New York Islanders took him in the 13th round in 1974, after a successful season of Tier II Junior in Brockville, Ontario.

When most people think of Neil, they think of the scout who became director of player personnel for the Detroit Red Wings, was hired in 1989 to be the New York Rangers' general manager, traded for Mark Messier in October 1991 and was president and GM in 1994, when the Rangers won their first Stanley Cup in 54 years.

When I think of Neil, I think of Richard Nixon.

I know you didn't see that coming. Neil's one of the funniest guys I've ever known. He lives for laughs, and the more juvenile and slapstick the humour, the better. He and John often went on for hours. I was always hyper-mature and took life way too seriously. I needed to lighten up. Still do.

Neil was able to make somebody laugh, no matter the situation, and his impersonations were legendary. Neil had

Nixon, the former U.S. president, down pat. Richard Milhous Nixon was elected president of the United States in November 1968, earned a second term in 1972, and was enmeshed in the Watergate scandal when John and Neil were freshmen at WMU.

By the time I had arrived, Nixon was out and Neil was in business. Not a day went by without Neil throwing up his two hands, flashing the peace sign and perfectly crooning, "I am not a crook."

One day, following a loss at Dartmouth, our disappointed team was trudging through Logan Airport in Boston when Neil decided to reach into his carry-on bag and pull out his Nixon mask. Who the heck knows why this was part of his game-day gear, but he never failed to pack that rubber Halloween mask, ready to entertain whoever was paying attention.

Trench coats were fashionable winter accessories at the time; nearly everyone wore one. Several players followed Neil around the airport, acting steathily as "Nixon's" Secret Service agents. Many travellers actually believed they were watching the 37th president board the plane, or so Neil wanted everyone to believe as he was whisked onto the jet amidst heavy "security." Neil even talked the captain into announcing the former chief executive's presence on board as one delighted lady shook his hand.

Today, that behaviour would land you in jail. In 1974, it was hysterical. That was Neil.

Speaking of writing, I've encouraged Neil to tell his story. He has lived such a colourful life; his book would make this one pale in comparison. He's another person the HHOF should consider inducting. Just look at his résumé: he was a scout who played a role in the construction years of the New York

Islanders dynasty; he was a central piece of the team that built the Detroit Red Wings dynasty, drafting Steve Yzerman and unearthing Nicklas Lidstrom out of nowhere; and he was the architect of the historic 1993–94 Rangers Stanley Cup championship team which ended New York's 54-year drought.

Everything he touched turned to gold . . . or silver in this case.

CHAPTER 21

Rookie Wrap-Up

On the ice, my first season as a hockey Bronco was unremarkable. Although it failed to meet my expectations, I finished second on the team among freshmen, with 7 goals and 12 assists while playing on the fourth line. I felt comfortable with my transition to college hockey and had total confidence in my game. I just needed to wait my turn.

Racially, it was a difficult year because I was getting hit on both sides. Off the ice, I was dealing with the racial tensions of the day and felt the pain of my race from a new perspective. I was essentially learning to be Black while trying to play a white man's game. On the ice, my opponents never ceased to find a way to remind me that I was different. As the first Black in the league, I faced challenges no teammate had ever had to endure. But with the NCAA rules about fighting (instant ejection from the game, with multi-game suspensions for repeat offenders), there wasn't much I could do about it.

Although my point production felt thin, I was playing a much bigger role on the team by the end of the season. The freshmen had to be patient, as Coach Neal understandably relied on his juniors and seniors. Kipp Acton led the freshmen with 11 goals and 12 assists, and Mike Brown emerged as a reliable offensive defenceman. In our first year competing in Division I, the Broncos finished 18–14–2 overall, with a record within our conference (the Central Collegiate Hockey Association, or CCHA) of 6–10.

With only five teams in the conference, we managed to finish in fourth place and sneak into the playoffs, where we dropped a bomb.

For our semifinal game, we were matched against heavily favoured Bowling Green. The Falcons were the CCHA regular-season champions and their roster was packed with notable players, including defenceman Ken Morrow and goaltender Mike Liut, who went on to enjoy stellar NHL careers. Ron Mason, who years later became highly regarded as coach and athletic director at Michigan State, was Bowling Green's coach and had the Falcons ranked eighth in the nation.

We rallied from two goals down and shocked them, 3–2, in overtime. And I helped key the comeback, as the *Kalamazoo Gazette* reported the following day: "Then Western, under siege, scored for the first time on a goal by Mark Beach off a 2 on 1 break with Kipp Acton. Bernie Saunders set it up when he poked the puck away from the Falcons at center ice and passed to Acton."

Gardiner scored for us in overtime, and the upset win is still considered one of the greatest victories in Western Michigan hockey history. The next weekend, we made the long bus ride—as decisive underdogs—to St. Louis University to play the Billikens in the two-game CCHA finals.

We tied the first game, 2–2, but the Cinderella story came to an abrupt halt 24 hours later, when we got pasted, 13–2. My freshman season was complete.

I headed back to Canada to train with a cloud of uncertainty blurring my future. I turned 20 on the first day of summer, June 21, unsure of whether I was going to remain a Bronco.

My brother was no longer a factor, as he was now living at home, vowing to never return to the United States. My partial scholarship at WMU left me with a financial burden, and I felt I deserved a full ride. And I still had a major junior mindset, still believing the Ontario Major Junior Hockey League was the best route to the NHL. Upon returning to Ajax, I contacted Punch Scherer of the Kingston Canadians and Sherry Bassin, who was now with the Oshawa Generals. I wanted to defect to a Major Junior A team as an overaged player.

In my mind, that was the clearest pathway to the NHL. Major Junior A rules allowed each team to carry one 20-year-old per season, so I wanted to explore the possibility of landing a spot on either team. Punch was interested, as he knew me from the Tony the Tuna story. But he researched my eligibility and told me league rules stipulated that overaged players had to have played in the league the previous season.

As a result, I wasn't eligible. So that was that.

I stayed in contact with Bill Neal over the summer, and when additional scholarship dollars became available, he increased my grant to a full ride. I was headed back to the 'Zoo.

Over the summer, I needed to work. Mom and Gail needed help with the bills at home, and I wanted to generate some pocket money for the upcoming school year. I landed a job on the automobile assembly line at General Motors of Canada in Oshawa, 15 miles west of Ajax, earning a whopping $6.43 per hour. That was twice my pay at Berkeley Pumps.

The job was brutal. You were given around two minutes to

complete, on average, four designated tasks as the cars inched by. As a summer employee, I replaced full-time workers who were on vacation. Each time a regular returned from their time off, I was moved to a new station. And each time I was moved, it took me a week or more to learn my new role on this unfamiliar portion of the assembly line.

The full-time employees kept newspapers close by; able to complete their tasks in less than a minute, they would enjoy the next minute by reading the paper. An apprentice like me needed the entire two minutes to complete my assignments, sometimes having to walk the line to get everything done. It was stressful and frenetic.

And, like clockwork, I would grow accustomed to my new role within about two weeks, getting to the point where I could build in a little breather—just in time to get rotated elsewhere again.

I completed three rotations and was working my ass off. Approaching my final week, I happened to mention my hockey background to a supervisor. His eyes popped out of his head. "Why the hell didn't you tell me this before?"

Before I could come up with an answer, I was reassigned to the "end of the line."

That phrase normally has a negative connotation, but not on an automobile assembly line. My new job was to drive finished product to a parking lot about a mile away. It was an area where they loaded the new vehicles onto the trains for transport. You know how, when you buy a brand new car, it already has a mile or so already recorded on the odometer?

That mile was me.

It was the best job ever. Those of us at the end of the line got to tune the radios and blare the volume. We drove to the designated area, parked the cars and then boarded a truncated bus that collected us in the parking lot and returned us to the factory.

Each of us planted our favourite beverage on the bus and caught a buzz as we "worked" the night shift. I am challenged to even call it a job. As legend has it, the most famous Oshawa General ever, Bobby Orr, and many others enjoyed the same worker's benefit.

Although it was a great summer job, better even than the Berkeley Pumps experience, it further drove home the message my father had already taught me: I needed an education. There was no way I could work on an assembly line for the rest of my life. Not even the cushy job on the end of the line.

EVERY CANADIAN HOCKEY player, and perhaps every Canadian, holds two fantasies from birth: playing in the NHL and hoisting the Stanley Cup. With the creation of the upstart World Hockey Association (WHA) in 1972, there were now two roads to a career in major-league hockey. I wasn't on the NHL's radar, but I had drawn interest from the WHA. Jacques Demers, who coached the Indianapolis Racers at the time, informed me they were planning on selecting me in the 1976 WHA amateur draft.

On Thursday, May 27, 1976, I woke up and rushed to buy the *Toronto Star*. The internet age had not dawned yet, so this was the main means to catch up on news. The draft had occurred the night before, so I went to find where the Racers had picked me.

To my dismay, my name was not anywhere in the *Toronto Star*. I had not been drafted. I kept a diary that year, and on

May 27, I wrote, "This is what could have been one of the biggest days of my life, turned out to be the biggest disappointment."

Interestingly, the Racers used their first-round pick to select Bobby Simpson, my former teammate on the Châteauguay Wings. Jacques made a career of sticking with people he knew and trusted. Simpson eventually played for the NHL's Atlanta Flames. The Cincinnati Stingers selected Barry Melrose that year, in the fourth round. Melrose, a rugged defenceman who became a head coach and then a very successful TV analyst on NHL broadcasts, eventually became close friends with my brother at ESPN. It's a small world.

As for me, I became a free agent.

The next day, the NHL held its draft. By this time, my friend Gary Murphy was the star of the St. Louis University Billikens, and many expected him to be selected. Unfortunately, he was shunned as well. After my disappointment from the day before, I became just as disheartened when I learned of Murph's bad news.

He had what I thought was a perfect NHL résumé. The outcome was discouraging, but to me it was only feedback. Motivational speaker Tony Robbins said it best: "There is no such thing as failure. There are only results."

I still had three years of college eligibility remaining, and I planned to become a much better player. Murph and I both doubled down.

CHAPTER 22

A Tooth for a Tooth

Dad's two major misdeeds were desertion and bullying. Gail sorely needed loving support from an emotionally present father. John endured a few incidents of unspeakable violence at the hands of our father, who had a dark side he fought to control.

Dad should have owned up to all of the incredibly poor decisions he made. On the other hand, he also deserves credit where credit is due. I give him high marks for his unwavering insistence that we obtain our college degrees.

As a typical Canadian hockey player, I developed an infatuation with Major Junior A and was a fistfight from making the Montreal Bleu Blanc Rouge and a phone call from signing with the Kingston Canadians. Who knows where I would be today if I had travelled down that rabbit hole.

I like to believe I still would have reached the NHL, but the key question is: To what benefit? What would I have done when my career ended? A life in professional sports is like quicksand. It can slowly suck you into the abyss.

Dad and John could barely coexist in the same room. John

never came to terms with Dad's ineptness and bullying. Those traits haunted John almost every day of his life and contributed to his depression. As badly as they affected John, I believe our father's incompetence affected Gail more. She was the typical daddy's girl. But she undoubtedly felt the weight of her gender, because sports were like gold to Dad, and consequently Gail had little currency of value to offer. And can you imagine the constant suffering, the sense of loss, she persistently felt because of my father's repeated absences?

Dad was a consummate liar who seldom carried through on a promise. However, he was true to his word when my hockey scholarship saved him $4,000 per year on college tuition. He rewarded me for that accomplishment by buying me a new car.

I have no idea how he paid for it. But I vividly remember meeting him in Oberlin, Ohio, late that summer after my freshman year to go car shopping. It was one of those dream days you never forget.

I had a blank cheque as we visited several local dealerships. I considered various options, including one of those wedge-shaped Triumph TR7 sports cars. But I finally chose a silver Datsun 280Z with a black leather interior. To me, the 280Z resembled a Corvette, only sleeker in design. I loved that car and grinned from ear to ear as I cruised onto campus as a sophomore for the first time, parking that car amongst all the other jalopies. I was the stud on campus, cruising behind the wheel of that sleek machine.

But the vehicle failed to bring universal joy. John resented it. He took it as a personal slight, because Dad had never bought him a sports car. That took some of the lustre off the reward.

I knew I had worked my ass off and earned that upgrade to a full college scholarship. Dad had promised me that car as incentive for my achievement.

And it wasn't as if John didn't have a car. Dad always provided us with transportation, but John drove the typical college beater. To John, my 280Z did not symbolize merit, but preferential treatment.

Consequently, we avoided the subject with a passion.

OVER THE LAST 40 years, I have occasionally looked back on my career and taken pride in two absolutes I brought to the teams on which I played: my steady scoring ability and a knack for scoring the big goal at critical moments in critical games.

I didn't notice the latter while I was playing, but over the decades, I came to wonder about this puzzling phenomenon. Why did I happen to score a lot of big goals? In a bid to improve myself in my post-hockey career, I became a self-help junkie. I read volume after volume on the subject.

Stephen Covey's renowned book *The 7 Habits of Highly Effective People* became one of my favourites. I must have reread it 10 times, and I came to realize I had gravitated to this book because I had practised one of its major principles long before I opened a page. Once I read the book, I learned it was describing something I had done my entire hockey career.

In stressful moments of big games, I would sit peacefully on the bench, awaiting my next shift. I didn't get nervous or tense. I would visualize myself making the pivotal play or scoring the crucial goal . . . before the moment occurred.

It isn't something I dared share with anyone. But I remember how I could feel it in my loins. Like I did in that huge upset of Bowling Green. I was the one who made the big play to turn the game around when we were down, 2–0, before Bob Gardiner provided the ultimate heroics in overtime.

In my sophomore year, we had a huge late-season game with Lake Superior State. Only four teams made the CCHA playoffs, and we were jockeying with the Lakers for the final spot. It all came down to a two-game series in Kalamazoo.

We fell behind in Game 1, and if we lost, we were done. Midway through the game, I drove to the net as the puck approached the crease. Goalie Pat Tims saw me out of the corner of his eye as he tracked the puck, and he thrust his stick and blocker towards me as I approached. I don't believe it was racially motivated; some goalies guard their crease more aggressively than others. When I arrived, he viciously cross-checked me in the face. My front teeth tumbled to the ice like Chiclets dropping from their cardboard box. As the blood pooled around me, the medical staff attended to the nerve endings dangling from the holes in my mouth. Teammates searched for the missing teeth on the ice. I was quickly escorted to the trainer's room for more detailed attention.

The jolt dislodged five front teeth. Included among the debris was the dark, decayed monster that had emotionally restrained me my entire adolescence. As I got stitched up, the medical personnel and I had to make a decision: they could provide immediate heavy painkillers and retire me for the evening, or allow me the opportunity to return to the ice without meds.

Really? There was no decision to make. Hockey mentality dictates getting back in the game. I wasn't trying to be brave; I was the typical hockey player with the typical mindset, impervious to pain. Think Bobby Baun of the Toronto Maple

Leafs in the 1964 Stanley Cup final, scoring a key overtime goal on a broken ankle. There are a cast of thousands who played with jaws wired shut after taking a puck in the face.

It was only five teeth, after all.

I returned to the game. The injury made it hard to breathe, and the way I was gasping, I was exposing the open wounds, which was causing more pain. I remember standing along the boards before a faceoff and hearing a poor, astonished young girl seated close to the glass, shrieking, "Oh my God, he lost his teeth!" Sometimes it is not good to get too close to the action.

We fell behind, but I pumped home a key third-period goal. Gardiner was on fire and scored three times to help us take a 5–4 lead. Lake Superior pressed and tied it late in the third, and regulation time ended with the score 5–5. Late in the 10-minute overtime, I recall myself peacefully awaiting my next shift, seeing myself leap over the boards to score the winning goal.

Moments later, I experienced what Covey calls the second creation (the physical accomplishment of the first creation, which takes place in the mind). With 3:18 left in OT, I corralled the rebound of my own shot and buried it behind Pat Tims. The packed Lawson Arena crowd made the building rumble while my teammates mobbed me on the ice.

We won again the next night to clinch the coveted playoff spot. I never dared discuss my ESP with anyone, but I became accustomed to the experience.

Here's how the *Kalamazoo Gazette* reported it:

Saunders' Goal Gives WMU Overtime Triumph
   After sustaining an injury that resulted in the loss of several teeth and required numerous stitches, Saunders came back to

*score two goals including the game-winner with just 3:18 left
to play in the 10-minute sudden death overtime period.*

The game became part of Kalamazoo folklore: the night
Bernie Saunders lost his teeth and scored the dramatic overtime goal.

For years after that game, seemingly every time I ran into a
fan, the first words out of his or her mouth was, "I was there
the night you lost your teeth."

The unintended consequence of that famous play was lib-
eration from my blackened front tooth, which had caused
me to suppress my smile for years. I visited the dentist the
following Monday, and Western Michigan University paid
the costly dental bill. Dr. Robert Costa gave me beautiful
dentures and changed my image for life . . . because I could
now smile.

THE BRONCOS FINISHED 17–19–1 my sophomore year, our
first losing season. And we were 5–11 in conference. But we
qualified for the CCHA playoffs again, and I received two of
the most coveted team awards: most valuable player and most
improved player.

To be the team's MVP as a sophomore was a tremendous
honour, but the recognition as most improved player touched
my heart the most. Self-improvement is my lifelong passion. In
37 games, I scored a team-leading 24 goals and 16 assists, doub-
ling my production from the year before and finishing third in
scoring behind two juniors, Tim Dunlop and Bob Gardiner.

Most important, I had established myself during a season
in which I became a fan favourite and a CCHA star at home,

but a lightning rod becasue of my Blackness everywhere else around the league.

The uniqueness of my existence was ever-present during college. Bob Wagner, the *Kalamazoo Gazette* sportswriter who covered the Broncos, wrote several feature articles on me over the years, the angle being the life of a Black hockey player. Here is what he wrote on Sunday, January 9, 1977, concerning some of the racial affronts:

BERNIE SAUNDERS IS A HOCKEY RARITY

In an early-season hockey game at Bowling Green, Western Michigan's Bernie Saunders was the victim of an especially brutal body check off the puck. "I remember that one," acknowledged Saunders, a six-foot, 185-pound sophomore right wing. "In fact, as I recall, there were quite a few runs at me."

Bernie Saunders is black, and that's a rarity in the turbulent world of hockey. "There are only two others that I know of playing now in college. One is Bill Wheeler at Michigan. There's another at St. Lawrence, but I can't remember his name."

Does being black warrant special attention from opposing players? Bernie shrugs his shoulders. "They're just testing me."

The racial taunts continued in the stands and on the ice, but with the no-fighting rule in college, it was a much different environment. I just tried to do what I read that many of my brothers have tried to do in the game and shrug it off as a cost of doing business.

In a non-conference game, I was lining up against an opponent at the start of a period, when this asshole greeted me by saying, "I can't believe I have to line up against a fucking [N-word]."

Hearing the term again chilled me to the bone, but this time, I almost wanted to laugh. I never engaged in trash talking, preferring to stare my opponent down. I didn't have my brother's nose-twerking action, but I developed what became known as the Saunders stare. I eyed this guy while thinking to myself, *Yeah, well, this [N-word] is about to drop a hat trick on your ass.*

And we proceeded to blow his team away. I played a great game and scored a couple of goals.

I never fought in the four years that I played college. As the team's leading goal scorer, it would have been stupid to let myself be goaded into a game suspension.

Rick Hummel of the *St. Louis Post-Dispatch* asked me in one interview about racial incidents that season. "There were a couple of times last year [freshman year] when it got kind of bad, but there's not much being said this year," I said. "I've had a little problem with Bowling Green. They like to bang me around a lot."

The other major factor was that I had grown so strong that it felt at times as if I were a man among boys. Sure, players targeted me, but if they wanted a piece of my ass, they were going to leave a chunk of their own.

I was one of the strongest players in the league.

CHAPTER 23

Jawing

When you think of great hockey towns, you probably think of Toronto and Montreal, Detroit and Boston. You think of Minnesota, where the game is so important, it's rightly called "the State of Hockey."

But nobody thinks of Kalamazoo, Michigan.

The 'Zoo, at first glance, does not scream "hockey mecca." But on many winter nights, the Lawson Ice Arena was packed with rabid WMU students pulling for their Broncos. And across town, Wings Stadium was jammed to the rafters with loyal International Hockey League fans screaming for the Kalamazoo Wings. Ted Parfet, the chief executive officer of the Upjohn pharmaceutical company, owned the Wings and ran it like an NHL team.

As a student and member of the WMU Broncos, I loved going to see the Wings on one of our nights off. They were coming off a couple of Turner Cup championships when the 1977–78 hockey season began, and were moulded in the image of the NHL's Philadelphia Flyers. They were the IHL's Broad Street Bullies. When it came to fighting in the mid- to late '70s, the IHL was the baddest of the minor professional leagues, and the K-Wings were the baddest asses of the IHL.

Coach Neal had taken a scouting trip to Europe over the summer with Bob Lemieux, head coach and general manager of the Wings. When they returned, they came up with the bright idea that the Broncos and K-Wings should scrimmage in preparation for the 1977–78 season, my junior year. It was hailed as a dream matchup all around town.

Since our season began earlier than the IHL's, we were already in shape for preseason competition when the minor-leaguers hoping to land with the K-Wings were just lumbering into town.

After emerging as a scoring leader in my sophomore year, I envisioned an even more successful third season, one that would keep me on track for an NHL contract. Although I appreciated the de-emphasis of fighting in college hockey, I did start to wonder if losing my pugilistic edge would hurt me as I prepared for the pros. By my junior season, I was a hulking mass who could physically punish almost any opponent.

Early in the scrimmage, the Wings' star forward, Mike Wanchuk, tried to stickhandle past me. This was my first test against pros, and I wasn't having it. I focused on the K on his chest and did what I was supposed to do: I hit him with a hard, clean check and left him in a heap on the ice. Seconds later, Len Ircandia, one of the K-Wings' notorious tough guys, did what *he* was supposed to do: he dropped his gloves and challenged me.

I dropped mine, and we started with the standard predatory dance. What I forgot was that Ircandia was a southpaw. As I danced left, he stepped right . . . and clobbered me with a stiff jab to the jaw. My knees buckled, and we wrestled until the linesmen intervened. I'm sure the two coaches started reconsidering this affair.

Nothing much else happened in the scrimmage, but I felt empowered knowing I had stood up to one of the toughest guys in minor-league hockey. My jaw came out of the game just fine—better than Ircandia's hand. He broke his wrist on my face and had to wear a cast for the early part of the regular season.

A very strange thing happened in the weeks leading up to our regular-season opener. We found ourselves glued to the TV set throughout the second half of October, when the New York Yankees and Los Angeles Dodgers met in the World Series.

The Saunders brothers were always Yankees fans. As kids, John loved Mickey Mantle, and Roger Maris was my favourite. But I found myself once again in the minority, because for some unknown reason, most of my teammates were rooting for the Dodgers.

Game 6 was played in Yankee Stadium on October 18, 1977. I woke up that morning thinking it was going to be Reggie Jackson's night. He wasn't Mr. October yet, but all day long, I walked the dorm saying, "Remember the name of Reggie Jackson! Remember the name of Reggie Jackson!"

Call it a premonition. I have no idea why, but I remember having this strong sense that Jackson was going to be the man.

And then we all tuned in that night for my Nostradamus moment. Reggie hit three home runs on three dramatic swings off three different pitchers. He painted World Series history with his bat and the Yankees won the championship, their first since 1962.

I don't want to weird you out or anything, but I strongly believe the universe speaks to us. On that day, the vibe was so strong, I could taste it. I wish I could use this talent with lottery tickets, but it doesn't work there. It's just that sometimes a signal comes in loud and clear and I can't ignore it. I believe we all underutilize our capabilities.

As fun as my Reggie prediction was in 1977, it didn't come close to what happened in 1984, when my brother met the beautiful Wanda Burton from Baltimore, Maryland (they married on August 10, 1986).

Why was this strange? In an amazing twist of fate, Wanda's mother happened to be Reggie Jackson's sister. No bull. Reggie is now family, and we affectionately call him Uncle Reg. Tell me that ain't eerie.

And no, I have never mentioned my Game 6 premonition to him. I can't imagine what it must be like to be Mr. October. If I could grow sick of people telling me they were there the night I lost my five front teeth, I can't imagine how Uncle Reg deals with the number of times people have approached him to reminisce about October 18, 1977.

I BECAME A CCHA Second Team All-Star in 1977–78, set a school record with seven shorthanded goals, and finished second on the team and seventh in the league in scoring. But the year was a disappointment, spoiled by a rebellion against Coach Neal by many of my teammates.

I was an innocent bystander to the debacle, in which there was fault on both sides. Too many players accused Coach Neal of being unfair, and some quit the team. The spat between players and coach dominated the season, and after a prolonged public affair, the university decided not to renew Coach Neal's contract.

I was not one of Coach Neal's detractors. He was an innovator, which I believe the game could use more of. In fact, his avant-garde penalty-killing approach was the main reason I broke the record for shorthanded goals. He installed a diamond-shaped 1–2–1 penalty-killing formation that allowed me, positioned at the top, the freedom to release into the neutral zone when we had clear possession of the puck.

This aggressive counterattacking style while down a man could be deemed risky, but Coach Neal taught us to never leave the zone prematurely; discipline was the key. Neil Smith was great at angling soft passes into the neutral zone, so I often looked for him to gain full possession of the puck before I took off. More often than not, I was able to use my speed to spring an offensive opportunity that caught the opposing power-play unit off guard. Many teams used a forward instead of a defenceman on the point, which was the mismatch that Coach Neal was seeking.

My seven shorthanded goals in 1977–78 are still a Broncos single-season record. And it was a product of Coach Neal's innovative thinking, inspired by that summer trip to Europe.

By the end of my junior year, my star had risen so high in the 'Zoo that I had become a local celebrity. I was recognized everywhere. The locals embraced this young Black kid who excelled at a sport where no Black had shone before.

To top it off, I was articulate and well-mannered, and I carried a 3.2 grade point average. So, when it came time to search for Coach Neal's replacement, the school formed a selection committee that included one player. And they selected me.

The committee that spring considered many of the same assistant coaches who had recruited me a few years earlier, and the swing from the recruited to the recruiter felt a little uncomfortable, at best. I tried to get Sherry Bassin to apply, but he had moved on to major junior hockey in Oshawa and was happy.

Astonishingly, when the committee interviewed the finalists, I carried the conversations. Yes, reluctant, reticent me. Most of the committee members weren't very conversant in hockey, so they knew to listen while I fired off questions in order to glean as much hockey knowledge and philosophy as I could from the candidates.

I had come a long way in three years.

Bill Wilkinson, who had tried to get me to go to St. Lawrence three years earlier, was a finalist, but Glen Weller from Michigan Tech won the job. He was not my top choice, but the other committee members loved him. At the time, Michigan Tech had emerged as a hockey hotbed under head coach John MacInnes, a hockey legend, and Glen, his assistant, was destined to share that pedigree.

Glen and I developed a great friendship over the years; he is as solid as they come. I believe if he had waited out the Michigan Tech job, or coached another established program, we would be talking about him in the same breath as Herb Brooks or Bob Johnson.

However, he wasn't best-suited to take on a role with a fledgling program like Western Michigan. I doubt I ever revealed to him I was the lone committee member who failed to select him. However, he is one of those people with whom I will remain in contact for life.

CHAPTER 24

Hoop Dreams

Dad was involved in our life, so it wasn't the stereotypical single-parent home that haunts Black families. Still, I barely knew my father.

So, after my disappointing junior year ended, I decided to settle this personal score. Having lived in the United States and begun to feel more comfortable in this setting, I wanted to spend time getting to know this man of mystery.

I had never even been to his residence. Yes, residence. I never pictured him living in a comfortable home. All my life, I had had this vivid image of my father living in a messy, one-room studio apartment—his work tools scattered all around . . . pictures of John, Gail and me proudly displayed.

Although my father had failed us on countless occasions, I still envisioned a man working his ass off to provide for his family back in Canada. Despite those painful Friday nights at the telegraph office when he failed to wire us money, I still painted a picture in my mind of a man agonizing over his mistakes.

I always felt he suffered along with us when he failed to provide.

Dad was born in Hamilton in 1928. Canadians are known

to be more tolerant than their neighbours to the south, but it still wasn't the land of milk and honey for Black Canadians. Both Mom and Dad had difficult lives as people of colour living in a predominately white world. I think that is why I always accepted their imperfections.

My father's job, as I grew to understand, was jack of all trades. He wasn't college-educated, but he worked white-collar jobs when we lived in Montreal. He grew up in Hamilton, Ontario, and his father was an immigrant from Jamaica who worked at the massive Dofasco steel mill. Granddad was cold and heartless, a man who toiled in hard labour and undoubtedly lived a hard life. Granddad was known to hide out in the basement and smoke cigarettes and drink rum when he was home. Dad and his brothers were no strangers to corporal punishment. So, Dad didn't have the best role model to follow.

Dad somehow managed to make friends with a wealthy lawyer in Elyria, Ohio, who had put him in touch with a couple of friends. These seedy lawyers were what you would refer to as slumlords today. As a side venture, they purchased local properties and rented them to low-income residents. My father was a handyman whose job it was to go in and fix up the places when the residents transitioned.

"Transitioned" being a euphemism for being evicted.

Dad had the perfect skill set because each place had its own unique needs once the tenants were displaced. He found that many of the places had been trashed. He gutted the apartments, repaired the plumbing or fixed the wiring, whatever was needed for the next occupant. Bernie Saunders Sr. could do it all.

Since he was an illegal alien, the lawyers paid him under the table. Based on this unlawful arrangement, my father managed to live illegally in the United States for more than a decade. The few times we visited him, it became evident he was paranoid of police. Whenever we drove with him and a patrol car inched near, he insisted we be still.

A more inquiring mind might have assumed he was a fugitive, as the man always became petrified. We just thought it was weird; we had no concept of illegal immigration. Dad survived as an undocumented immigrant for years before he eventually received his green card. In 1986, Ronald Reagan's Immigration Reform and Control Act granted Dad and three million other illegal aliens amnesty and legal entry into the United States.

To this day, I get a little queasy when I see a patrol car in my rear-view mirror. But then again, most Black men do.

I had one year left at WMU, so rather than return to Mom and Gail in Ajax, I made a consequential decision to devote the summer to my father. He promised to pay more in salary than I could make on one of my jobs back home. And he insisted I would have ample time to remain dedicated to my conditioning program. The deal sounded so ideal, I convinced Murph to join me.

Murph, who had received a free-agent invite to the St. Louis Blues' training camp, and I planned the perfect summer: spend time with Dad, make money, have fun hanging together and double down on our workouts.

Things started out well. Murph and I tore down dilapidated apartments for Dad's company. The job didn't suck and the pay was nice. Murph and I joined a summer hockey league, which complemented our usual off-ice conditioning regimen. And most important, it afforded me the time to get to know this enigmatic parent. Dad was kind and engaging, the type of man who could charm the pants off most everybody. He just didn't have a good relationship with responsibility.

Most surprisingly, Dad's digs were really nice. He lived in a large Tudor-style house set back from the street behind a long circular drive that accessed his and two other houses. His two-storey home had four bedrooms and a basement. It had a large barn in the back, filled with his heavy machinery. The building doubled as a garage, with a basketball hoop playfully watching over the sliding doors.

Dad's home was neat and tastefully furnished. The only part of my boyhood image of Dad's accommodations that I got right were the several framed pictures on the walls and countertops: John and me in hockey regalia, Gail from her beauty pageants and modelling shoots.

This was the antithesis of a bachelor pad. It was a comfortable home.

Midway through the summer, I had to attend Neil Smith's wedding. Neil was marrying a girl from Escanaba, Michigan, he had met at WMU. Don't fret if you haven't heard of the place. It's way the hell up there, a 14-hour drive to the Upper Peninsula of the state. (Michiganders pronounce it "You-Pea.") To get there, you have to cross the Mackinaw Bridge, take a left turn at Sault Ste. Marie, and keep going and going and going. If you hit Green Bay, Wisconsin, you've gone too far.

I left Murph in Oberlin, Ohio, with my father and made the long haul myself.

The wedding was great. I got to see my brother and several of my Broncos teammates. Bob Gardiner was Neil's best man, and John was a member of the wedding party as well.

The bunch of Broncos in attendance, including that insepar-able trio and me, partied all weekend, and Sunday morning came way too soon. I decided to return non-stop, so when the Datsun 280Z pulled into my dad's circular drive, I was think-ing only about hugging my mattress.

Murph, who was outside shooting hoops against the barn, had other ideas when he saw me pull in. "We have to talk," he said impatiently.

I replied that whatever was on his mind would have to wait until I got some rest, but he insisted we talk immediately.

We retreated to our upstairs bedroom for privacy. Murph explained he had spent quite a bit of time over the weekend with Wendy, the next-door neighbour. She was more than 20 years older than Murph, so I knew he didn't mean anything romantic. But since Murph was such a friendly guy, he and Wendy had hit it off. Murph enjoyed her company while I was on the road. At some point over the weekend, my father became extremely jealous and intervened.

Things got heated, according to Murph, and a verbal alter-cation ensued. At which point, Murph uncovered the truth: Wendy wasn't the next-door neighbour. Wendy was my fath-er's partner. She and her two sons normally lived in the big house where we were staying. The four were essentially a family. Dad had them living surreptitiously in the house he also owned next door, while he spent the summer with us.

Now the whole summer was a fraud, my whole life a ruse. All the wasted years I had spent, sadly visualizing him living in this one-room apartment, were a joke. The reason why Dad never came home was because he *was* home—and parenting two other boys instead of John, Gail and me. His two white sons even called him Dad.

I confronted my father, furious that he could so badly hurt Gail, John and me. My father tried to do what he did best: lie and try to make me feel sorry for him. But I told him exactly what he needed to hear from a child in agony. I packed my bags to leave, but he begged me to stay. In the end, I did, as WMU's training camp was only a couple of weeks away. But I was numb.

Murph left for St. Louis. It was too uncomfortable for him to stay.

I spent the remaining time remembering situation after situation in my life when I had given my father the benefit of the doubt. This new reality was torture. I could forgive his other sins, but family was the ultimate to me. All those years while we were starving for fatherly direction, Dad lived in Ohio, parenting two other boys.

That reality left a scar that will never heal.

It took me more than a year to tell John and Gail, as I knew the news would hit them harder than it hit me. I told John one day when he was really down from his depression. I often tried to coach John out of his latest funk. We were driving to Moncton, where he had started a new job in television. The moment seemed right, so I told him late at night while we traversed a dark highway.

John was stunned. He had me stop the car. He got out and wailed.

Understanding Dad's dirty little secret helped clarify so much in John's mind. My brother had felt the pressure to be perfect, so uncovering Dad's imperfections soothed some of the pain. We saw the majestic northern lights for the first time that evening, and I quietly hoped that it was a sign from the heavens.

The revelation supported John in some ways, and I tried to help him put it into perspective. But Dad had been so hard on John, it was difficult for John to forgive the hypocrisy.

John pledged to never get over it until he saw my father in his grave.

We never had a basketball hoop.

CHAPTER 25

Senior Seniority

I accept my life and fate. God has been good to me. But there have been certain times in my life when situations forced the Mini-Me sitting on my left shoulder to want to cry foul.

After accepting and trudging through the strong hierarchical system at Western Michigan—where, under Coach Neal, the law was unequivocally "seniority rules," we underclassmen waited patiently for our turn in the catbird seat.

When we finally got to the front of the line during my senior season in the fall of 1978, it became crystal clear that new head coach Glen Weller had a different vision. As part of his rebuilding program, he had just completed his first recruiting summer and intended to showcase his prized recruits.

While Bill Neal had annually mined Ontario for talent, Coach Weller had broken new ground by reaching out to British Columbia, as he had done while at Michigan Tech. He landed Ross Fitzpatrick from Penticton, Terry Olson from Victoria, and Bob Scurfield from North Vancouver, among other prized rooks.

All were highly talented, no doubt. But in the season when I needed to be most aggressively showcased to attract NHL scouts, I was demoted from day one of camp. It reminded me of Steve Falkner's sudden appearance four years earlier, in my final season of Junior B.

Coach Weller loaded up the early games with a ridiculously weak schedule: McMaster, Windsor, a conference game against Ferris State, Wilfrid Laurier and St. Scholastica. Coach Neal had scheduled a "can't lose" game to start each of my first three seasons, but then immediately jumped into more highly competitive opponents. Coach Weller had scheduled five powder puffs in a row.

As talented as the new recruits were, I knew I just had to be patient.

We opened the season against McMaster, and I was buried on the third line. I wasn't a happy Bronco. The freshman thoroughbreds jumped out of the gates these first five games, but when we finally began playing legitimate CCHA competition . . . surprise, surprise: the surge stalled. And from that point on, Coach Weller promoted me to the first line, where I remained the rest of the season.

It was an arduous year. As a collegiate athlete, there is no worse feeling than being a senior when the team decides to retool and change its long-standing approach. I did my best to be a leader on the team, as it wasn't anybody's fault, but it was an anticlimactic season.

One positive development was the emergence of a second talented Black in the CCHA. I took pride knowing that Larry Marson, Mike's younger brother, had game, too. Larry skated for Ohio State and tallied 59 points in 37 games as a rookie. *The Hockey News* featured us in an article celebrating the fact the CCHA boasted two Black scoring stars.

The irony of Marson's arrival was that Ohio State had a

tiny rink with screens instead of glass. The rink was an embarrassment to college hockey. I hated playing there because the fans could shout right through the screen and I could hear every word. It was one of the toughest buildings for me to play in until Larry Marson arrived on the scene.

When I was sheared three years earlier, I decided that hazing had no place in a college dressing room . . . or anywhere, for that matter. As captain, I wanted to discontinue this barbaric and ridiculous tradition. Striving to live by my values, it would have been hypocritical to continue a tradition I was starkly against. As a result, I tried to terminate the humiliating tradition.

However, I was overruled. The other upperclassmen wanted to enact their revenge. I could not change people's minds. So, the shaving and ornament painting continued. Brownie took over the shearing duties, but Boomba Bernie chose not to participate. But by my taking this personal stand, the cycle was broken a few years later.

My entire senior season was like this: just a little bit off. In sports, there's a fine line between playing freely and pressing. I was pressing. My patented slapshot from the top of the faceoff circle was inches off. I remember hitting five goalposts in those first few games.

To this day, more than 40 years later, I can remember one game when I darted left around a defenceman, then shifted right to elude the goalie while getting hooked from behind by the trailing defenceman. I found myself flying past the *completely* open net with both legs in the air . . . attempting to roll and redirect the puck towards the empty cage to the left. The sheer force from my surge sent me sprawling into the opposite corner. I lay there, exasperated, as I peered back to see the puck resting unattended against the near goalpost before the goalie recovered and smothered it.

While on my knees in the corner, I dropped my head in disgust. But the WMU fans jumped to their feet and gave me a drawn-out standing ovation. They appreciated my effort and style. It warmed my heart and helped me get my game back on track.

I've never forgotten how special my relationship with the WMU fans was over my four years. I became a local celebrity in Kalamazoo, a favourite son. My name was cheered the loudest during pre-game introductions and after I scored a goal. It certainly helped me endure this difficult senior year.

Neil Smith's return to campus did, too.

Neil had graduated a year before me. Having been drafted by the Islanders in 1974, he decided to turn pro after graduating and attended their training camp in September 1978. He didn't get far. He played for a few teams in the Eastern Hockey League and the IHL, trying to catch on, before he quickly realized his pathway to play in the NHL was closed.

Now, he was in Kalamazoo, having played in a handful of games for the K-Wings, looking to land a day job. He had no money, so he moved into the dorm with Matt Dietz and me. It was funny, watching him migrate from job to job that winter, trying to figure out what he was going to do with his life.

Each time he would get fired, he would return with a mock dejected frown. It became our signal for a night on the town, a chance to duck out and commiserate. Neil's presence helped to take the edge off a frustrating end to my college career.

Without a doubt, the most wearisome few days of this entire season came during a brutal Michigan snowstorm. A year earlier, we had endured the Blizzard of 1978, one of the state's heaviest snowstorms on record. That storm was on my mind when, during a break in WMU's schedule, I took advantage of a rare chance to see one of John's games in Toronto. John, now married and living in Ajax, was playing hockey for Ryerson, whose campus was in downtown Toronto. Since our hockey seasons overlapped, it was nearly impossible for us to see each other play.

But since this was the one chance I had, I jumped into the 280Z despite it starting to snow. And snow. And snow. I was in the Datsun when they were calling this the worst storm since last winter's blizzard. Highway 401 was a sheet of ice. The stretch from Windsor to London had black ice beneath the snow, forcing me to crawl for miles.

To say the least, I had risked my life to see John's game. I was hours behind schedule but remained determined to make it to the Moss Park Arena in downtown Toronto. And I did, pulling into town minutes before the opening faceoff. I parked, ran into the tiny arena and noticed my brother alongside his usual defence partner, Frank Sheffield. Frank, the team captain, is also Black, which made Sheffield/Saunders likely the only all-Black defence pair, well, in the history of hockey. They were dubbed the Ebony Connection.

John glanced over towards the entrance to the small arena. He caught sight of me rushing in, all dishevelled and shaken from the trek, and he flashed his patented crooked grin. That smile made the dangerous drive well worth it.

John often told me his coaches wanted me to attend all his games because he always played his best when I was present.

Before I even thought about finding a seat, the puck dropped and the game began. In the opening seconds, the puck slid back to Sheffield. According to John, Sheffield fed him a bad pass and the puck ricocheted into John's corner, where I stood. John, with his back to the play, tried to corral the puck. His opponent ran him from behind, driving him face-first into the glass. Before you knew it, John had thrown a flying elbow, dropped his gloves and started throwing haymakers.

It was 22 seconds into the game. It was college hockey, so, because of the fistfight, John was ejected.

As the officials escorted John and his foe off the ice, John glanced over his shoulder towards me, staring dumbfounded from behind the glass.

"You fucking asshole," I mouthed silently.

Years later, when he was inducted into the Ryerson University Athletics Hall of Fame, John told that story. Everyone roared. I laughed, too. It was funny, years later.

I risked my life to witness 22 seconds of my brother's career.

Back in Kalamazoo, we finished 17–19–0 and missed the CCHA playoffs for the second straight season. Although I was disappointed with my final year as a Bronco, I had achieved most of my personal goals as a collegian:

- I led the Broncos in scoring with 51 points and won the team MVP award for the second time in four years.
- I finished as the team's leading goal scorer for the third straight year.
- I finished as WMU's all-time leading scorer.
- As the first Black captain in Western Michigan hockey history, I became only the second Black captain in NCAA hockey history—Richard Lord was the first, in 1949–50 for Michigan State.
- I became only the second hockey player inducted into the WMU Athletic Hall of Fame, behind Neil Smith.

But my greatest accomplishment? I earned a college degree. Not by skating through a worthless curriculum, but by earning a degree that could lead to a career after hockey. I took my academics seriously and graduated with a bachelor of business administration, with an emphasis in marketing.

I was the first in the family to receive an advanced education. I was proud of my BBA, but now it was time to earn my NHL.

CHAPTER 26

Welcome to the Jet Set

My brother was my de facto first agent, and he got to work on my behalf early in my senior season. As my final few games as a Bronco approached, John had already sent letters to every NHL and WHA general manager.

Our goal was to get me a tryout after graduation.

John Ferguson, GM of the WHA's Winnipeg Jets, was one of those who bit. Ferguson's scouts flew out to watch me play over the Christmas break in the Cornell Holiday Festival tournament, where I was the lone Bronco selected to the all-tournament team, and apparently, they liked what they saw.

As soon as the season ended, Ferguson asked me to report to the team—he wanted me in Winnipeg immediately. I was still attending classes during my final semester, and the Jets were in the midst of their 1978–79 WHA schedule. It didn't make total sense, but I hopped on a plane and flew to frigid Winnipeg.

I was fewer than 40 days from the end of the semester, and I had hoped to complete school over the summer. But plans are meant to be changed. I arrived late in the day, watched the Jets lose a lacklustre game that night and prepared to join the team for practice the next morning.

You have never been cold until you have faced the winter wind in Winnipeg. It goes right through your bones. My hotel stood adjacent to a mall, with the Winnipeg Arena on the other side. For the game that night, I left my hotel and walked through the mall to avoid the freezing temperature.

I awoke for breakfast, eagerly anticipating practice. No one had instructed me what to do or when to show up, so I assumed someone would call or come by the hotel. I waited in the lobby, but nobody showed.

When I returned to my room, the red message light on the phone was flashing. Seconds later, the phone rang. It was Ferguson's secretary, wondering where the hell I was. It was 9:30 a.m., and I was supposed to be there for the 10 a.m. practice.

I raced towards the arena, panicked. When I reached the mall entrance, I tugged on the door. It was locked. The mall was closed. Inappropriately dressed, freezing and feeling like an idiot, I raced through the frigid streets and got to the arena late for my first pro practice.

The players were already on the ice when I got to the Jets' dressing room. The equipment manager took time to outfit me with the proper gear, and I was lacing my skates and ready to jump out there when the door flew open. One by one, the players stepped back into the dressing room.

Ferguson had just fired head coach Larry Hillman, and he was running the practice. I was a Montreal Canadiens fan as a kid, so I knew all too well about Fergy's toughness as an NHL fighter, his intimidating demeanour. Seeing him in person for the first time, with his steely face and jagged nose, I braced for the verbal tirade that would begin as soon as the players marched to their stalls and took their seats in the silent room.

Mr. Ferguson, marching in last, went around the room, blasting each player about everything from his toughness to his mother. One by one, he spared nobody. When he got to me, midway through his outburst, he screamed even louder, putting his face inches from mine, eyes bugging out of their sockets.

"And you! Here you are at your first practice and you're late?" he bellowed. "I ought to send you back to where you came from right now."

He kept screaming at me, spewing typical hockey expletives. He was uncontrollably mad and treated me like any other dumb rookie who was late to his first practice. I was scared and felt extremely stupid.

After that rude introduction, I pulled myself together and the tryout was a resounding success. I had little difficulty adapting to the quicker pace of play, which several of the Jets noticed. A few players commented on my ability. Terry Ruskowski, one of the Jets' top players, was particularly welcoming. He stopped me to compliment my hockey sense after I threw him a crafty area pass. The *Winnipeg Free Press* reported, "The Jets have been impressed by tryout Bernie Saunders. The product of Ajax, Ontario, had 26 goals and 22 assists in 36 games at Western Michigan University last season. He has been followed by John Ferguson for the past two seasons."

It was a great experience, and I was pleased I had impressed the club. There was no mention of my race in the media or in the locker room the entire time I was there. I was just a hockey player and I couldn't have felt more accepted.

Since the WHA season was winding down, Ferguson and I agreed on the pragmatic thing to do: I would return to campus for the final five weeks of the semester so I could graduate, and I would launch my pro career the following season in the WHA with the Jets.

Fergy wanted me to play a few IHL games for the K-Wings, too, and the *Free Press* actually reported that the Jets had assigned me there. Everything pointed to me returning to Winnipeg in the fall and launching my pro career in the WHA with the Jets.

SHORTLY AFTER I arrived back in Kalamazoo, K-Wings GM Bob Lemieux called. Injuries and suspensions had left his team a few players short, and he needed me. I was in my dorm room, working on a homework assignment, when Lemieux asked if I would play for the K-Wings that night in Fort Wayne, Indiana.

It was March 15, 1979. Lemieux instructed me to meet the team bus on the highway. The team had played on the road the night before, and they were on their way to Fort Wayne. I drove my 280Z to the rendezvous location, parked it at the truck stop on Interstate 69 and settled into my seat on the bus to prepare for my first professional hockey game.

I played great, scoring my first pro goal in my first game. My goal gave the K-Wings a 3–1 lead. Unfortunately, the Komets rallied in front of a packed home crowd and beat us, 6–5. I had a three-point night with a goal and two assists.

In preparing to be dropped off at the truck stop on the ride back to Kalamazoo, I started thinking about how late it was, and the alarm clock ringing to wake me up in time for classes the next morning. A few minutes later, while chatting with a teammate, I began to sense that the ride was taking longer than it should have. "Where are we going?" I asked.

"We're headed to Milwaukee," he replied. "Game tomorrow night."

Milwaukee? Tomorrow night? I suddenly realized Lemieux had penned me into the lineup for the entire road trip, not just the game in Fort Wayne. You would have thought he would mention that minor detail. I didn't even have a toothbrush or change of clothes. But that was Lemieux. I never made it to class the next morning and ended up playing three games on the trip, recording five points.

Lemieux was trying to settle on a playoff roster, and he wanted me on it. But I wanted to finish school. So, Lemieux put me on waivers, but with conditions. According to the *Kalamazoo Gazette*:

> *Saunders, who scored five points in three games within the week for the Wings, was placed on waivers with a string attached. "We put right on the TWX message that Bernie does not plan to report to any other club because he wants to remain in Kalamazoo and finish his education," said Wings general manager Bob Lemieux.*

Living in Kalamazoo afforded me the opportunity to get my feet wet in the pros without having to leave my dorm. Between the games with Kalamazoo and my audition in Winnipeg, I gained instant feedback on what I needed to make a successful jump to the next level.

Unbeknownst to anyone at the time, major-league hockey was on the threshold of a historic transformation. Remember when I complained about my poor timing and rules tending to change on me at the most inopportune time? Here we go again . . .

The WHA, coming off its seventh and final season, and the NHL announced a blockbuster merger, a consolidation of franchises. The WHA's four healthiest clubs—Edmonton Oilers, Hartford Whalers, Quebec Nordiques and Winnipeg Jets—joined the NHL. The Cincinnati Stingers and Birmingham Bulls dropped down a notch to the Central Hockey League. The Indianapolis Racers, who did not make it past November 1978, simply folded.

Sports is no different from any other business when it comes to the loss of jobs. This contraction of teams meant I faced more competition for a big-league contract. On a positive note, though, being a free agent allowed me to talk to any team I desired.

The WHA had been a cut above the American and Central Hockey Leagues but a definite step below the NHL, as evidenced by the many average NHLers who had defected to the rival league and become WHA stars. I'd left my tryout with the Jets in March of 1979 intending to sign with them. The master plan was to graduate from college to the WHA, and later advance to the NHL. But now that the WHA was gone, that plan had to be scrapped.

My first move was to hire an agent. John had served me well, but it was time to hire a professional. I considered a number of agents and chose Art Kaminsky. Art was a pioneer, one of the first full-time sports agents. He attended Cornell, befriended Ken Dryden and represented him when he turned pro in 1971 with the Montreal Canadiens. Eight years later, Kaminsky was representing many top players in the NHL. He was as high-profile an advocate as I could find, and in the beginning, he did his thing. I attracted keen interest from the Detroit Red Wings and New York Islanders, as well as the Nordiques and Jets. It was an extremely exciting time.

After careful consideration, we decided to sign with Quebec. First, we considered each team's roster, and together we felt I had the best chance of making it with the Nordiques. Second, we were attracted to the fact that their head coach was Jacques Demers, my former Junior B coach and a man well known for his loyalty to former players.

Kaminsky negotiated a three-year deal with the Nordiques. It was a two-way contract, which meant I made $45,000 a year if I played for the Nordiques, or $20,000 if I was sent to the minors. I also received a $5,000 signing bonus, which was a chunk of change back in the day.

The paperwork arrived in my Kalamazoo mailbox on May 29, 1979. My roommate, Matt Dietz, signed as my witness and it was official: I was under contract with an NHL team.

A first dream fulfilled.

CHAPTER 27

Zapped

I left home for my first NHL training camp with a unique going-away gift: my bank account was mysteriously $2,000 light. I had deposited my $5,000 bonus cheque, hadn't touched the account, but when I got ready to leave for Quebec City, my statement said I had a balance of $3,000.

Huh?

I immediately looked into the matter, and it didn't take me long to determine that my mother had forged four cheques drawn on my account. As bad as that sounds, the worst part for me is that she did it *four times*. For some perverse reason, I was willing to grant her one moment of weakness. But for her to discover my box of extra cheques and reach into it to forge my signature four different times was beyond inexcusable.

She carved off 40 percent of my signing bonus. And $5,000 could buy a brand-new car in 1979. Mom knew that I had signed an NHL contract and must have decided she deserved a finder's fee.

When I first confronted her, she lied. She then quickly admitted it when I pinned her down with the raw evidence. I asked her how she could do such a thing, but all she said was that she had fallen behind on the rent. And that she had to do it.

John was infuriated and once again flew to my defence. He confronted her, enraged, but she gave her typical rationalization, saying she needed the money.

"You've stolen from Bernie, somebody who's been loyal to you!" John screamed. "You no longer have three children. You have two."

And for years, John avoided contact with Mom at all costs. He became estranged from both our parents.

Maybe there was a little Stockholm syndrome at play. But at times like these, I tried to remind myself that my parents weren't perfect people. We weren't the Huxtables, but my parents were my family and I loved them, and I felt their love in return. I still couldn't imagine how a parent could steal from his or her own child. Why she couldn't openly come to me, I will never know. I guess she figured I was rich now and could afford it. Who knows? I just believe that if you carry this stuff inside, then it wears on you like a disease.

All I could do was to let it go and try to turn these events into a positive. I promised myself I would never pass a negative torch to my children, which enabled me to turn these painful experiences into positive life lessons. Mom was the one who was always there for me. She just made some amazingly poor decisions at times.

The incident did make me feel worse about leaving Gail home alone with Mom, because she was too young to protect herself from my parents' failures. But I had to forge ahead and make my own way in the world. And hockey is where I learned to deal with the volatile world around me.

Naively, I headed to Quebec thinking I could win a roster spot with the Nordiques. Although some of the players in camp were celebrities I had watched on TV for years, I wasn't awed by the competition. I flew up and down my wing, scored goals in scrimmages and played with boyish freedom. What excited me the most is that I found the higher calibre of play made things easier for me, not tougher.

Hockey is organized chaos, and the game actually becomes more predictable when the players you play with are more intelligent. Playing with players with higher hockey IQ results in everybody executing at a higher level, making fewer mistakes.

That helped a player like me considerably. In this environment of increased predictability, I found it easier to anticipate the play on offence, disrupt the flow and, with my speed and instincts, cause a little chaos. I also learned that my ability to complement my linemates' tendencies paid off more handsomely at this level.

Heads started turning my way immediately.

"Rookie defenseman Pierre Lacroix, defenseman John Baby, left wing Bernie Saunders (the No. 1 all-time scorer at Western Michigan) and Terry Johnson have all drawn raves," reported the *Syracuse Post-Standard*. "Saunders, who never missed a game in four years at Western Michigan, has impressed everybody here. The 6-foot, 190-pounder is the lone black in camp."

I had a great training camp. Grand illusions of sticking with the big boys began to creep into my head. That is, until my roommate, a guy by the name of Kevin Zappia, who starred at Clarkson University, got a call from a family member. This relative in Syracuse, New York, reached out to Kevin not long after another one of my strong scrimmages.

Zap was told that the Nordiques had announced their

first round of cuts, and Zap and I were on the list of players assigned to the AHL's Syracuse Firebirds, Quebec's top minor-league affiliate. The cuts were listed in the newspaper, but the team hadn't bothered to tell us yet.

That would be unheard of in today's internet age, but it was a different world back then. The Nordiques wanted to get fans of their AHL affiliate excited about their team, and I understood that. But cutting me so quickly, given how I was playing, was disappointing. I had hoped for an honest look and a chance at a roster spot.

Nevertheless, I understood hockey politics. I reported to the Firebirds, prepared to spend a full season in the AHL. I marshalled the confidence gained from my scrimmages in Quebec City and got off to just as fast a start in Syracuse. I began to separate myself from the pack, as a *Post-Standard* article reported on October 4, 1979: "Best looking line in scrimmages was trio of Kim Davis, Bernie Saunders and Steve Coates."

A few days later, the *Post-Standard* published a story with the headline "Love of Hockey Has Helped Saunders Endure Flak." It was the first of several features on me that discussed the life of a Black hockey player and the racism I was already enduring in preseason games.

"The incidents of racially-tinted name-calling and blatant intimidation have occurred all too frequently during Bernie Saunders' short lifetime," the story read. "But as one of hockey's few black players, Saunders obviously makes an inviting target."

The reporter had watched me work on my marquee move, slog through sideboards drills by myself, and spend those extra hours alone on the ice after practice. He captured my hunger for improvement and the intensity of my personal workout program: "Daily he's been the last one off the ice, spending extra time each day perfecting his shot or pushing himself through a series of energy-draining wind sprints."

Without a doubt, my first pro camp had a major impact on my career for another reason: the Nordiques in camp employed a stretching trainer, which to their credit was an innovation in 1979. Players were required to attend stretching sessions before going onto the ice.

Since the methodology was in its infancy, the trainer had us bouncing during the exercises, which is known to be taboo today. As a result, I badly pulled my groin during one of the sessions in Quebec and needed to be iced and bandaged before play. In four years at WMU, I had never missed a game and was considered a physical thoroughbred. But now I had suffered an injury that affected not only my first pro season but the rest of my career as well.

The human body is an incredible machine, because each part works in concert with the others. One needs this balance to excel. My right groin injury eventually caused an injury to my left knee. To this day, I don't skate because my groin pops out of place whenever I make a quick striding motion.

But I couldn't afford to let a nagging groin slow me down, so for that entire season, I did my best to fight through it. I was one of the early preseason stars of camp, so when the Nordiques made a few more cuts from their NHL camp and Syracuse's AHL roster swelled, something had to give.

But I was shocked to learn one of the somethings would be me.

The *Post-Standard* reported that the Firebirds needed to pare their AHL roster down from 24 to 20 just before the regular season began, and that prompted some last-minute housecleaning, "thus sealing the fate of Bernie Saunders, Rob

Garner, Les Hudson and Ken Kuzyk. Saunders, Garner and Hudson were dispatched to Cincinnati of the Central Hockey League, while Kuzyk was assigned to Nova Scotia, as part of considerations owed Montreal by Quebec."

What we all learned was that the NHL–WHA merger, which prompted the demotion of Cincinnati and Birmingham to the CHL, included an agreement that the four WHA teams absorbed into the NHL would stock the Stingers.

The Syracuse media criticized my reassignment, since I had already emerged as a top scorer for the Firebirds. In fact, the local media was constantly at odds with the Nordiques for what the writers widely interpreted as consistent boneheaded blunders.

The Nordiques were in their first year in the NHL and just did not have their act together. As Chuck Bellinger of the *Post-Standard* wrote about one roster move midway through the 1979–80 AHL regular season: "It was a shocking personnel move, regardless of the many other strange and mysterious maneuvers the Nordiques have pulled this season, moves which included Norm Dubé's exile to Nova Scotia (where he is now the AHL's leading scorer), and Bernie Saunders's preseason demotion to Cincinnati."

Just like when I was cut three times in junior hockey, my reassignment from Syracuse to Cincinnati led me to believe that nobody could comprehend that a Black hockey player could excel at this level. Racial injustice comes in many forms, including unconscious biases. In many instances, I believe people lacked malicious intent; they just presumed I was incompetent because I was Black. I was a freak.

I appreciated the support from the fans and media, but no matter, I was off to *WKRP in Cincinnati*.

CHAPTER 28

Visceral Memory

I joined the Stingers on October 13, 1979, in Fort Worth, Texas. The head coach was Al Karlander, an NHL journeyman with the Detroit Red Wings who had played college at Michigan Tech. Karlander's difficult charge was to mould a collection of prospects from four different new NHL franchises into a cohesive team. This peculiar arrangement had doom written all over it.

The team had already opened the season by losing two early road games at Indianapolis and Oklahoma City when I arrived. Unfazed by my unfair demotion from Syracuse to Cincinnati, I pulled the Stingers' black and gold jersey over my head and went back to work. I scored my first Central Hockey League goal on one of my first shifts, and later in the game, I scored my second goal, the winner in a 4–1 victory over the Texans.

Although my second goal was the winner, my first CHL goal pleased me just as much because it was a product of the extra effort I brought to every game:

Midway through the first period, a defenceman collected the puck and shifted around me, heading towards the blue line. Normally, that defenceman wouldn't have to worry about the forward behind him, because most in that position take a wide, lazy turn before heading back towards the play. Coaches hate this because it wastes valuable time. Through years of sideboards training, I did a quick stop, reversed my direction and accelerated in hot pursuit of the defenceman.

Before he reached his blue line, he hesitated. He was looking to make a pass that wasn't there, and he held the puck longer than he should have. He wasn't thinking of me as he searched for a second option. That split-second hesitation allowed me to catch him from behind, lift his stick, steal the puck and quickly reverse direction. I accelerated on the breakaway so quickly, I was on top of the goalie before he knew it. He stopped my first shot, but the rebound landed at his right pad and I banged it home.

"Saunders is a story by himself," the *Fort Worth Star–Telegram* reported, adding:

> *The first black player ever to compete in the Central Hockey League and one of a very small group to play professional at any level, the 23-year old graduate of Western Michigan not only matched Stan Gulutzan's early goal, he scored what proved to be the winner during Cincinnati's three-goal eruption in the final stanza.*

I don't know how accurate that statement was about my breaking the CHL's colour barrier. Former Dallas Black Hawks forward Dirk Graham also played in the league that season, so it was either him or me. But now you can see why I related to Willie O'Ree. At almost every road game, fans and opponents would remind me that they had never seen a Black

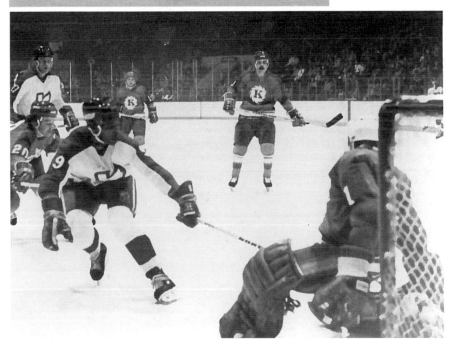

John (*left*) and I (*right*) were reunited in Kalamazoo briefly. Here, we're with coach Bill Neal (*second from left*) and Neil Smith (*second from right*). Who could have guessed that, years later, John would be broadcasting the game when Neil won the Stanley Cup with the New York Rangers? (Courtesy of WMU Archives and Regional History Collections)

Get the goalie leaning to my forward hand and stickhandle to the back hand while slipping the puck "one-handed" into the area that the goalie just vacated. I see this play being done today, but not many pulled it off back in the day. (*Kalamazoo Gazette*)

BERNIE SAUNDERS

The most pleasant surprise of the Cincinnati Stingers' season has been the play of Bernie Saunders. Throughout the first two months of the campaign Stinger coach Al Karlander has been sure of one thing: that Bernie Saunders will patrol his right wing and fill the net.

After grabbing early-season scoring honors for both the Stingers and the CHL, Bernie Saunders has caught the eye of many people in professional hockey. After all, Bernie is the first to admit that the jump from a "small college" such as Western Michigan to professional hockey is not easy. However, Bernie realizes that scoring has never been a problem for his game.

"Every level of hockey to which I've moved, I've always been able to score," Bernie noted. "It's always taken a period of time to adjust. For instance, I wasn't a big scorer my first year of college, but things turned around my second year and I was the team's leading scorer."

Saunders may never have gained a college degree had it not been for the foresignt of his father who insist-

ed on an education instead of junior hockey for young Bernie. The decision turned out to be a wise one as Saunders closed his collegiate career as the second leading scorer in Western Michigan history.

An invitation to Quebec's training camp followed but Bernie soon realized just how big that aforementioned jump is in reality.

"I knew that it would be hard for me to jump right into the NHL," Bernie admitted. "But, I hoped for a longer look. Quebec simply wanted me to come to the minors and prove what I could do when given a chance. Hopefully, I've gained their attention."

Although Bernie didn't make the Nordique roster in training camp, he still traveled a circuitous route before arriving in Cincinnati. Saunders was first sent to Syracuse by Quebec where he would work with Michel Parizeau, the Nordiques' coach in Syracuse. However, when the season rolled around, Bernie was riding a plane to meet the Stingers in Oklahoma City.

Naturally, there was some apprehension on Bernie's part about leaving Syracuse, but that was quickly resolved by his play with the Stingers.

"I had just started to settle in Syracuse when I was told I would be coming to Cincinnati," Saunders said. "I had come to know all of the players and the coach fairly well and thought my future was there. But, when Quebec sent more players there, I knew my playing time would be cut.

"So, when I came here, I just put my nose to the grindstone knowing I'd get some playing time. I'm very happy in Cincinnati and would rather be here than any other city in the CHL or AHL."

Saunders' torrid scoring pace has gained notoriety with the player changes endured by the Stingers. Bernie hasn't yet had the chance to work with steady linemates and knows the situation is frustrating for the Stinger players and management.

"Playing with Dave Debol was so easy that it was an adjustment when Dave was recalled," Bernie noted. "But, Byron Shutt and I work well together because we both come from the forechecking style of hockey played in college. And, Dale Yakiwchuk, our center, is a fine hockey player, so it shouldn't be much longer before we put it together."

Like any professional athlete Bernie's pride has been tested by the Stingers' recent hard times. Although it's sometimes difficult to remain an optimist during a slump, Bernie Saunders sees the light at the end of the tunnel.

"Losing grows on you and nobody on the team enjoys it," Bernie noted. "But, we have a good nucleus so as soon as we all settle down and play our game, instead of pressing, we'll be all right."

I had several feature articles done on me wherever I travelled. This one was done in the Cincinnati Stingers' program. (*Faceoff*, **official publication of the Cincinnati Stingers**)

Top: John (*second from right*) was good friends with Jim Valvano (*left*), the famed North Carolina State basketball coach. We enjoyed annual golf trips before Jim's tragic death. I loved trading coaching philosophy with "V," as he was one of the most intelligent people I have ever met. Here, we're with Mel Sole (*centre*) and Don Harrison (*right*). **(Courtesy of Bernie Saunders)**

Above left: "*Le Petit Noir.*" My first year in Junior B playing for the Châteauguay Wings under Jacques Demers. (*Châteauguay Sun*)

Above right: Mom, aka Hurricane Molly, holding her two rambunctious boys.
(Courtesy of Bernie Saunders)

Top left: Jonathan and Shawn (being held by John) were smitten with hockey from the crib. Jonathan played at Miami University and Shawn at the University of Massachusetts. Andrew (who I am holding in the back) charted his own path away from hockey, having been dragged to practices and games. **(Courtesy of Bernie Saunders)**

Top right: I practised the Guy Lafleur slapshot for years, and it was a key element in my scoring tool kit. **(Courtesy of Bernie Saunders)**

Middle: When I signed with the Kalamazoo Wings of the International Hockey League in 1981, I told J.P. LeBlanc that I expected to score 50 goals and 50 assists. Injuries plagued the year, but I enjoyed helping Brent Jarrett win the IHL scoring title. **(*Kalamazoo Gazette*, photograph by Duane Scheel)**

Bottom: When I made it to the NHL, it just felt like it was where I was supposed to be. Until it didn't. **(Courtesy of the NHL)**

Top: John started off as the goalie for State Farm Insurance. I cried in the stands until the coach let me join the team a year early. (Courtesy of Bernie Saunders)

Bottom left: John enjoyed all his assignments at ESPN, but none better than those with the hockey crew. Here he is with Darren Pang, Steve Levy and Barry Melrose. (Courtesy of Bernie Saunders)

Bottom right: For John's 60th birthday present, I commissioned a talented Canadian Black artist, Taha Clayton, to paint this piece, which I titled *Celebration of Life*. The painting represents how John and I enjoyed success in life as a result of playing hockey. The patches on our jerseys are to remember Gail. (Courtesy of Bernie Saunders)

John helped build ESPN into the sports goliath that it is. The network loves to throw a party. I was his "date" at the ESPYs one year. (Courtesy of Bernie Saunders)

My three sons. What is the measure of a man? You are looking at it. My boys (*from left to right*), Andrew, Jonathan, (me) and Shawn, make me so proud, each in his own unique way. (Courtesy of Bernie Saunders)

The worst year of my career was 1980–81. The Nordiques didn't have an AHL farm team, so players like me were loaned to Halifax, where I watched from the bench as the Montreal Canadiens' Guy Carbonneau and Dan Daoust blossomed. (Nova Scotia Voyageurs handout photo)

My workouts were ahead of their time and became the subject of a couple of feature articles. (Courtesy of Bernie Saunders)

Some people ask me why I didn't follow in John's footsteps after hockey— the Gumbel brothers did fairly well. Simple answer: I sucked. Speaking has never been my forte. Put me in front of a camera, and I get worse. Here I am as the expert analyst on WMU hockey with good friend and legendary broadcaster Robin Hook.
(Courtesy of Bernie Saunders)

I held a surprise 60th birthday party for John in Manhattan. John could never let me one-up him; he countered with a surprise 60th birthday party for me in the Bahamas. Everyone wore "Bernie Puck'in Saunders" T-shirts. **(Courtesy of Bernie Saunders)**

Above: Patented play: Chuck Durocher hit me with another lateral pass at the goalmouth, right on my tape for me to deflect the puck into a wide-open net. Notice the ice spray: I'm stopping (thanks, Sherry) so I can be in position to bury the rebound, if there is one. There weren't many.
(Courtesy of Bernie Saunders)

Right: I never felt comfortable during my second stint in the NHL, with Michel Bergeron breathing down my neck. That's me in the middle of the picture.

Left: My Hall of Fame photo, which hangs from the rafters at WMU's Lawson Ice Arena. **(Courtesy of Bernie Saunders)**

Bottom: John, our close cousin Loretta, Gail and me. John and I tricked the girls into standing as our goalposts as we played ball hockey in the basement. The girls thought they were playing hockey with the boys as John would narrate, "Oh, he dinged one off the goalpost!" **(Courtesy of Bernie Saunders)**

I played on the Howard S. Billings junior varsity team at the same time as I played for the Châteauguay Midget travel team. Gerry Magee, on the left, was one of my best friends. (Courtesy of Bernie Saunders)

Jacques Demers (*centre, with arms raised*) gets a job with the Chicago Cougars in the newly formed WHA. Jacques was our coach and neighbour, and he consulted Dad on the idea of living in the United States. (*Châteauguay Sun*)

Willie O'Ree, John Saunders and P.K. Subban. P.K. could have led the NHL into the "dark ages," but his expressiveness has been squelched at every turn. He could have helped the other players line their pockets with cash. Ask any professional golfer.
(Courtesy of ESPN Images; photo by Scott Clarke)

Jonathan (*middle row, second from the left*) helped found a hockey program in Nairobi, Kenya, that was eventually showcased in a Tim Hortons commercial. I posed for a picture with them when I visited. (I'm in the back row, third from the right.) Could hockey ever look like this? (Courtesy of Bernie Saunders)

Top: This was the turnover that started WMU on the way to our biggest win of my freshman year. I stole the puck in the neutral zone, reversed direction and generated a two-on-one with Kipp Acton (22). That's Ken Morrow, another freshman, behind Acton, getting caught up ice. Bob Gardiner later tallied the historic overtime goal.
(Courtesy of WMU Archives and Regional History Collections)

Left: Pam had a massive stroke in 2016 and I have become her caregiver. She is one of the bravest people that I know, and I thank her for her love and companionship.
(Courtesy of Bernie Saunders)

There weren't many collegians graduating to the NHL when I first attended WMU. I became the first Bronco. But many would follow, including Mike Eastwood (*second from left*), Keith Jones (*middle*) and Glenn Healy (*right*). Jamal Mayers (*not pictured*) was the third Black player at WMU behind me and John (*second from right*). **(Courtesy of WMU Archives and Regional History Collections)**

The Black Flower unleashing another patented slapshot. **(Photo by johngilroyphotography.com)**

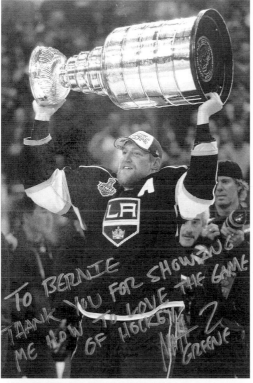

Two of my players won the Stanley Cup with the L.A. Kings: Scott Parse and Matt Greene. Mike "Doc" Emrick made me feel like part of the celebration as he announced that fact while Matt (*pictured*) hoisted the coveted trophy. **(Getty Images)**

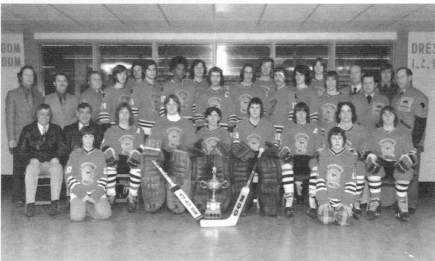

Sherry Bassin (*back row, far left*) had a team philosophy when he coached the Pickering Panthers that racism should be a "we" problem. Although it embarrassed me, I enjoyed the support of my teammates. Imagine if Akim Aliu's teammates refused to play when his coach called him the N-word for playing rap music? That's what hockey needs. That's what the world needs. **(Courtesy of Bernie Saunders)**

My boys from the Ackley Dorm sixth floor: (*front row, second from the left*) Matt Dietz, me, Kipp Acton and Mike Brown. **(Courtesy of WMU Archives and Regional History Collections)**

I felt I had to do something for myself to signify my disappointment with my hockey experiences. My resolution was to raise the Black Power salute every time I scored as my silent protest against the game. I'm on the far left. (*Kalamazoo Gazette*)

hockey player before. I heard the typical unoriginal filth on nearly every stop.

I just blocked it out. From day one, I became the star of the Stingers. Karlander played me on a line with two other collegians in the New England Whalers' system, Dave Debol from the University of Michigan and Byron Shutt of Bowling Green. Before long, teams were matching lines and shadowing us.

"The Debol line with Shutt and the league's leading scorer, Bernie Saunders, already has caused the opposition to make adjustments," wrote the *Cincinnati Enquirer*.

Tuesday night, Fort Worth coach Ron Ullyot wanted to put NHL veteran center Rey Comeau on Debol and let Willie Trognitz chase Saunders. There was a lot of jockeying of lines when Saunders tied the score at 1–1 after 12 minutes of play. "Hey, that's fine with me," Karlander said of the matchups. "If he (Ullyot) wants to turn one of his best scorers (Comeau) into a checker, that's great. And Trognitz will chase Saunders all night."

For most of my time in Cincinnati, I led the CHL in scoring—until I suffered the knee injury resulting from my messed-up groin. That slowed me down.

I also played against my second Black opponent, although I didn't know then that the light-skinned Graham was Black. In one 5–4 win over Dallas at Riverfront Coliseum, I scored a hat trick and Graham had a goal and an assist. A CHL game dominated by two Blacks . . . and I didn't realize it until years later, when Graham showed up as the 10th Black to play in the NHL.

Dirk went on to an illustrious 12-year NHL career with the Minnesota North Stars and Chicago Blackhawks. I loved his hard-working, honest approach to the game. He played five seasons in the CHL and IHL before getting his long-overdue NHL opportunity. And he made the most of it.

I've never talked to Dirk, but I wonder if there were nights when his Blackness went unnoticed becasue of his light skin. I don't want to minimize his experience, but there is an advantage to being fair-skinned. Being dark-skinned, I rarely got a night off on the road from my colour. Unlike Graham—or goalie Grant Fuhr, who wore a mask—I stood out like a charcoal snowball and faced racial hatred at nearly every stop . . . even sometimes during a home game.

My SECOND BRUSH with the U.S. Olympic Team came in my first month with Cincy. As in 1976, the 1980 team was a collection of amateurs just hoping not to get slaughtered by the competition at Lake Placid. Team USA arranged to play 18 games against CHL competition, home-and-home sets against each of the nine teams in the league. Head coach Herb Brooks insisted that the games count towards the CHL standings so that "the professionals didn't take a night off" against his young collegians.

Even before their Miracle on Ice, it was clear they were a talented bunch. In these 18 games against pros, they went 14–3–1. They were already drawing a lot of attention among the country's hockey purists when they arrived in Cincinnati on November 14, 1979.

Having recently graduated from WMU, and now playing on a line with two other young collegians, I was prepared for this game to be played at a blistering pace. And it was. Our line was able to match the young, high-tempo national team stride for stride. It was hockey at its finest, exactly what Brooks's team needed to prepare for the Olympics. He had his players flying, and we were every bit as quick. All these years later, I remember the night, but not because it was a beautifully skated game in which Team USA beat us in overtime.

I remember it because of one play, one moment, still embedded in my soul.

On this particular play, I lined up Mark Johnson, the U.S.A.'s most talented forward, and I punished him with a bruising bodycheck. Johnson was an amazing talent, but he was tiny. If you saw him with his helmet off during the national anthem, you would swear someone's younger brother had slipped out onto the ice.

Johnson had just distributed a pass, and had taken another stride when I arrived, perhaps an instant late. He was relaxing, not expecting to be hit after he passed the puck.

It was one of those plays that bordered on a penalty, but no call was made. He crashed to the ice in a heap and was not a happy camper as he stumbled back to his bench. Having witnessed the scene, Brooks jumped up on the bench, placed one foot on the dasher boards, pointed directly at me and, with the veins in his neck bulging, shouted a series of insults that included a racial epithet. All these years later, I am not comfortable sharing the specifics of the incident.

I will say this: I had no problem with Brooks being angry. I had a big problem with what he said.

Here's the thing: Herb Brooks became a national hero, a giant in the eyes of the hockey world when the 1980 Olympic Team won the gold medal in Lake Placid. His premature death in a 2003 automobile accident at the age of 66 was a tragic, sad moment.

Nobody wants to pick on a legend, especially posthumously. It also happened 40 years ago during a much different time, when intimidation was a big part of hockey culture. But I also believe you must own up to your own stink. It happened, and it hurt. As I followed Team USA's triumphant march to the gold medal, all I could think about was Herb Brooks with his foot on the dasher boards, pointing his finger, spewing hate because I had thrown a borderline-late check.

I prefer Badger Bob over Herb Brooks.

Let's discuss this right now. That doesn't make him a racist, and I am not calling him one. I want to emphasize that. If someone murders, then they are a murderer. But I do not think that, just because Herb Brooks used a disgusting, bigoted language, he should be immediately and permanently branded a racist. He was racist in that moment, but I have no idea how the man lived his life. It could have been the only time in his life that bigotry percolated to the surface.

I'm not letting Mr. Brooks off the hook, either. I didn't know him, and I just don't know his personal story. What I do know is this: Herb Brooks was a fierce competitor, a legendary hockey coach with a brilliant hockey mind.

On November 14, 1979, in an exhibition game on his way to history, he took things too far. He treated me like dirt. I'll bet he boarded the team bus that night and thought nothing of what he said. It was a different time, and nobody knew how to deal with me.

I entertained the idea of not including this one essay in the book, because I feared that my story would be defined by this one chapter. If that happens, I will have failed. But I decided that I have to be honest with myself. The reality is that Brooks was not the first coach to spew racial obscenities from an opposing team's bench. He was not the last. The only reason why this incident is momentous to me is because it won't go away. The experience is forever green in my consciousness. Three months later, Team USA shocked the world in Lake Placid. Their inexplicable victory saturated the news for months. Today, the media commemorates the Miracle on Ice every February, which forces me to relive my exchange with Brooks in Cincinnati—over and over and over.

I moved on with my life and rarely think about my hockey career. But this incident is a trigger. A key to the catacomb that unlocks the passageway to my visceral memory, returning my consciousness back not only to that night, but to my entire career. It forces me right back to the torrential downpour of angry fanatics pounding the glass, mimicking primate gestures, spewing the N-word. It is a nightmarish curse.

Do you . . . believe . . . in miracles?

Ugh.

CHAPTER 29

Birmingham Bull

A week after the loss to the U.S. Olympians, a few of us were hanging out in a restaurant one morning on the road when Paul Stewart sat down, beaming.

It was obvious from the huge grin on his expressive Irish face that something great had happened. Stewie loved to yap, loved to tell stories, and boy, did he have one on this day.

"I've been called up!" he shouted. "We're in Boston."

The night before, the Nordiques and Bruins had fought a few times in Quebec City, and now Stewie was being asked to provide a little pugilistic artillery for the rematch.

Stewie couldn't have dreamed of a better NHL debut.

He was born in the Boston suburb of Dorchester, Massachusetts, and grew up in an Irish Catholic section of the city called Jamaica Plain. Stewcat dreamed of an NHL career watching games as a kid in the old Boston Garden, and after punching and gooning his way around a variety of minor leagues for five years, that's exactly where the Nordiques asked him to show up.

As we ate breakfast and gossiped about the call-up, Stewie grew more animated. He planned to make his presence felt in the Hub, and he promised an NHL enforcer's version of a hat trick.

"I'm gonna fight O'Reilly. I'm gonna fight Secord. I'm gonna fight Jonathan," he exclaimed. We all laughed at Stewie's hyperbole. Terry O'Reilly, Al Secord and Stan Jonathan were three of the Bruins' toughest forwards and three of their better players. I was just happy to see Stewie getting his first NHL shot . . . especially in his hometown.

I wanted to know what happened in Boston the morning after Stewie's first game, so I grabbed a newspaper and searched for the NHL game summaries. The Bruins had beaten the Nordiques, 7–4. And Stewcat was splattered all over the box score: Paul Stewart and Terry O'Reilly, two minutes each for delay of game at 11:54 of the second period . . . Paul Stewart and Terry O'Reilly, five minutes each for fighting at 14:44 of the second period . . . Paul Stewart, five minutes for fighting, and Stan Jonathan, 10 minutes for deliberate injury, at 3:40 of the third period . . . Paul Stewart and Al Secord, five minutes for fighting at 18:37 of the third period.

At breakfast with us the day before, Stewie had pre-selected his smorgasbord choices for his meal at the Garden. And he got them all.

I was shocked when he moved across the aisle to become an NHL referee, but I guess it made sense. He knew the rule book better than anybody, having broken every one.

I love Stewie. He was a friend and a mentor during my early CHL days and we often roomed together. Unbeknownst to me until years later, the Nordiques brass asked him to keep an eye on me as we travelled to destinations below the Mason-Dixon line. He doubled as somewhat of a personal bodyguard. And I needed one.

The CHL was awesome. In most of the minor leagues, players endure long, gruelling bus rides to grey, unexciting cities like New Haven, Connecticut, and Binghamton, New York. The CHL travelled by air to appealing destinations like Dallas and Oklahoma City. Cincinnati itself is a major-league city. If you had to be relegated to the minors, this was the place to be.

Weeks after my arrival in the Queen City, we flew off on another road trip. The itinerary included Birmingham, Alabama, way down in the Deep South. If you study American history from a Southern perspective—from below the Mason-Dixon line—you learn about the Jim Crow experience. You learn that Blacks were once seen more as slaves and possessions than as human beings.

As a Black trailblazer, I steeled myself for my first game in Birmingham, our next stop. We actually were scheduled to play the Bulls in consecutive games over the weekend.

The games had an established storyline. The year before, during the WHA's last gasp, Tony McKegney had signed a huge contract with Birmingham. McKegney had completed his successful junior career with the Kingston Canadians, and as a highly touted prospect had been selected in the second round of the 1978 NHL amateur draft by the Buffalo Sabres.

He figured to be the first Black star in the NHL, but he opted for the Bulls, who were signing a slew of young players for big money. McKegney's WHA contract was for $75,000 a year and a $75,000 signing bonus.

But soon after he signed Tony, the Bulls' owner, Johnny F. Bassett, decided to renege on the deal. According to Bassett, the season-ticket holders revolted.

"I'm just not gonna put out that kind of dough for players

anymore," Bassett was quoted as saying back in June of 1978. "Plus, I had a lot of season-ticket holders calling up and complaining because he is black. It is the most negative reaction I've had since I've been in Birmingham. I didn't know it was here anymore. It's very discouraging. I gave him permission to go to Buffalo. I'd rather he go there than come here."

McKegney accepted his release and signed with the Sabres. "I never really considered my colour as being a major factor in hockey," he said when he agreed to terms with Buffalo. "I thought all those feelings were over with 10 years ago."

I always thought this was an unfortunate quote, given my experiences, but according to the book *Breaking the Ice: The Black Experience in Professional Hockey* by Cecil Harris, on top of everything else, Tony claims that he was being misquoted on the topic.

Guess who became the first Black player to play in Birmingham following the Tony McKegney controversy? Yep.

The Stingers' front office was aware of the risk and felt it important enough to hold a preparatory meeting with me before the first game.

My imagination conjured up visions of a sniper gunning me down from high in the balcony. I always got a little jittery before games, but this night was different. My life could be in jeopardy. The shit started to fly the second I appeared in warm-ups. Fans began banging the glass and kicking the boards as I skated past. I was really scared.

And then something strange happened. My line scored . . . and the highly partisan Birmingham crowd erupted in a standing ovation, a shockingly strange version of Southern hospitality that I could not understand. I'd just made a nice play against their team, and they were *cheering* me? Surreal.

Later in the game, I got a repeat performance: standing ovation number two. On a night I feared I might be joining my maker, I was instead being treated like a rock star—well, a country and western superstar, given the setting.

As often happened after road games, we visited the local watering hole, where we mingled with the friendly natives. And they explained to me what had just happened.

The Tony McKegney incident was appalling to many of them. They claimed John Bassett never received "hundreds" of letters from the Birmingham season-ticket holders. Maybe he received a few, but certainly nothing close to what was portrayed. These fans were disgusted at being depicted as bigots, and they wanted to prove their innocence. They wanted to make me feel as welcome as possible, even though it meant cheering an opponent.

That night restored some optimism to my psyche. As difficult a journey as this was becoming, it was one of many heartwarming stories of humanity. There was one other moment from this season that was seared into my brain, and it was anything but heartwarming.

I remember the assassinations of Martin Luther King Jr. and President Kennedy, even as a small child living in Canada. I remember 9/11, when the Twin Towers fell. And I will never forget December 3, 1979: the night of the Who concert at Riverfront Coliseum.

Because the rock band was scheduled to play the Coliseum that night, we were forced to practise that morning at a seldom-used indoor/outdoor rink on the Kentucky side of the Ohio River. We had a light skate and were free for the rest of the day. I wasn't a huge Who fan, so I decided to stay home.

Later that night, the tragic news came over the television:

11 people had been killed at the concert. The problem was that nearly 15,000 of the 18,000 seats had been sold as general admission, and people were lined up on a landing, awaiting admittance. When the Who appeared on stage for a pre-concert sound check, the fans thought the concert was starting.

Because it wasn't, the doors weren't unlocked yet—except for two that were inadvertently open, which produced a human stampede as the excited fans rushed to obtain a preferred seat.

People fell to the ground in the chaotic rush, and some were literally crushed. Our trainers told us that our locker room became a sort of MASH unit tending to severely injured concertgoers, some of whom died of asphyxiation.

The band completed its sound check and was never informed of the tragic events. The concert went on as scheduled, despite the calamity. But the Cincinnati City Council wouldn't get fooled again. Just 24 days later, it passed a new law banning "festival seating" and "general admission seating."

To this day, it sickens me to think back to that city's horribly painful night. The idea of human beings trampled under the weight of their own, and then having the personal experience of entering a dressing room that a day earlier had been transformed into a morgue.

We are supposed to be an intelligent species.

CHAPTER 30

Black Is the New Orange

Christmas break was approaching, and I was still among the top scorers in the CHL. My groin had slowed me a little, but the big story around Cincinnati was the health of the Stingers. The team's relegation to the CHL from the WHA had failed to inspire fan interest. Published reports suggested the organization was hemorrhaging money. We were attracting fewer than 2,000 fans per game into the Coliseum, which seated 17,556 for hockey.

It wasn't working, and the story of the team disbanding leaked the day of a game against Oklahoma City. We knew the rumour was true. Guys had their cars packed, ready to pull out of Cincy immediately after the game. We were lame ducks, and a paltry 949 fans witnessed a 10–1 drubbing that preceded officials from the franchise bluntly announcing the team was closing its doors.

The Cincinnati Stingers were defunct at 11–21–1, having played only 33 of their 80 scheduled games.

Gilles Leger, the Nordiques' director of player personnel, flew to Cincinnati to talk to us in person. After he congratulated me on a great start to my career, he told me I was being reassigned back to Syracuse, where Firebirds management was eager to add me back to their roster.

Leger explained that the CHL's style of play matched the NHL's Campbell Conference, and that the Nordiques wanted to see how I would do in the tighter-checking AHL, whose style more closely resembled the Wales Conference, where Quebec played. He said I needed to prove I could score in the AHL the way I had in the CHL. And if I could, they would promote me to the NHL.

I packed up the 280Z on December 20, 1979, for the long 580-mile drive to Syracuse, where the Firebirds were playing the New Brunswick Hawks the next night. This trip reminded me of the day I drove to WMU to start my college career: a cold, damp day with me battling the flu. I felt miserable as I drove on this dark, drizzling night, but I was eager to take the next step in my hockey journey.

That 580-mile drive took forever.

The Firebirds played in the Onondaga County War Memorial, a monument to the two world wars. Built in the centre of the city, it was a relic even back in the 1970s. It was a rudimentary multi-purpose building in a colourless blue-collar town. The War Memorial shouted "minor league" so loudly that it was the perfect backdrop for many of the scenes in the quintessential minor-league hockey movie, *Slap Shot*.

The Firebirds' uniforms weren't so colourless. Did you ever get drunk late at night, wolf down a midnight pizza and heave it all back in the toilet the next morning? The colours that would have floated in your bowl must have inspired the orange, green, yellow and white atrocities that made it look like the circus just came to town when the Firebirds hit the ice.

The next day, I was ready for my AHL debut. I pulled one of

those gaudy jerseys over my head, wearing the number 12 I had worn in my freshman year at WMU. Make no mistake: numbers are important to players. I had worn 20 in Cincy, the only time I was handed a number that had no significance to me.

There was a buzz in the air in the War Memorial when I returned, since my controversial preseason departure to Cincinnati had been met with criticism. I scored on my first shift, starred in the game and had the fans chanting my name.

Here's how the *Syracuse Post-Standard* critiqued my AHL debut:

SAUNDERS A HIT FOR FIREBIRDS

A Star Is Born: *Judy Garland starred in the original movie, Barbra Streisand took the top role in the recent remake. If last night was any indication, Bernie Saunders might be the leading man if a third version of the film is ever made.*

The Syracuse Firebirds debuted their newest hockey player last night, much the way Hollywood premieres its blockbuster movies during the Christmas season.

Needless to say, he was a big hit. Right winger Saunders arrived yesterday from Cincinnati, where he had led the now-defunct Stingers in scoring. Donning a Firebird uniform for the first time, he played to rave reviews against New Brunswick. His two-goal, one-assist performance combined with Gary Carr's sparkling effort in goal, helped spin a 4–1 Syracuse victory. By the end of the evening, the War Memorial crowd of 2,133 was cheering Saunders on every shift.

If anyone theorized that Cincinnati was a fluke, I quickly disproved the notion. I GAGed (goal a game), scoring 11 goals in my first 11 games in Syracuse, a hotter pace than any of the AHL scoring leaders midway through the season.

Playing hockey is like breathing to me. It is the only time in my life when I feel totally at peace. I found the lifestyle adjustments around the games much more difficult.

The day-to-day routine in the minor leagues was predictable: one mid-week game, usually Wednesday, and two or three between Friday and Sunday. The alcohol almost always flowed following a game night. Mondays usually were off-days or limited to a very light skate, with time spent mending on a trainer's table. Most players shot over to the local lounge for "lunch" after practice. Pool, darts, Pac-Man, beer. And lunch often rolled into dinner, and the day was capped with more nightlife.

At first, it was fun, like being on vacation. But a few weeks into the routine, I began asking myself, "Is this it?" Alcohol and hockey became almost synonymous.

I hate to sound arrogant, but I felt a little "above" the fray. After all, I had obtained a college degree and craved mental stimulation. Many teammates were playing a much different game, gambling on their futures. Most lacked a college education and had placed all their proverbial eggs in one basket. I felt I had packed a parachute, but I could hear an audible time clock ticking in the background. If I let too much time expire following graduation, I would become much less marketable in the business world.

I was 24. I didn't want my value to depreciate.

I promised I'd give it three years. Instead of drinking beer all afternoon, I began reading more, pledging to read two books per month. In a bus league like the AHL, I had plenty of time to fulfill that goal. On one bus ride to Springfield,

Massachusetts, I was reading the Max Ehrlich thriller *The Reincarnation of Peter Proud,* an eerie story of a murder and subsequent reincarnation.

Ehrlich was describing a bridge scene in Springfield just as our bus drove across the actual bridge. A shiver shot up and down my spine as I heard someone from the back of the bus yell, "Hey, has anyone read *The Reincarnation of Peter Proud?*"

Reality and fiction merged, making it feel as though I was a character in the book.

I was not extremely social in Cincinnati. The person I spent the most time with was Paul Stewart, who took me under his wing. When the Stingers folded, I was assigned to Syracuse and he was sent to Birmingham. Although Stewie and I were apart, I sensed a camaraderie that had not existed in Cincy because there weren't players from four different franchises on the roster.

Although Rob Garner had been one of my teammates in Cincinnati, it wasn't until we got to Syracuse that he and I began establishing a friendship. I told him on one bus ride that my biggest challenge as a rookie was in the kitchen. My mom made all the meals at home, and I ate all my meals for four years in the WMU cafeteria, so I had never learned how to cook.

Garner insisted that I buy a set of pots and pans, which I never did in Cincinnati. He taught me how to broil meat and how to bake a potato. I was a quick learner. Following this culinary training, I was inspired. For my next pre-game meal, I enjoyed a well-done porterhouse steak.

I was very proud of myself, and very fired up for the game.

The player benches at the War Memorial were undersized, not fit for the bulky frames of professional hockey players.

During the first period, I heard one annoyed teammate ask, "What reeks?"

I smelled this awful stench, too, but could not place it. Later in the period, another teammate groaned, "It stinks in here. I think it's garlic."

At that moment, the source of the odour hit me. It was me. Chef Bernie had been a little too liberal with the seasoning on his steak, and once I started sweating in the game, the stench from my digested meal poured from my pores. I never confessed, but I did consider this culinary lesson number two: you know you've used too much garlic when you can smell your own stink.

What didn't stink was my new line. Head coach Duane Rupp put me on a unit with Roland Cloutier and Louis Sleigher, both promising French-Canadian players. Sleigher's English was pretty good, Cloutier's was limited, but our communication on the ice was superb. They were already playing well together when I arrived, so I adapted to their style.

That was one of my strengths. Coaches liked the fact that I would modify my style to play with anyone, without affecting my production. That's a big reason why I found it easier to play the higher I climbed up the hockey mountain. I felt I could play off anyone.

Playing with Debol and Shutt in Cincy was the best. Dave played centre while Byron and I flanked the wings. But both were called up at times and I had to adapt to another centre, Dale Yakiwchuk—we called him Yickity Yak. Yak was a big-time talent with minuscule focus. He had a completely different approach on the ice than Debol. Nevertheless, I adjusted to Yak and we thrived.

Now, in Syracuse, Rollie was perfect for me, too, a slick

left-handed centre who always thought pass before shoot. As his right wing, I learned to get myself open around the net, knowing he would somehow find me—sometimes in spectacular fashion.

Louis was a right-handed shot who preferred the left side. He had one of the strongest moves to the net from the top of the circle you'll ever want to see. When he decided to turn the corner towards the net, there was no stopping him.

Around the league, word quickly spread about the Firebirds' new line.

"Sleigher scored three goals and assisted on goals by Cloutier and Saunders as the Birds put on an offensive show resembling the 'Shootout at the OK Corral,'" the *Syracuse Post-Standard* reported. "Sleigher and Cloutier both finished the night with five points, while Saunders ended up with three. It was a masterful performance by the newly formed trio, which could end up being one of the most potent lines in the American Hockey League."

Cloutier and I worked so well together, we were called upon to kill penalties. And as I had done with Dan Stothers at WMU, Rollie and I turned the penalty kill into an offensive exercise. Cloutier never made it to the NHL, which is a shame because he was such a great puck distributor. He could have made it if he had ever been paired with the proper NHL linemates. He was tiny, but he had a heart of gold. Sleigher was eventually promoted to the Nordiques and later landed with the Boston Bruins.

Playing with those guys, an obvious pattern was developing. Wherever I played, my line became one of the top trios in the league. And while I was playing an offensive role, I was still highly trusted in defensive situations.

Everything was going great until February 3, 1980. I was still nursing my right groin, which I'd first injured in training camp. The injury had stalled my hot start in Cincinnati and was not going away. And in our game that night at the War Memorial against the Rochester Americans, I injured my left knee again. The doctor diagnosed it as a cartilage tear and prescribed surgery. I would be out for the rest of the year. Devastating news.

I stumbled around on crutches for a few days, but after a while, I found I could put weight on the injured side. I've always hated how crutches rip apart your armpits, so I ditched them and endured a tender limp. I reported to the orthopaedic surgeon's office for a pre-op visit the day of the surgery, and when I hobbled in unaided, he asked, "Where are your crutches?"

"I trashed them," I replied.

He was shocked. If I could walk without crutches, he said, then no surgery would be performed on that day. And he cancelled my operation.

I have always appreciated his decision. Surgeons make a living by cutting; that's what they get paid to do. But this wonderful doctor was not about to operate on me if he saw me moving the way I was, without crutches.

Remember, MRIs were in their infancy in 1980. Less invasive arthroscopic surgery was still experimental. Had my surgeon operated, he would have had to cut my knee completely open, through muscle and tissue, to repair a tear in my cartilage. He would have left me with railroad tracks on my kneecap, and I would've faced a whole lot of extensive rehabilitative work in the months ahead.

Instead, I rehabbed my sore knee religiously beginning that day, and I was back on the ice less than two weeks later.

It was critical that I get back in the lineup, because life in the minors for a player can be strangely counterintuitive. Normally, a player would be rooting for his team to do well in his absence. But in the minors, everyone is trying to climb over everyone else to get to the next level.

While I was out rehabbing my knee, Porterhouse Rob Garner was thriving in my spot with Cloutier and Sleigher. I was happy for Rob but irritated that, when I finished rehab and fought my way back into the lineup, Coach Rupp kept Rob with Rollie and Louis together as a unit. Without question the right thing to do, as Rob had earned it.

Midway through my first game back, however, we were trailing and the team needed a boost. Rupp juggled our lines and put me back into my regular slot. From Jim Kosciolek of the *Syracuse Herald-Journal*:

> *Stymied by the absence of their injured hero for the past five home games, the Bernie Saunders Fan Club was out in full force at the War Memorial last night to welcome the popular right winger back. Saunders' personal booster organization even had a section-wide banner proclaiming its name. They chanted, "Ber-nie, Ber-nie, Ber-nie" most every time their man hit the ice. . . . Duly inspired, Saunders scored two goals and added one assist to help the Firebirds reach third place for the first time this season.*

I was back in the lineup, back on my line and back on track. My newfound celebrity produced another development, which was predictable to me: Firebirds crowds began to swell.

News of our exciting team and its Black star spread around town. Fans were drawn to my "take no prisoners" style, and the Bernie Saunders Fan Club was created in appreciation of my exciting way of playing. Between shifts, I could look up from the bench and see a throng of rabid fans in the right corner, with a banner spanning the entire War Memorial section: *Bernie Saunders Fan Club*.

Attendance began to spike, to more than 3,000 fans per game. One headline in the *Post-Standard* acknowledged what was happening in Central New York: "Saunders Has Big-Time Ice Appeal."

As I look back, I made a strategic error when I was a free agent. Had I signed with the right U.S.-based team, especially one with a large minority population, I believe I could have been a major hit . . . a marketing bonanza.

To be fair, I was not oblivious to this concept when I signed with Quebec. I had zero interest in making it to the NHL as a circus clown. Nonetheless, my popularity could have been a nice accessory had I succeeded the proper way in the right market. I honestly believe I could have helped advance the game in its efforts to appeal to a broader audience. We will never know.

What I do know is that when teams arrived in Syracuse, one of their top challenges was to slow my line down. When we faced the Springfield Indians one night in early March, the morning headline read, "Birds Scalp Indians in Wild Shootout, Sleigher, Saunders, Cloutier Pace 8–6 Triumph."

The age of the Black player is still off on the horizon. But this period brought the first sprinkling of talent. Ray Neufeld, another talented Black forward in his rookie season as a pro, scored for Springfield that night. Neufeld played more than 10 NHL seasons for Hartford, Winnipeg and Boston from 1980 until 1990.

Comparisons are unfair and fodder for sports talk radio, but as a rookie in 1979–80, Ray scored 23 goals in 73 AHL games. I scored 23 goals in 38 games. With his numbers, Ray got promoted to the NHL the very next season.

I was one of the hottest scorers in the AHL. The Bernie Saunders Fan Club was eagerly awaiting my first bite at the apple.

CHAPTER 31

Stairway to Heaven

My fan club didn't have to wait long.

It was March 18, 1980, when Firebirds general manager John DenHamer called me into the team's offices at the War Memorial. He had a smile on his face.

I was going to the Show.

DenHamer told me the Nordiques wanted me to fly to Chicago to join the team on its western road trip. The Nordiques were playing the Blackhawks on March 19, 1980, and I was expected to be in the lineup for my first NHL game.

The GM complimented me on my AHL success. He noted my point-per-game scoring pace, the best on the team, and the fact that my torrid pace had me among the league leaders. He noted my all-around play. "From the day you arrived," he said, "you've done everything the Nordiques asked. We hope you never come back."

I called my brother, John, shortly after I left DenHamer's office. After I conveyed the news, there was what had to be 30 seconds of silence. I don't have the vocabulary to express our feelings. We were so close, it felt like we'd both gotten the call. I cried. I could feel his tears through the phone.

All of Toronto could hear his pride when John reported my promotion on Citytv later that evening.

YOUR FIRST GAME is like your first kiss: it's something you remember forever. My NHL debut was in the historic and cavernous Chicago Stadium—the Madhouse on Madison. One of the best buildings in the league, against an "Original Six" team. I had grown up watching Blackhawks legends like Bobby Hull, Stan Mikita and Keith Magnuson.

Chicago Stadium's visiting dressing room was underground, behind the Blackhawks goal. To reach ice level and the ocean of ruby seats, we had to climb a steep flight of decrepit wooden stairs, battered from years of razor-sharp hockey blades gouging each tread. I remember my legs feeling like Jell-O, and I don't know how I made it to the top. I was extremely nervous, which was unusual for me. But this was it: the rungs led to my first game in the NHL. A dream fulfilled.

My first shot on goal was on Hall of Famer Tony Esposito. Tony is left-handed, meaning that, unlike the vast majority of NHL goalies, he wore his catching glove on his right hand. My marquee move was designed to hit the far side of the net past a goalie's blocker.

I remember skating down the boards the way I always did but failing to generate a full head of steam since it was late in my shift. I reached the top of the circle and fired a wrist shot towards the far post, since I lacked the time to rifle my patented slapshot. Esposito effortlessly gobbled up my shot and gazed back at me through the large, round eyeholes in his iconic white goalie mask as if to say, "Son, you are going to have to do a lot better than that here."

Nonetheless, it was my first NHL shot on goal.

The Blackhawks' uniforms are likely the most antiquated in sports. Beyond the team's culturally insensitive nickname, the red, white and black jerseys feature the head of a Native American in war paint. It is beyond offensive, and I think of my Indigenous buddies every time I see the jersey.

Throughout my debut, the Blackhawks' jersey might as well have been adorned with the profile of Uncle Ben. Several times when I motored past the Chicago bench, the N-word trailed in my wake. And it wasn't a lone voice.

You know how sports fans do the wave by jumping to their feet, section by section, and throwing their hands in the air? I was greeted with the verbal equivalent, from the Chicago bench. It felt like every Blackhawk chimed in, although I know it couldn't have been everyone. What made it hurt worse was the fact that two of the Blackhawks in the lineup, Terry Ruskowski and Rich Preston, were guys I had met the season before in Winnipeg, when I was welcomed so graciously.

I doubt those two were among the voices I heard that night. But I must admit I was shaken with the realization I would have to deal with such racism in the NHL. The incident itself didn't surprise me, as things like that routinely happened. But until this moment, I had naively believed it wouldn't happen once I reached the NHL.

I was probably highly sensitized by the fact I was playing my first game and reacted like a bride enduring rain on her wedding day. But when I climbed those stairs before the game, I felt like I was ascending to paradise. Afterwards, it felt like I had just crossed the Edmund Pettus Bridge.

The Blackhawks beat us, 5–2, in a hard-fought game. It was a disappointing loss for the Nordiques, who were engaged in a battle for a playoff spot with just a few games left. It was such a bittersweet moment for me because of the racial vitriol, but I acquitted myself well. The pace was notably faster than in the AHL, but I had no problem with the adjustment.

"Saunders pleasantly surprised me," Demers was quoted as saying in one of the French papers whose reporter travelled with the Nordiques. "But the loss is too bitter to find solace in his positive performance after a game like this."

Assistant coach André Boudrias was a little more expressive when asked about my debut.

"For me, I find it encouraging that a little guy shows up from nowhere, and for whom nothing has been easy since his beginnings in hockey," Boudrias said, "hockey being a sport reserved for whites. They certainly never shied away from constantly reminding him (of his race)."

Boudrias was paying respects to my struggle as a Black hockey player. His reference to "a little guy" was not referring to my size, but to the idea of my rapid ascension to the team from seemingly out of nowhere. As for me, I was happy with my performance but shaken by the astonishing jeers.

From Chicago, we flew to Denver and a game against the Colorado Rockies at McNichols Arena. Not only did I play well, but I was one of the best Nordiques on the ice in our 6–2 victory. On one play down low, I deked goalie Bill McKenzie and had him beat with a wide-open net staring me in the face. But I got hooked from behind and sent the puck clear across the empty net and off the far post.

I've had many a nightmare over that one. I couldn't know it at the time, but ringing one off that pipe was the closest I would come to scoring an NHL goal.

In the second period, Stewie got into it with a feisty forward named Bobby Schmautz. Stewie was in the lineup to keep an eye on Schmautz, who had a vendetta against our tiny, talented centre, Robbie Ftorck.

When Schmautz, who never did get to Ftorek in the game, jabbed the blade of his stick directly towards Stewie's eye, Stewie became livid. The referee and linesmen kept things in check, and both players were ushered to their respective penalty boxes. When they were released two minutes later, they re-engaged and started a dangerous stick-swinging exchange.

Stewie was making the point that you should never use your stick as recklessly as Schmautz had done when they first squared off minutes earlier. Eventually, the referees broke up the sword fight and both players were tossed with game misconducts. Stewie had done his job.

To leave the ice at McNichols, visiting teams had to skate across the ice from their bench and exit down a hallway. That T-shaped hallway came to a dead end, with the visitors' dressing room to the right and the Rockies' dressing room to the left. From my vantage point on the bench, I could see straight down the hall. When the officials escorted Schmautz off the ice, he walked down the hall and took a left towards his dressing room.

As I watched Stewie leaving next, I shouted to anyone within the sound of my voice, "Stewie is going to take a left!" Sure enough, instead of taking a right towards our locker room, he charged the other way. He wanted to settle the score with Schmautz.

Chaos ensued when both teams realized what was happening. Suddenly, I was in the middle of a bench-clearing brawl—under the stands. I had witnessed, and a few times been in the middle of, minor-league games where Stewie did similar things. For whatever reason, I always seemed to be an accomplice to Stewcat's mayhem.

A Western Michigan alum attended the game and stopped by to say hello afterwards. He said he had been hoping just to see me play a few shifts and was astonished to see me playing so much, and so well.

I knew I had shown well. The game was confirmation that I could not only play but thrive at this level. The reporter from *La Presse* in Montreal agreed:

> *No play on words intended, however, we did notice a bright light shine in the darkness; the performance of Bernie Saunders. He missed a few scoring opportunities and skated with ease as well. Maybe the best Nordique in the first period.*

For me, the most uncomfortable part of writing this book is the fear of sounding egomaniacal. This is especially true when describing something as subjective as my performance in a particular game. The press clippings are invaluable. After this game, the writer could have reported that I looked comfortable playing in my second game or something along those lines. Instead, he describes me as possibly the best player on our team in the first period and skating with ease.

I felt relaxed and believed I had finally arrived. To be fair, the Rockies were a weaker team, so let's not get too crazy. But the NHL never intimidated me. Plus, I had bad puck luck in this game. If my shot had been a fraction of an inch to the right, who knows how the story is written from there.

CHAPTER 32

Friendly Fire

I don't have a racist bone in my body."

As Blacks, we hear it all the time. A friend will "slip" and say something racist in front of us, and then quickly try to reel it back with this stale apology. That's one of the many complications of racism: it is multi-faceted and nuanced. Pure racists sometimes are the easiest to deal with. There are people who don't believe they are racist when in fact they are. And there are people who aren't racist but who commit racist acts. It goes on and on.

The main subject of this next story is a teammate I won't identify. I contacted him, seeking permission to use his name, and he respectfully declined. It's ironic that when you are a person of colour, you are sometimes forced into situations where, despite being offended, you're asked to protect the offender.

To tell you the truth, I understand the player's reticence, because it is unfair to apply today's standards to yesterday's ills. Wearing a blackface costume 25 years ago doesn't make you a racist. But neither does it absolve you from responsibility for something you did ages ago.

The paradox is, it becomes much more difficult to tell my story objectively as I attempt to protect as many perpetrators as possible.

But here goes . . .

When we landed in Los Angeles the day after our victory—and my stellar performance—in Denver, we had a day off. It was our only day off on this four-game, five-day trip.

Several of us went on an excursion, and there was a slip of the tongue that not only offended me but hurt me deeply. My teammate used the N-word in front of others, which stripped me of my humanity. The two of us discussed the offence later in the evening, but by then, we had started drinking, and I was never satisfied with how the conversation ended.

There was just no end to it. I was facing racial attacks on nearly every stop and was reeling from the Chicago experience; I was probably extra sensitive. This more recent incident, coming from one of my teammates, put me into a further funk. I couldn't even relax on my day off.

Some 25 years later, long before I thought about writing a book, I received a phone call. It was from my teammate, whom I hadn't spoken to in years, calling to apologize. During the conversation, he told me he understood how much he hurt me that day. He explained he did not want to leave this Earth without making peace with me.

I was shocked to hear from him. I was shocked to hear him making amends. I probably did not provide the response that he wanted during this call, but the gesture touched my soul. I often wonder if people understand the amount of pain racism can cause. The apology told me all I needed to know about this man, who was a teammate I respected and liked. Just as I had remembered him when we played, this was a stand-up guy.

In real time, the whole racial issue was difficult for me to untangle. Today, I do not believe this person is a racist. As I have said several times, my sudden emergence as a rare NHL prospect who was Black was difficult on everyone. No one knew how to act or react.

But put yourself in my position. It's tough enough being a prospect, trying to make it into the NHL, without being one of the few Blacks in the game. As racial barbs were flung at me from every angle, they all seemed racist at the time. More important, they all hurt.

When a soldier in a firefight gets struck by "friendly fire," it doesn't matter that the bullet came from members of his own troop. It still wounds.

I was programmed to handle all the shit from the stands and from my opponents, but when it came from within, it stung extra hard.

This was one of the handful of events that made an important contribution to my decision to leave the game. But as I told my former teammate on the phone, he is a hero, not a villain. He is one of the few people that understood the amount of pain he had caused me back in the day. We were these big, burly professional athletes flaunting our macho image to the world. And yet, he had the empathy to understand my struggle.

His phone call is a gift I will always treasure.

CHAPTER 33

Blood in the Water

The first thing out of Demers's mouth when we got to Los Angeles was that nobody was allowed in the hotel swimming pool. That seemed a reasonable team rule, since swimming tightens the muscles and causes sluggishness. We had played on consecutive nights in Chicago and Denver, and the trip concluded with games in L.A. and Vancouver.

I went to my room, unpacked my bag and then headed to the restaurant for lunch. The restaurant overlooked the pool, and as I ordered my meal, I peered over to do some people-watching. The first thing to catch my eye was the sight of five teammates, splashing around in the deep end.

I couldn't stop laughing. Not less than an hour earlier, our head coach had instructed us not to swim. I was an impressionable rookie with only two NHL games under my belt, but I already realized my coach didn't have total command of this crew.

After playing so well in Denver, I couldn't wait to carry the momentum forward. Surprisingly, I didn't dress against the Kings, and no one offered an explanation. We lost, 4–1. The following night, I watched from the stands again, as we beat Vancouver, 6–2. We then headed home.

I was now euphemistically known as a healthy scratch, or what the hockey world calls a "black ace." You can't make this stuff up.

I was still in the press box when we beat the Blackhawks at home. Then we headed to Philadelphia. "You don't want to play in this one, Bernie," Boudrias whispered in my ear shortly after our lineup was announced and I found myself scratched yet again.

The Flyers were no longer the Broad Street Bullies of the mid-'70s. But they were atop the NHL standings and still a rough-and-tumble team, and the Spectrum was still one of the toughest NHL buildings to visit. But make no mistake, the coach wasn't just alluding to the Flyers' style of play before their 5–2 victory. Throwing a Black person into that pool would have been like dumping blood into a shark tank.

My appearance in the game would have put the entire team at risk.

When I say that the colour of my skin is a key reason why I didn't last in the NHL, this is a perfect example. I was a good fighter, but I typically fought players like me who were there to play hockey, not the enforcers. In this game, I would have been subjected to abuse and intimidation from the baddest asses in the NHL. Let me be clear, I was not a strong enough fighter to fight at that level. Paul Stewart, Curt Brackenbury and Wally Weir were our heavyweights and the ones supposed to take on the other teams' goons.

I wish that I could have played in Philadelphia as just another rookie.

* * *

WHEN I GREW up dreaming of playing in the NHL, I expected everything to be first class: the coaching, the players, the facilities, even the coffee. When I finally arrived in the late '70s, I was disappointed to discover certain elements that failed to live up to my fantasy.

For example, I expected the coaches to take me under their wing and invest in my improvement, encourage me when appropriate and redirect when necessary. You know, coach me. Don't get me wrong, I didn't expect to be coddled. But I somehow expected a certain level of professionalism. Nobody talked to me.

The Nordiques had a particular protocol on game days. The team would have a light morning skate, and then the lineup would be announced. One of our assistant coaches worked out the scratched players once the regulars who were playing that night vacated to the showers.

I hated those workouts because it felt like the assistant coach was trying to make a name for himself. With only a few players on the ice and little recovery time after each drill, the practice after the morning skate would become exhausting. I actually found myself praying I wouldn't get inserted into the lineup following those mini-practices because I was drained.

Nonetheless, I stayed prepared in case something changed. Most players in the lineup take an afternoon nap after the morning skate, to best prepare for the exhausting three-hour torment their bodies were about to endure. So, even in games when I was scratched, I took my normal afternoon nap and arrived at the stadium as if I were in the lineup.

On the road, however, the procedures depended on the itinerary. When we arrived in town the day before the game and we were able to schedule a normal morning skate, everything remained the same. However, there were times when we arrived in a city late and did not have time for a morning skate. In those instances, everyone skated during pre-game warm-ups.

This meant that the two or three players travelling with the team who were healthy scratches would undress, shower and watch the game from the stands after taking part in the warm-up.

Most dressing rooms have stalls with storage compartments under each built-in seat. When a team arrives in a town, the equipment staff lugs the 25 player bags into the room, neatly hangs each player's gear in his stall, and stuffs the empty duffle bag and any extra paraphernalia into the compartment under the seat. This keeps the room neat and tidy.

Following the pre-game warm-up, when the team returns to the locker room, whoever's equipment bag is sitting on the floor in front of his stall isn't dressing in the game.

That was the communication process: put your shit back in the bag.

I don't know if this is common in the NHL or was unique to the Nordiques, but I found it to be incredibly embarrassing. If you saw your bag in front of your stall, you didn't dare make eye contact with anyone. You felt the empathetic glances from some teammates out of the corners of your eyes. At the same time, you could sense the relief from others who were glad it was you, not them, having to pack up.

Now, I am sure some will criticize me, as this was the big leagues after all. But I expected a more professional and humane approach. This was a shit show.

Learning to be a healthy scratch, I wasted my time roaming the other NHL buildings and evaluating the food. I dreamed of authoring a hardcover coffee-table book titled *The Concession Stands of the NHL*. There is a lot of idle time when you are not in the lineup, so your mind drifts and wanders.

FOLLOWING OUR 5–2 loss to Philly at the Spectrum, we flew to Detroit. We had a day off before a date with the Red Wings in the shiny, new Joe Louis Arena, 150 miles from Kalamazoo and WMU. I had played in the Great Lakes Invitational Holiday tournament at the Detroit Olympia the year before but had never seen the Joe, which had opened only three months earlier.

My girlfriend and several friends from Western Michigan drove over for the game. Although the team was at a hotel adjacent to the Joe in downtown Detroit, I reserved a room for my girlfriend a few minutes away across the Detroit River (and the Canada–U.S. border) in Windsor, Ontario.

We had a morning skate scheduled, so I took a taxi from the hotel in Windsor to the Joe. When we reached the border crossing, I was asked for my identification. Crap, I had left my credentials back at the hotel . . . I was going to be late for practice.

I feebly explained to the U.S. border security agent that I was an NHL player and I played for the Nordiques. Upon hearing this, the look on the officer's face said, "Are you crazy?"

He was not amused. Nobody had ever seen a Black hockey player before, especially in Detroit. Sensing something amiss, he ushered me into that back room that everybody fears. I started to panic.

Incredibly, in one of those amazing twists of fate, Mike Brown's friend worked in the customs office and happened to be checking in for his shift. He recognized me and vouched for my story. I had only met the guy once in my life, when he visited campus, but he remembered that Mike and I were WMU teammates.

After a sigh and a laugh and a few signed autographs, I made it to practice on time. I told you I had great timing! And I guess this was one time I was lucky to be Black. Do you think Mike's friend would have remembered me if I wasn't?

I guess this was one of those good days. I got to the rink in time to participate in the morning skate, and later found out I was in the lineup for the first time in nine days—especially exciting since my friends were making the drive in the hope of seeing me play.

My lucky day took a nasty turn, however. When the puck dropped, I found myself sitting at the end of the bench. I was in uniform, but Jacques was not playing me. The Nordiques slogged through another lacklustre performance, and the game turned into a laugher. The 9–7 loss sounded like a low-scoring football game.

I sat in exile on the bench, closer to a young kid in the stands on the other side of the glass than to the game. But well into the third period, just as I was resigning myself to the fact that I would not see the ice, Jacques tapped my shoulder.

I was cold and stiff, and now engaged in my third NHL game. The Red Wings had a huge team, with players like Willie Huber and Peter Mahovlich (both 6-foot-5) and Vaclav Nedomansky (6-foot-2). On my first shift, the puck bounced along the boards on my side and I had to capture it to clear the zone. At the same time, one of Detroit's redwoods flew down the boards and pummelled me. He hit me so hard, I could hear groans of sympathy from the fans. I got up, shook off the thunderous hit and trudged back to the bench.

Detroit was my worst NHL game, and I was disappointed. It felt even worse knowing I had friends in the building to witness the debacle. But my instincts are to always find a lesson in defeat. In this instance, I knew I needed to adapt to limited ice time, to figure out how to come off the bench in relief.

I had never done that before in my career, and I felt I had flunked my first test. I was crushed, both literally and figuratively. But there was no time to dwell on it. We flew home for a game the next day against the talented New York Islanders. I was in the lineup for my fourth NHL game, still feeling bruised by the lack of ice time the previous night in Detroit.

I arrived at a simple solution: to keep my legs warm, I decided to continuously shuffle them while sitting at the end of the bench. That way, they would be semi-warm if Demers tapped my shoulder. I never wanted to hop over the boards again with that dead feeling in my legs. If I was going to be a potted plant, then I was going to be the best potted plant in the NHL.

We played a dismal first period and I never saw the ice. We were already in the dressing room when Jacques burst through the door, furious. He did his thing, yelling and screaming at everyone. When he looked over at me, he scolded me for making noise at the end of the bench.

I hadn't realized it until Jacques started screaming, but my leg shuffling made a distracting noise. The benches at le Colisée had a wooden floor, and Demers interpreted my tapping sounds as an attempt to draw attention to myself to get him to put me in the game. Jacques was under a lot of pressure to hold on to his job, and was operating with a short fuse.

The Islanders beat us, 9–6. I didn't play at all until the third period. But I did enjoy one affecting moment, thanks to Islanders rookie defenceman Ken Morrow.

Back in college, WMU's nemesis was Bowling Green. Ron Mason coached the Falcons at the time and had built a hockey powerhouse. Among the future NHLers on that team was Morrow, the tall, bearded, lanky defensive defenceman who was a key member of the 1980 U.S. Olympic Team.

Only five weeks earlier, Morrow was part of the Miracle on Ice. He had a gold medal. Now he was playing with Mike Bossy and Bryan Trottier, Denis Potvin and Billy Smith.

Morrow and I had battled in the CCHA for four consecutive years. He was one of the evolving "big" men in the game (think Larry Robinson). I remember several times against Bowling Green when I thought I had Morrow beaten, only to have him recover with his incredibly long reach. Kenny had one of the best poke checks in the game. You can learn a lot about a guy when you face him in the trenches. He was tough, but never dirty. He wasn't mouthy. I never met him away from the rink, but he always played with class.

The touching moment with Morrow occurred before the game, a brief instant in my life that has had a long-lasting effect. When he spotted me during warm-ups, he made a point of approaching me at centre ice.

"What took you so long?" he asked, grinning. He was basically telling me I deserved to be there alongside him in the NHL. Here was a guy who had just won an Olympic gold medal, was on a team poised to win a Stanley Cup and was on top of the hockey universe. He didn't have to do that. But he did anyway. It was a nice gesture from a fellow competitor, something I'll never forget.

I was reassigned back to Syracuse the next day. The Nordiques had four games remaining in the season and were out of the Stanley Cup playoff hunt. What I did not realize until much later was that my promotion had been part of a plan. Later, I discovered that they gave me a taste of the NHL to reward me for my breakout year in the minors, but they always planned to return me to Syracuse for the AHL playoffs.

I had played so well in my first two games at Chicago and Colorado, but I got no feedback. They didn't tell me anything. Which is why I couldn't understand why I then ended up being designated to rate the quality of the concession stands for four straight games. And since I didn't understand French, the newspapers were no help.

CHAPTER 34

Black Is Beautiful

I was disappointed to be returned to Syracuse, not understanding Quebec's master plan. I thought that with four games left, and little at stake for the Nordiques, there would be an opportunity for me to display my NHL potential.

On the brighter side, I was happy to have the experience behind me. It did nothing but confirm that I could thrive at the game's top level, and I couldn't wait for another shot.

When I arrived back in Syracuse, the difference in mood was palpable.

The Nordiques were a beaten team winding down the season, splashing around in the pool. The Firebirds were embroiled in a fierce battle with the Rochester Americans for the coveted third spot in the AHL's Southern Division.

Avoiding fourth place was critical, because the fourth seed would have the unenviable task of facing the heavily favoured New Haven Nighthawks in the first round of the Calder Cup playoffs. The Nighthawks were a powerhouse, the top team in the AHL, with 101 points, a whopping 25 ahead of second-place Hershey. Nobody wanted to face New Haven.

I got back in time for the regular-season finale in Rochester. We were one point ahead of the Amerks and needed only a tie to clinch third. Rochester had to win. The outcome of this game had special meaning to our coach, Duane Rupp, and our GM, John DenHamer. The tandem ran the Amerks the season before, but both had been fired. They craved payback.

We played hard, dominated the game, outshot them 35–25, but trailed 2–1 with less than a minute left. The Rochester War Memorial crowd of 5,603 was roaring, certain that the Amerks were sending us to a best-of-seven headache with New Haven.

Rupp pulled goalie Gary Carr and put me out there in this critical offensive situation, and we attacked. I tied it at two with 20 seconds left in regulation, silencing the boisterous crowd. And since Rochester had to win, when they pulled goalie Ed Walsh in the final minute of overtime, Rupp put my line back on the ice.

We prevented the Amerks from scoring with six attackers, and we counterattacked the empty net. And after Blair Stewart and Rollie Cloutier had shots blocked in a furious goalmouth sequence, I backhanded a third rebound into the empty net to win it.

Our cramped visitors' dressing room was a scene of delirium after the game. The Rochester writers wanted to hear from Rupp and DenHamer, who were enjoying such sweet revenge. Rupp, who played on two Calder Cup champions in Rochester and another in Hershey, called this game his biggest thrill in hockey.

"This is even better than my Calder Cup," he said.

DenHamer was more succinct.

"Black is beautiful!" he shouted.

DenHamer was an advocate and meant no harm. But after my demotion back to the minors, after hearing the filth from the Blackhawks' bench in my NHL debut, after enduring my teammate's unfortunate N-friendly fire, and after enduring another gruesome night of racial obscenities from the Rochester mob, DenHamer's microaggression churned my stomach.

I assume he wasn't aware that I had endured another long evening of "Kill the Black guy" attitude from the partisan crowd. The Rochester fans were merciless that night. The typical out-of-town abuse I endured varied from game to game, and this evening's verbal garbage was at a KKK-rally level. DenHamer's effusive phrase, though well intentioned, took a little of the lustre off the evening for me.

And the honest truth is, I don't recall if there was much viciousness from the Amerks on the ice that night. As Willie O'Ree wrote in his book, it felt at times as though my name was "N-word." Hearing the obscenity was like being shot by a stun gun every time I heard it. But it happened so often on the ice, I had to block it out. That night in Rochester, I was trying to win a hockey game; there was no way I was going to succumb to personal pain.

I know I was supposed to be a big, burly hockey player, but it hurt me deeply every time it occurred. It got to where there was no place to hide, not even while celebrating a sweet victory in the solidarity of my own dressing room.

It is why a letter published in the *Rochester Democrat and Chronicle* means so much to me, even 40 years later. Somebody felt my pain.

Here it is:

SOME FANS STILL BIGOTS

Maybe I'm naive, but I had hoped that we white people had come a long way in overcoming our prejudices in the past few years. Well, I guess not. As if watching the Rochester Amerks lose a decisive hockey game to the Syracuse Firebirds on Easter Sunday wasn't bad enough, I was subjected to some of the most ignorant dribble from the mouths of fans that I've ever heard.

Bernie Saunders is a fine hockey player for Syracuse. In fact, it was this talented center who scored the tying goal with just 20 seconds left in regulation, and the winning goal in overtime. While I don't expect Rochester fans to exactly embrace Saunders as their hero—after all it was he who defeated the Amerks—I never expected to hear what I heard that night in the stands at the War Memorial.

Saunders is a black man—one of the few playing professional hockey—and was the target of many catcalls from all corners of the arena whenever he entered the game. What kind of person talks this way? I'd love to hear their explanations, but I'm afraid those explanations would be as articulate and intelligent as the jeers that prompted this letter.

This kind of talk shouldn't be allowed. War Memorial rules prohibit abusive language. Is this not abusive? I had hoped things had changed. Those bigots in the stands have shown me how wrong I was.

David J.Caiazza

Thank you, David, for speaking up.

CHAPTER 35
The Sports Reporter

Expectations were high for my older brother, John. He was attractive, bright, charming, well mannered and articulate. Sometimes it made me want to puke. Everyone predicted early in our lives that, as the first-born, John was headed towards success and stardom.

Sadly, because he suffered from depression, John saw life as a cup half empty. John believed that because he was the oldest, our parents were stricter with him than they were with me. Parents tend to use the first-born as a guinea pig. However, I used to remind him he never had to wear hand-me-down skates. Plus, I never pushed the envelope with our parents the way he did. Birth order brings advantage and disadvantage.

While I was completing my career at WMU and earning my degree, John found himself on a negative path. He didn't have a career goal, he had flunked out of school and his young marriage was failing. In addition, he had finally come to terms with the realization his hockey career was kaput. We didn't know what he would do with his life. As his younger brother, I felt John's pain as my own and worried more about him than myself.

Although John didn't last long at Western Michigan, it was

where Neil Smith unintentionally introduced him to broad-casting. Neil majored in communications arts and sciences. He hosted a show on the graveyard shift at the campus radio station, WMUK. For fun, Neil invited John onto the show so that they could perform the same on-air slapstick comedy rou-tine they did all the time on campus.

The two had a blast. The show clicked.

When John flunked out of WMU and returned to Ajax, he took that ounce of on-air experience and leveraged it into part-time work on the local country and western radio station, CHOO. He juggled his time on the air with classes at Ryerson University in Toronto and earning a paycheque at the Bayly Engineering plant, producing latex rubber gloves.

John had no idea what to do. Zippo. He had painted him-self into a corner. He had no career goal, no degree, a failing marriage, and the realization that his hockey career was over. Otherwise, he was good.

John's greatest asset, clearly, was his verbal skill. He could talk a famished kid out of a Fudgsicle. So, I suggested that he turn this innate gift into a vocation. I convinced him to record audition tapes and mail them to stations around the area. We already had the blueprint, as he had sent my bio to every NHL and WHA general manager when I wanted to turn pro.

As they say, the rest is history.

John's rise in the sports broadcasting profession was meteoric. He made brief stops at a few radio stations but quickly transitioned to TV, which landed him in Moncton, New Brunswick, and then Toronto. Before long, the *Toronto Sun* ranked him the most popular sportscaster in the city. John had gone from country and western radio to the pinnacle of his profession in Canada in a matter of years.

That's a first-born for you.

After conquering Canada, the United States came calling, and John was off to Baltimore, Maryland. Before long, the locals there loved him as much as they had at his other stops. It wasn't lost on me that John had vowed to never return to the United States after the cultural mishaps that occurred during his brief time at Western Michigan.

But John had become a much different person. He covered the Baltimore Orioles baseball team and became friends with Eddie Murray and Cal Ripken Sr. and Jr. Along the way, he met a local broadcaster who was just starting her career, as he was just starting his: Oprah Winfrey. For a brief moment, John became so firmly entrenched in the Baltimore scene that I considered moving there myself.

And then, in 1986, ESPN came calling. The sports behemoth was a young and upcoming network when they reached out to John, and he was hesitant . . . until they flashed the contract offer in front of his face. He was off to Bristol, Connecticut, and broadcasting for a fledgling network to a national audience from the middle of a barren field. Good thing I didn't move to Baltimore. John became one of the original talents at ESPN.

How do you explain his dazzling success? John had the uncanny ability to be himself. He had a sincerity about him. Most people, when a camera shines on them, become someone else. They freeze, or they overact, or they try to be sincere and simply look phony. When I tried, I turned into a blithering idiot—I did colour commentary on WMU Broncos broadcasts with Robin Hook for four years. I was awful.

My brother looked into a camera and became *your* brother in *your* living room. Just by describing the day's sporting news while not attempting to be the news, John became your best friend, refreshing and informal. When he and I were out, people recognized him and reacted as though they bumped into an old friend. There weren't many encounters with star-struck fans, just warm and friendly greetings along the line of "Hey, John, I just saw you in my living room. How're you doing?"

Most people assumed John's job was easy, probably because he did it effortlessly. That amused me, because I knew how difficult his job was, and how his prodigious talent made it look simple. He didn't need a teleprompter as a pacifier. He became a master of live TV. John barely shrugged when producers and directors screamed frantically into his earpiece while he was addressing a national audience.

Paradoxically, John did not fully appreciate how talented he was. I remember one Saturday afternoon when I was living in Kalamazoo. I was watching the Michigan football game when he called me. I kept one eye on the game and we were five minutes into our casual conversation when he said, "Bernie, hang on a second."

This was before cellphones, so I held the receiver to my ear and turned to the TV just as the announcers on the football game said, "Let's go back to our ABC studios for an update with John Saunders."

I didn't realize it, but he was chatting with me while he was on national TV! As I patiently waited on hold, he whipped off a classic update, voiced over a few highlights and threw the telecast back to the game in Ann Arbor.

Seconds later, he was back on the phone: "So, what I was saying was . . . ," acting like he had just left for a moment to grab a snack.

"How do you do that?" I asked, incredulous.

The question befuddled him. "What's the big deal?" he said.

REMEMBER I TOLD you I was a victim of bad timing? I don't really believe I'm a victim, for several reasons. To me, the world is a blank canvas, and we each paint our own personal masterpiece. The universe brings to us exactly what we can achieve. Plus, we all have a path and a journey, and I wouldn't trade mine for any other.

Having gotten that off my chest, I suffered an unfortunate chain of events during my career that really sucked.

Following my rookie season, I was on cloud nine. With an NHL hockey career at my fingertips, I felt I was operating in my centre ring. I had done everything the Nordiques asked, and Quebec City embraced me. There was a Bernie Saunders buzz in the air. At the end of the season, the front office told me I had secured a roster spot for the following season.

John was on fire, as well. He was the star at Citytv in Toronto. We had both reached the pinnacle of our professions, and we finally reunited that summer, living together in Toronto. Life was good.

The Saunders brothers ruled the city. True to form, I worked out like a maniac in preparation for my first full NHL season. In the evening, I would meet John after his broadcast for a night on the town. We were on top of the world, feeling nothing could stop us. Well, not unless something really weird happened.

Cue record-scratch sound effect.

Something really weird happened . . .

"Bernie, are you sitting down?" John asked over the phone in a voice I knew was not delivering good news. My immediate thought was someone had died. "The Nordiques just smuggled the Stastnys out of Czechoslovakia."

John read from the wire stories. In a scenario that could've been stolen from a Hollywood movie, Nordiques officials had snuck the two Slovak brothers, 24-year-old Peter and 21-year-old Anton, away from their team at the Europa Cup tournament in Innsbruck, Austria. After their team's final game, the Stastnys were whisked to a waiting car that drove them to Vienna. There, they sought political asylum at the Canadian embassy.

These two world-class forwards were joining the Nordiques, and both had signed for a reported $250,000 a year. Their addition meant I plunged two spots on the depth chart.

Nobody had died, but my NHL career might have.

CHAPTER 36

Ransacked

Focused and determined, coming off a rookie season that opened eyes and turned heads, I arrived in Quebec City for my second NHL training camp. Unlike a year ago, I was now a known entity, told by the Nordiques I had essentially earned a spot on their 1980–81 roster.

The Nordiques understood that my numbers were phenomenal. It wasn't just 23 goals; it was 23 in 38 games with Syracuse after I went from CHL scoring leader, to my team folding, to my ass being shipped to the tighter-checking AHL, to not missing a beat and ending the season as one of the 1979–80 season's most dominant minor-league goal scorers.

I scored in bunches, including hat tricks in both leagues as a rookie. I scored on the power play and the penalty kill. I scored several game-winning goals, one in overtime. In Syracuse, my 1.05 points per game would have landed me fifth in AHL scoring had I been there the full season.

This was where I was meant to be.

Today, most players train 12 months a year and arrive in peak shape for quickie training camps with short preseason schedules. But NHL training camps in the 1980s were designed to skate the summer vacations out of most players.

The coaching staffs delighted in crafting brutal workout schedules, called two-a-days, in the early part of camp. A morning scrimmage followed by another in the afternoon—two intense sessions that left players exhausted. The best way to resuscitate after one of these days was to get as much salt back into your system as possible. And we're not talking Gatorade. We're talking ice cold Molson Canadian or Labatt's Blue.

Terry Johnson and I hung out together at camp. We were both free agents signed by Quebec in the summer of 1979 who had spent a few games with the big club in 1979–80, but the rest of the season in the minors. He and I played together in Syracuse after I arrived from Cincinnati. TJ reminded me of *Sesame Street*'s Big Bird. He was tall and wiry, and wore a goofy, friendly grin beneath his curly hair. He was a towering western Canadian whose formidable strength appeared to be produced from heaving bales of hay rather than pumping iron.

TJ and I became close, possibly because we both came from "nowhere," were both considered underdogs and were both turning heads in Quebec City.

After one gruelling set of two-a-days, we walked towards the hotel elevator, off to find dinner and resuscitation. We passed a room with the door propped open and saw the Stastny brothers sitting on their beds, blankly staring at the TV, clearly bored.

TJ stopped, walked back to the room, poked his head in and asked Peter and Anton if they would like to join us. The brothers seemed extremely shy. Their English seemed suspect. But when TJ raised an invisible beer bottle to his mouth, their eyes lit up. They were in.

We found a local watering hole for the evening and a funny thing happened: the more we drank, the better their English became. We didn't think they could speak a word of the language, but they became quite conversational after several pops. At one point, Peter disappeared. Several moments later he returned, carrying a tray full of shots.

"Canadian beer? Water!" he complained. "We drink wodka."

It was hysterical. A now-comfortable Peter couldn't understand why the bartender wouldn't sell him a full bottle, so he cheerfully settled for a tray loaded with shot glasses. We laughed, drank vodka all night and bonded with our two new European teammates.

The next morning arrived way too quickly. Although I was usually very responsible and rarely let the night before affect my morning after, I was a mess. I've always been able to consume high quantities of beer without suffering the following morning, but liquor was different. I was hungover, and I could tell TJ was sluggish, too. We just tried to survive the morning scrimmage.

Not our new Czechoslovakian friends. They were flying around the ice as if they'd tucked themselves into bed the previous night at 10 p.m. It was so ironic. Here TJ and I were, two underdogs trying to secure NHL jobs, struggling after way too many. And there were the Stastnys, with their huge guaranteed contracts, unaffected by our little impromptu party.

This training camp had a different vibe than the camp from the Nordiques' inaugural NHL season. Jacques Demers had been fired as head coach. General manager Maurice Filion decided to step behind the bench and do both jobs, and he promoted Michel Bergeron from the Trois-Rivières Draveurs of the QMJHL to be his associate coach.

There was a buzz in the air with the Stastnys in town. The United States had won the gold medal at the Olympics in Lake Placid six months earlier, while the Russians had been the overwhelming favourites, but those who watched very closely believed the Czechoslovakians were probably the best team. And that was because of the Stastnys.

The Quebec media focused on the brothers, but I was not ignored. I had a microphone in my face constantly. Writers who had reported on my promising rookie season began hanging around my stall. And when Michel Blanchard from *La Presse* in Montreal summarized the prospects, he reminded the fans to watch for me: "Bernie Saunders: Young player of the future. Might deserve a post on the team. Done very well with Syracuse and in the few games that he played with the team last season."

Most NHL teams structure their camps by inviting 40 to 50 players from throughout their system. They start with a series of scrimmages, make a substantial first cut, and then begin a four-to-six-game exhibition schedule to assess the remaining players.

But the Nordiques were forced to improvise because le Colisée was undergoing an expansion and the construction project was running behind schedule. Camp began with three intramural teams. The plan was to make cuts, reduce the teams within the camp to two, and then have the remaining players play a few NHL exhibition games—all on the road.

I picked up right where I'd left off in Syracuse and was on top of my game. I flew up and down my wing and was one of the top players in camp. At one point, I got word through the grapevine that management wanted to see me fight. I can't remember how, but there was an unambiguous message sent my way that it would help my chances if the brass could see what happened when I dropped my gloves.

Fine. Next scrimmage, I made it a point to play more aggressively. I planned to fight the first player who hinted at a challenge. And sure enough, while skating towards a loose puck and fighting off a checker in heavy traffic, I felt a slash from behind across my forearm. It stung.

I instantly dropped my gloves and challenged the assailant. As we squared off, I realized it was none other than Marc Tardif. Crap. I loved Marc's game when he played with the Montreal Canadiens. I had watched him as a kid, and he was my instructor one summer in hockey school.

We had a good scrap—call it an even bout—and nothing much happened other than I felt embarrassed at having fought my former teacher. When I read a translation of the account in one French paper recently, it suggested the brass also wanted Tardif playing more aggressively. So maybe the whole thing was a wash.

I refused to be deterred by the Slovak invasion and was one of the stars of the camp. During the three-team intramural tournament, they kept stats as if it were a regular-season schedule. And the final camp leaderboard looked like this:

	Goals	Assists	Points
Anton Stastny	6	8	14
Peter Stastny	6	8	14
Bernie Saunders	8	3	11
Michel Goulet	5	6	11

I led the entire tournament with eight goals and was tied for third in scoring, behind only the Stastny brothers. And yet, as the Nordiques prepared for their NHL exhibition games, I was told to report to the team offices the next morning . . . at a shopping mall. One of those average-looking, one-level malls with a flat gravel roof.

The club, you see, had had to vacate its offices at le Colisée during the renovations. So, the management rented office space in this plaza. While people strode past us with shopping bags in their hands and quizzical looks on their faces, five nervous Nordiques prospects—Gary Carr, TJ, Louis Sleigher, Reg Thomas and me—sat on a long, wooden bench outside a colourless storefront awaiting our cruel fate. It was a scene so ridiculous, it somehow felt appropriate.

I was devastated. It was difficult to process as I sat there, trying to figure out what had gone wrong. I had shocked the organization my rookie campaign with a breakout performance in the Central and American Leagues and backed that up as the leading goal scorer in training camp. Yet, I knew this mall visit meant I was being "shopped" to the minors. The Nordiques were not even going to reward me with one NHL exhibition game.

One by one, the first three guys were called into the office for their 30 minutes with Filion. The GM/coach sat behind a makeshift desk in a makeshift office and informed each player he was getting reassigned.

After each meeting, the player strode sadly out from the storefront and told those of us still waiting outside what Filion had said to him. Reg Thomas and I were the only two players left on the bench. I must have been sitting there for two hours when Thomas, the ex-WHA veteran, emerged and told me they were sending him home.

"They told me to go home and wait," he declared mournfully.

"Home?" I asked. "How is that even possible?"

Thomas, disgusted, just shrugged. He said he was headed back to his farm just outside of London, Ontario.

Finally, it was my turn. Having sat there for two hours, I had rehearsed and re-rehearsed the questions I had for Filion. Every player before me had talked to him, so I'd had four chances to hear what he told them. I knew what I wanted to say, and what I needed to ask.

I have always had the mindset of taking bad news constructively. To me, there is never failure, there is just information. I planned to ask Filion where things had gone wrong, what the club felt my deficiencies were, what the coaches wanted me to improve upon in order to get back to Quebec, and how I could turn what they saw as weaknesses in my game into strengths.

But when I was invited inside the offices, Filion had bolted. He must have slithered out a back door. He was nowhere to be found!

The Quebec Nordiques left it to one of their assistant coaches, André Boudrias, to sit me down and formally announce my demotion. To his credit, he didn't try to bullshit me. He had nothing negative to say, nothing to explain.

"I thought you had made the team," he said. "The other players thought you had made the team."

Boudrias looked as shocked as I was. All he could suggest was that I return to the minors, work hard, stay positive, and everything would work itself out.

A part of me died in that moment. My pride was the only thing that held back the tears. I could not believe my ears, and could not believe I wasn't talking to Filion.

Filion would not face me man to man.

The Quebec writers were always hounding the players

and the front office for news, and this day was no different. Normally, I hated that the press never left us alone. But years later, I was glad that reporter Maurice Dumas was there to accurately describe the scene.

I was smart enough to keep my mouth shut when he approached, and I left the mall without saying a word to him. But I appreciated how he captured the scene in *Le Soleil* the next morning:

Bernie Saunders remained silent for several minutes after Andrés Boudrias had invited him for a meeting in the office of Maurice Filion. He didn't utter a word and probably had minor-league miseries on his mind. He proved to be the Nordiques' best sharpshooter during training camp. "Saunders has talent and we're keeping an eye on him," Filion said.

The French- and English-speaking papers all reported on the unfairness of my demotion. Between the anonymous comments from befuddled teammates and the hollow explanations from voices within the administration, the Bernie Saunders Controversy became the story of training camp. From Albert Ladouceur at the *Journal de Québec*:

THE SACKING OF SAUNDERS: A SURPRISE

The sidelining of Bernie Saunders, at this stage of the training camp, even before any exhibition games, comes as a real shocker. Saunders ranked third amongst the scorers, behind the Stastny brothers.

A strong athlete, this [player of colour] wasn't afraid of the corners and was skillful on defence, without being perfect.

According to some of his teammates, Saunders has been treated unfairly.

A member of the organization was said to be stunned by the pulling of Saunders: "There are others who should have been shown the door before him," he said.

The subject of this controversy doesn't understand the strange decision from Nordiques head office. "I thought I was doing a good job during the training camp," Saunders said. "Team management did say that my last season in the minors proved to be an asset. I would've liked to take part in an exhibition game. It's possible that my playing style is not appealing."

Saunders, a graduate from an American university, will be heading back home. "I'll take some time to reflect and will make a decision in regards to my future in hockey."

The treatment was so unfair that even the press and my teammates rallied to my defence. Players were coming up to me, asking what was going on, as if I had some influence over this illogical decision.

I enjoyed the respect of my peers, just like when I was fighting off the racial affronts in Pickering, but I didn't want this attention. I just wanted to play. I just wanted to fit in without standing out.

André Bellemare, of the Presse Canadienne wire service, voiced equal surprise at my departure, and asked Maurice Filion where I was headed.

Some were a little surprised to see Saunders' name on the cut list since, after a week of training camp, he had done well. The coloured player from Montreal was third in scoring only behind the Stastny brothers . . .

It is not clear where the left winger will play this winter, having counted 36 goals in 67 games in the minors last season (with Cincinnati and Syracuse), but Filion is confident that a team will retain his services. Nor can Saunders be recalled by the Nordiques if the need arises, especially if injuries continue to decimate the ranks of the Quebecers.

Albert Ladouceur of *Le Journal de Québec* focused on the fact that Filion had no way to explain how the third-leading scorer in the club's intramural tournament had been demoted. "Another year in the minors will help him to polish his game," Filion said. "Some guys are ahead of him. We have no particular criticism to communicate to him. It's just a group of facts."

Filion was talking to the press, but he wasn't talking to me. However, the fact that Filion had no criticisms made me feel worse. With constructive criticism, I would have been happy to go back to the minors and "polish my game." There was almost nothing I wouldn't have done to get myself back into an NHL jersey. But nobody ever offered any feedback, positive or negative. Players kept telling me how unfairly I was being treated, but nobody in management would talk to me. Boudrias was the only go-between, and he always just rallied to my defence.

And there was one big problem with my ability to go back to the minors and "polish my game": the Nordiques didn't have a minor-league affiliate.

The Nordiques had nowhere to send me!

Quebec's working agreement with the Syracuse Firebirds had terminated, and the Nordiques failed to secure a working relationship with another American League farm team. They were trying to place a team in Saint John, New Brunswick, but hit a snag with the local arena. Consequently, this fledgling NHL franchise had nowhere to train its prospects.

Just think about that: no development program.

That's why Boudrias had instructed me to go home, stay in shape and be prepared for a call. He said the Nordiques would let me know in a couple of weeks where I would be assigned. He mentioned that the team had a desire to "loan" me to another AHL team, but he also said I might be assigned to the Eastern Hockey League.

The EHL??

This ordeal was a transformational moment for me. I was idealistic and naively believed that the NHL would be hockey heaven. That if you worked hard and performed on the ice, you would be rewarded for your effort. I believed the NHL was a meritocracy. I led a group that included two future Hall of Famers in Goulet and Peter Stastny in goals, and I had ranked third in points. What more could I have done? I had always played the game with such unbridled passion, and it felt like they were robbing me of that, cutting out my heart.

The obvious question that I am asked is this: Did the fact that you are Black have something to do with this?

I am not labelling these people racist. But to be fair to myself, with all the other racial abuse taking place, everything felt racial in real time. When you are in a prejudiced rainstorm, it's difficult to distinguish between the drops. Although I didn't believe then—and don't believe now—that any of the executives were blatantly racist, I do believe my treatment was substandard because of my race.

Plus, I had another strike against me. The French–English strife lingered in the background and didn't work in my favour. Said Reg Thomas after his release became official, "I wouldn't be surprised if, before the end of the year, they trade three or four English players for two or three French players. Honestly, I don't think there's an English player there that is happy."

Time out. I want to put these events in proper perspective. The Stastny brothers were hustling their asses off. Michel Goulet, Dale Hunter and Lee Norwood were all motivated to make the roster and were skating in midseason form. But veterans like Marc Tardif, Buddy Cloutier and Robbie Ftorek were probably just playing themselves into shape. So, my gaudy stats must be put into perspective. I get that.

I'm not saying I was better than any of those players because I outscored them in training camp. My simple argument is the leading goal scorer in an NHL training camp deserved a much better fate than getting cut before the preseason even began. And I do believe that I would have gotten more respect if I were white.

I have tried not to speculate. But I do believe that I would have benefited from playing in at least one exhibition game without everything on the line. I also believe I would have kept scoring, and that history would have been written much differently had I been treated fairly. All I wanted was a fair shot. But life is not fair.

This is why I relate to Herb Carnegie, because I had done everything to prove myself and yet, like Mr. Carnegie, they told me to go back to the minors and do it again.

WHEN I DROVE back to the hotel from the mall, I was in a daze. A mantra in the Black community is that we have to be twice as good to get half as much. Even Michelle Obama mentions this in her bestseller *Becoming*. I had outscored everyone in training camp, and that wasn't good enough. How many more goals did I need to score? The sting of injustice ripped through my soul. I decided to immediately pack my belongings into my compact Datsun 280Z. It was going to be a long drive back to Michigan, literally and figuratively, and I wanted to get an early start. Packing the night before would save me an extra 45 minutes in the morning.

Since I had expected to be in Quebec City for the long haul, I had brought most of my belongings to camp. The Datsun was stuffed. Even the passenger seat was loaded, and there was barely any room to see out the side and back windows.

When I awoke early the next morning, the car was empty. Ransacked. Almost everything I owned was taken. I was sick. It felt like my whole life had been stolen.

I had plenty of time to stew during the long drive back to the States. In retrospect, there were only two valuables I considered irreplaceable: a monogrammed bible my aunt and uncle had given me as a kid, and my WMU class ring. I reported the incident to the Quebec City police and pointed the silver sports car south.

Two irrevocable losses in two horrible days.

CHAPTER 37

The Honeymooners

It was an excruciating two weeks in Lansing, Michigan, where I stayed with my girlfriend. From September 24—the horrible day I spent driving home after the painful day at the mall—until October 6, I was a player without a team.

Michigan State allowed me to skate at their rink, and I kept in shape at a local gym. Finally, two weeks after my demotion, the Nordiques called and told me they had assigned me to the Nova Scotia Voyageurs. The news was both good and bad.

The good? It was the AHL, not the Eastern League. The bad? The Voyageurs were the top farm team of the Montreal Canadiens, Quebec's provincial rival. Rollie Cloutier and I were dispatched to the Vees in Halifax, and Reg Thomas was headed there, too, having eventually signed as a free agent after Quebec released him.

The Canadiens were known for their powerful developmental system, and the Voyageurs were stacked. Prospect after prospect emerged from Montreal's top minor-league team, and it became clear to me from the moment I arrived that I was not going to get much ice time. Talented players in the Canadiens system like Dan Métivier were buried behind blue-chip prospects like Dan Daoust, Craig Laughlin, Yvan Joly and Guy Carbonneau.

If Métivier was not going to be featured, why would the Canadiens spend any time developing me, or any of the Nordiques' prospects, over their own players? It made zero sense.

We three exiled Nords—Thomas, Cloutier and I—became one line. On most AHL teams, we would have been the number one unit. In Halifax, we were number four, playing fourth-line minutes. Thomas played the point on the power play, and Rollie and I killed penalties, but with my limited minutes, I plummeted from a top-10 AHL scorer to a role player . . . almost overnight.

There would be no Bernie Saunders Fan Club in Halifax.

Demers, who had been demoted to an organizational scout after being fired as head coach, occasionally kept his eyes on us. Whenever he visited, I voiced my concern that my production was being artificially reduced. Jacques tried to be positive and assured me the organization understood.

Two of Quebec's young defence prospects, my buddy Terry Johnson and Lee Norwood, were assigned to the Hershey Bears of the AHL. And what's pathetic is that we were luckier than most of the other prospects, who were dispatched to the Erie Blades of the EHL.

My girlfriend wasn't making life any simpler. She was dealing with her own version of societal abuse. She was a criminal justice major at WMU and had just taken a job at nearby Ionia Correctional Facility. Working in the slammer was her entry-level experience. As dejected as I was with my status in the Nordiques organization, her situation was worse. She was a tiny Black lady, closer to 100 pounds than

110, patrolling a prison wall with a rifle or walking through jail cell blocks, having to endure suggestive catcalls from the ill-mannered inmates.

For me, thinking about her job, and her fears, in the prison was agonizing. Being hundreds of miles away from her only exacerbated the tortured helplessness. One day, I asked her to pack her bags and come live with me in Halifax. It just made sense. I was unhappy and she was unhappy, so why not be unhappy together?

She agreed, so we united in Halifax. I had someone to support me through this debacle of a start to my second pro season, and she got out of prison.

At first, it was great. Less than a week after she joined me, I got home from practice to find my dirty laundry washed, dried, ironed and folded. My underwear was stacked in my dresser drawer as if it were fresh out of the package.

"This could work," I remember thinking. Suffice it to say, I never received the starched-underwear treatment again. But it was cute.

She provided the support I needed, and it was great having her there by my side. Being a hockey wife is an odd existence, but since several other players lived in the same apartment complex as us, she got to know the other wives. We became good friends with the Thomases and the Gormans.

But my girlfriend's parents were not happy with the arrangement. They issued an ultimatum: either we got married or she was to return home. We had wedding plans, but not exactly on that timetable. So, we got married on Monday, November 10, 1980. It was an off-day for the Voyageurs, what seemed like a slapstick wedding with the nuptials performed by the justice of the peace in Halifax.

A week before the wedding, I was on the phone with John. We talked for a good half hour, but somehow, I failed to mention the nuptials. Later that day, John spoke to Mom, who asked what he thought about the exciting news. A shocked John immediately called me back, wondering why I had omitted such a relevant piece of information from our previous conversation.

I had a funny relationship with John. I knew I could never win an argument with him, so whenever I had made up my mind on something I felt he would try to talk me out of, I wouldn't share that news with him. I had been conditioned to survive on my own, and I felt I knew myself best. I had to live in my own skin.

On the other hand, if I needed an opinion on a subject about which I was unsure, he was the first person to whom I turned.

John and my parents rushed to Halifax the next week to attend the wedding, if you could call it that. No one from my fiancée's family attended. We planned to have the justice of the peace in Halifax make it official that day, and then organize a wedding celebration during the off-season in Lansing.

We both recognized the absurdity of what we were doing, and both let out reflexive sardonic chuckles before we said the ceremonial "I do." We were planning to have a small celebration later in the day with my family and our friends who attended, but if this situation wasn't preposterous enough, I got a gag wedding gift from the Nordiques: an immediate recall to the NHL.

You can't make this up. The organization had reserved a plane ticket and instructed me to meet the team in Quebec City immediately. I had to catch a flight that afternoon.

So, the bride spent her wedding night with my brother, parents and uncle. I spent my wedding night in Quebec, preparing for a game at le Colisée against the Chicago Blackhawks the following day. It was the most ridiculous wedding day imaginable. The whole thing was a farce. We both deserved better.

The Nordiques' start to the season was as rocky as mine. With le Colisée's renovations not scheduled to end until late October, the team opened with a treacherous nine-game road trip. After a 1–3–2 start, Filion replaced himself behind the bench with Michel Bergeron, who only had a few months' experience as associate coach. After the trip ended 1–6–2, the team came home for three games but slid into a deep 1–9–4 hole.

All else had failed, and that's when the Nordiques called for me. To their credit, they were giving me a shot to give the club a jolt, although my offensive production had dropped dramatically with the Voyageurs. When I was promoted, Albert Ladouceur from *Le Journal de Québec* referenced the Bernie Saunders Controversy following my unfair demotion and my fourth-line playing status in Halifax.

Saunders Recall

Managing director Maurice Filion has announced the recall of black right winger Bernie Saunders. The latter had been excluded from the team during the second round of cuts at training camp. At the time, he ranked third among scorers and his exclusion was the source of many comments.

During 13 matches with the Voyageurs, Saunders scored three goals and made one assist, although he was primarily used when the team was shorthanded. It's important to note that when he played for Cincinnati and Syracuse last season, he scored 36 goals and made 28 assists in 67 games.

The groom was in the lineup on November 11, skating against the same team that had welcomed him so ungraciously the year before. But this stint would be very different. A year ago, my first NHL games were a reward for a breakout rookie season in the minors. But it was preordained that I would return to Syracuse for the playoffs. This was a make-or-break call-up. Although Coach Bergeron never talked to me, I knew the pressure was on me. I wasn't there to find my NHL sea legs; I was there to spark a failing expansion team.

We tied Chicago, 6–6, and I played a regular shift on a line with Robbie Ftorek and Marc Tardif. The review in *Le Journal de Québec* said our line fared well. I wore number 22, which brought a smile to my face when I found it hanging in my locker because it was Willie O'Ree's number. I'd worn 25 the previous season.

After the game, reporters and cameras swarmed around my locker. The press, still intrigued by the Bernie Saunders Controversy, applauded my overdue promotion. There was a sense of excitement that I could be the missing piece of the puzzle. The team (0–8–3 in its previous 11 games) performed better with me in the lineup, and we picked up an important point against the Blackhawks. It felt exactly the way I had visualized it all my life.

We trounced Winnipeg the next night, 5–1, for the team's first victory in a month. I got an assist on Tardif's goal, the eventual game winner, but I was pressing in a way I had never experienced before. I could brag about my assist being a no-look, behind-the-back gem, but I must be honest: it was a bullshit assist.

I came flying through the neutral zone down the left with the puck, trying to make something happen. As a right winger, why I was on the left side is a mystery. I cut towards the middle at the blue line—a rookie mistake. The left defenceman stepped up and clobbered me with a clean hip check. The impact caused my stick to ricochet backwards, which catapulted the puck back towards the left boards . . . directly onto the trailing Tardif's stick. He took two strides and drove a slapper into the lower right corner.

That was my only NHL point. A gaffe turned into a goal. But the review in the UPI wire story made it sound like I made an intentional play: "Tardif spurted over the Winnipeg line after taking a pass from Bernie Saunders and blasted a low drive past Jets goalie Markus Mattsson."

See what I told you about history?

Most important, we gained a win—Bergeron's first as an NHL head coach. Unfortunately, I also drew a penalty for interference in the first period, and Michel was unhappy. He believed rookies should be seen, not heard, and that they should never be in the penalty box. The only times I heard from him directly were when he reprimanded me for the penalty during the game, and at practice the next morning. I never felt that he was on board with my promotion.

The press was in my corner, but as in every other situation, they treated me like an anomaly. While I do not in any way put myself in the same category as Willie O'Ree or Herb Carnegie, I relate strongly to them because of how often race instead of hockey became the focal point whenever the subject was me.

Days after my recall and the tie with Chicago, Jean

Beaunoyer from *La Presse* in Montreal published a feature article on my promotion. But the slant of the article had little to do with my solid play or quick ascension from the minors. Nope. The storyline centred on the all-important question of why a Black person would want to play hockey. I tried to provide polite, thoughtful responses.

With all due respect to my forefathers, whenever I fielded questions like that, I felt as if I were breaking the hockey colour barrier myself.

RECALLED BY THE NORDIQUES

"A Black Cannot Have Guy Lafleur as an Idol"—Bernie Saunders

Very few Blacks don a uniform in the National Hockey League. We have always been able to count on the fingers of one hand the rare specimens who have managed to get into a few games. This year, there was only one player of colour in the league: Tony McKegney of the Buffalo Sabres. The second is now Bernie Saunders, recalled from the Nova Scotia Voyageurs last Tuesday for the game against Chicago.

When we talk about him in the media, we always hesitate to mention that he is a player of colour. When we met, I confess I struggled to talk to him about the Black phenomenon in hockey. We imagine many things that have nothing to do with reality. Saunders was particularly comfortable talking about Black people, and he taught me a lot.

"I know that I am more noticed than the others," he said. "When I do well on the ice, it's even better than the others, and when I do badly, it's worse." . . .

The inevitable question was why a Black person plays hockey.

"I am a Canadian with a Canadian mentality. Blacks are usually associated with warm-weather sports. When you are a Black American, your idols are Black and their names are Willie Stargell, Wilt Chamberlain and Ron LeFlore. Here, a Black cannot have Guy Lafleur as an idol. Currently, McKegney is likely to influence many young people and give them a taste for hockey, because sport is part of the culture of Blacks here and elsewhere."

Saunders speaks of his race with the pride of a new generation. His brethren in the NHL or the AHL, he knows them all, and can recite their journeys and their stories. No hang-ups, no taboo, we talk about prejudices:

"The story that Blacks have weak ankles is a joke, the way we say francophones have big noses. Nevertheless, the physical structure of Blacks is different. Their legs are longer, thinner, and that is why Black people win so many marathons."

And people's reactions?

"You often hear racist insults in the stands and even on the ice by players who want to get me unhinged. But I've learned not to pay attention. In Quebec City, however, I did not hear anything like that."

Saunders understands French, is still struggling, but intends to take the courses the club gives players to integrate better in the city. A fine conversationalist, remarkably polite, Saunders would like to open the door to young Black Canadians who only have Stargell, [Ellis] Valentine and LeFlore to look up to.

"I want to succeed so much that I have missed a few goals, but if I am trusted, it will come. We are in a multicultural country and I would like to see Canadians from different cultures become more interested in hockey."

248

Having played in college instead of Major Junior A, I had been totally off the radar, so the reporter saw me as though I was a member of the Jamaican Olympic bobsledding team. And yet, in my mind, I was a typical athlete trying to reach the pinnacle of my profession. The writer mentioned my polite demeanour, but I wanted to scream because the question that I always hated most is why a Black person would want to play hockey.

I wanted to tell him I was just a normal kid from the same hockey-crazed country as him. When I was born, I lived in Montreal, right on the island in Notre-Dame-de-Grâce. Later in life, I lived across the Mercier Bridge in Chateauguay. To tell him that my childhood was just like his childhood . . . watching the Canadiens on *Hockey Night in Canada* in those breathtaking red, white and blue uniforms, the horizontal striping across the chest accenting the famed *CH* crest.

I wanted the writer to know that for me, just like for him and so many Canadians across the country, Saturday night was magic. At 7 p.m., our black-and-white television showed a view from an airplane flying low over the Atlantic Ocean, a large city fast approaching, and an emcee decrying, "From the sun and fun capital of the world, Miami Beach, we bring you *The Jackie Gleason Show*, starring Jackie Gleason and Art Carney and *The Honeymooners*."

And away we would go to another hilarious hour with the plump, self-effacing Gleason and his sidekick, Carney. The side-splitting hour passed by in minutes. It was the perfect appetizer for the main course.

After Mr. Gleason said good night, the *HNiC* logo appeared to the *da-da-da-DA-da-DA,* before Ward Cornell or Dick Irvin introduced the game of the week. *Hockey Night in Canada* was a national institution that had millions of Canadians glued to their TV sets. It was *Monday Night Football* before *Monday Night Football* existed. If another country wanted to invade our land, Saturday night would be the time.

With that in mind, why wouldn't I want to play hockey? Why was it so puzzling? Guy Lafleur was my favourite because he was so many other kids' favourite. John and I never missed a Saturday night. But the reporter only saw the pigmentation of my skin.

Nothing in my professional career befit my dreams. It felt more like my hockey *nightmare* in Canada.

MY SIX-GAME STINT went well. We went 3–1–2, and some teammates made a point of telling me they felt a palpable improvement in the club's mood that correlated directly to my arrival.

With the team responding, it looked as though I was finally at home for good. We lost to Buffalo after beating Winnipeg, but then topped Washington, 6–2, and Detroit, 2–1, before tying Calgary, 3–3.

The acoustics in most NHL rinks don't allow players to hear many individual voices. On the ice, you hear a dull roar. I recall a few difficult walks down runways where the vitriol flowed. There were several racial catcalls in Buffalo, which was surprising, since Tony McKegney was there. But overall, I was trying to bask in my new life in the NHL. John attended the game in Buffalo and was overjoyed to see his little brother skating as an NHL regular.

But the truth is, I failed to play as well as I had under Demers the year before. Bergeron was breathing down my neck, the pall from the Bernie Saunders Controversy wouldn't lift, and I was pressing.

I did my best not to let the background noise undermine my performance. But I took four minor penalties in the six games, one each in the last three games. After my penalty in the tie with Calgary, I got reprimanded by Bergeron again. This last time, he was livid.

Although I didn't draw many penalties throughout my career, I will take full responsibility for the mishaps, but it would have been nice to be given a little grace period. Plus, his criticism felt like a red herring for his apparent dislike for me.

What ate at my stomach the most was that the last infraction shouldn't have been mine. I converged with one of our defencemen while backchecking, and when he poked at the puck, his stick caught the Flame's skate. The referee saw the trip, but incorrectly fingered me as the offender. Charles Thiffault, who joined the club as assistant coach when Bergeron was promoted to head coach, was the players' new firewall from Bergeron, so I talked to him about it the next day. Thiffault was one of the early advocates of video as a coaching tool. We watched the replay, and he agreed.

But I was still guilty in Bergeron's eyes, the only eyes that mattered. I know it sounds like whining, but it happened. On top of all the racial crap I had to contend with, I also had to deal with good, old-fashioned bad luck.

The Nordiques locker room was the most dysfunctional I have ever occupied. It drew a lot of press, and I can confirm that it wasn't pleasant. You had the French–English strife that was played up in the papers. If Buddy Cloutier were to say hi to me today, it would be the first word that we spoke. The Stastny brothers dominated the scene, stealing all the headlines from the other egos. The tough guys were at war, battling to wear the team belt. Bergeron was his cantankerous self. And then throw in this quiet Black guy. When I think back, it's comical that I ever thought it could work.

At one point, a veteran player who had just bought a new house approached me with a proposition. He wanted me to rent his apartment, an amazing place tacked to the side of the bluff, literally hanging off the cliffs overlooking the St. Lawrence River. From the street, the unit looked small. But when you entered the foyer, you approached a staircase that traversed a dramatic precipice.

The building was gorgeous. The view was indescribable. I couldn't wait to move in with my new wife and start my new life in the NHL.

My teammate asked me to commit, but I told him we had to wait until the Nordiques brass signalled that I was there to stay. It seemed a fait accompli to most, especially my team-mates, but I didn't want to jinx things, so I asked him to wait. He grew impatient, so he approached management to ask about my status, since he needed to rent the place and felt that I was a lock to stay.

I got the call later that afternoon—via speakerphone, and I could tell there was more than one person on that call. I could also tell the news was not good. And I could tell the voice on the phone was Maurice Filion's.

In the friendliest of tones, he thanked me for my play and told me I was being sent back to Halifax.

My heart stopped. I was so pissed at my teammate for for-cing the issue. The decision was probably already made—I'll never know for sure. But I needed somewhere to direct my anger. I was headed back to hell. The Nordiques had checked the Bernie Saunders box. Although the team had responded to my presence, with only one assist in six games, the Nordiques had placated the media and fans by calling me up, so it was safe for them to send me back down.

The honeymoon was over.

CHAPTER 38

Whirlwinds

I accept 100 percent responsibility for my fate and have no one to blame but myself. That six-game stint was a whirlwind. It felt like it was over before it began.

After hanging up the phone from Maurice's call, I sat quietly in my room in the Auberge des Gouverneurs, trying to gather my thoughts. Once again, I was not provided with any concrete feedback, so I lay on my bed in silent speculation. Before I arrived, the team had a record of 0–6–2 under Michel Bergeron. While I was there, we went 3–1–2. My head was in a daze.

I never got comfortable with Michel Bergeron behind the bench, and it felt like he never got comfortable with me. I got that penalty in my second game and quickly found myself in his doghouse. I already felt a lot of pressure following the Bernie Saunders Controversy. The penalty had heaped more pressure on top of that.

Bergeron just never made me feel welcome. During one practice, we were running a basic drill. It was a warm-up exercise where the coach gathers pucks behind the net. Three forwards skate towards him from the near blue line, and he passes the puck around the boards, where the strong-side winger is supposed to gather in the puck, pass it to the centre and initiate a breakout towards the other end.

When the other lines approached, Bergeron feathered a soft pass around the boards to the pivoting winger and everything flowed perfectly. With my line, it was different. When I approached, he practically took a slapshot in order to ring the puck around the boards like a pinball. It careened so wildly, it bounced as it ricocheted around the corner. I did everything I could to stop it, but it was impossible. The puck sailed down the ice. When I failed to contain it, Michel stopped practice and yelled at me as if I had ruined a routine play. He never did that with any other winger that day.

One of the many difficulties of my race is putting life's pitfalls into perspective. I live in South Carolina. Yesterday, I returned from the beach to find my patio furniture in the pond behind my house. My mind immediately considered the possibility that I had been the victim of a racially motivated attack. But my friend kept insisting there were other possibilities. Although it was a relatively calm day and none of the other neighbours had been affected, maybe some type of mini tornado or whirlwind appeared in my backyard. And that is a viable possibility.

That's what it is like when you live in Black skin. That's how my hockey career felt many times. Put yourself in my skates. You are dealing with all of these incidents of overt racism from the people in the stands, on the ice and in your dressing room. And then something else really bad happens to you. Where do you think your mind would go? I don't believe that the Bernie Saunders Controversy was an overtly racially motivated event today, but years ago as I was facing racial hatred all around me, why wouldn't my mind go there? Then I got called back to the team all of a sudden and the new coach was making me feel unwelcome. What would you think?

The reality is that my second NHL stint coinciding with Bergeron's promotion was a perfect storm. I got called up when my hockey confidence was as fragile as it had ever been in my life and I felt like I was being asked to turn around a failing NHL team, on my wedding day. Meanwhile, le Petit Tigre, as Bergeron was known, was being promoted to his first NHL assignment. He had just been plucked from the QMJHL and was a new NHL assistant coach, but after a six-pack of games was promoted to head coach and asked to turn around a 1–3–2 team full of characters, egos and dissension. This was not a perfect union.

Here's how the situation was depicted in the *Philadelphia Daily News* on January 15, 1981: "A muddled coaching situation, which had General Manager Maurice Filion foolishly taking on both jobs after firing Jacques Demers, appears to have been stabilized since the naming of Michel Bergeron early this season. Bergeron, a long-time success with the Three Rivers junior team, is an avowed separatist, but his more immediate problem is separating the egos from his team's performance."

Most people personalize things when bad things happen. In my mind, I had three strikes against me before entering the batter's box: I was Black, there was the French–English issue and Michel would go on to be known for his infamous aversion to rookies.

Sports Illustrated ran an article on Bergeron on January 30, 1989, emphasizing this point: "Short-fused coach Michel Bergeron likes rookies the way W.C. Fields liked children: parboiled and fricasseed." The *SI* article talked about how Tony

Granato felt afraid to make a mistake . . . which is exactly how I felt. It's difficult to perform under those conditions. When you're scolded *not* to get a penalty, guess what is likely to happen?

But when you dissect those three internalizations, it is difficult to support the accusations with any credibility. I personally witnessed Bergeron giving rookie Dale Hunter the kid-gloves treatment. During training camp, I arrived for my scrimmage early and found Michel and Dale on the ice following an early session. I watched in disbelief as Michel worked with Dale on power turns. The next day, the headlines in the papers read, "Dale Hunter Est Prêt." With my limited French, I knew that meant Dale was declared ready to play in the NHL. Michel Goulet was another rookie on the team who did pretty well for himself. Bergeron later coached newcomers Brian Leetch and Tony Granato with the Rangers. So, it would be hard to get the anti-rookie claim to hold up in a hot-stove debate.

The "anti-anglo" claim is easily dispelled as well. There is a long list of non-French players who thrived under Bergeron. I mentioned Dale Hunter. Peter Stastny is another, and he skated into the Hall of Fame. The only complaint I can register in this regard is that Michel never talked to me, other than to yell at me during practice. André Boudrias was fired when Michel got promoted, so Thiffault became the go-between, or the "good cop." Life can be circularly cruel because I believe it would have helped my career dramatically had I been able to learn French in high school. I don't regret much about my life, but I have always regretted not learning the language of my native province.

The race card is harder to dissect. I can comfortably put Michel in the same category as many other people who didn't seem to know how to deal with a Black hockey player. However, Tony McKegney played for him with the Nordiques in 1983–84 and 1984–85, and did a second tour in 1989–90. Tony scored 24 goals and recorded 51 points in 75 games that first season. Scotty Bowman, probably the best coach in hockey history, reached for a baseball equivalent when he spoke on this subject: "I can take a lot of aggravation from a .300 hitter, but none from a .200 hitter."

I had one assist in six games. My bad.

So much for conspiracy theory. That's the thing about being Black. My backyard incident does appear to be racially motivated, so my instincts were correct. But sometimes it really is just a whirlwind. Maybe Bergeron was just a tough SOB and unsatisfied with my performance. There were many other recipients of his wrath. Michel almost boasted how, as a coach in juniors, he ran Pierre Aubry out of Trois-Rivières because his parents had the audacity to approach him about moving their son to a different position. Or for hounding his leading scorer, Jean-François Sauvé, to the extent that his parents paid Michel a visit.

Now, I understand I was not the same calibre of player as Leetch or Granato—not even close. Hunter and Goulet were treated differently in Quebec as well. But I was showing a great deal of promise and could have used a little love myself. It was just such a difficult time for me, as Michel's style was the opposite of what I needed.

Michel made a name for himself on his style of coaching. Herb Zurkowsky wrote a feature article on him for the *Montreal Gazette* that said, in part, "It's easy to like Michel Bergeron. He's humorous. . . . But it's easy to hate Michel Bergeron. He's irascible, tempestuous, cantankerous, strict, occasionally an s.o.b. and always a tough disciplinarian who rules with an iron fist. Often it's Michel Bergeron's way or the highway." That was a reporter writing a pro-Bergeron article.

Independent of his coaching style, my disappointment is that Bergeron never took the time to get to know me as a player . . . or as a person.

Although I wish I could have gotten a longer look, I take full responsibility. Blaming others is futile. When I got sent back to Halifax, I was mad at myself for needing to rely on the subjectivity of my performance. All my career, I was accustomed to coming out of the gates like a cannon, filling the net. I needed objective measures of success in this situation. I failed to do that in the NHL, and it cost me dearly.

As a proud goal scorer, the NHL is the only league in which I was shut out.

IT SHOULD ALSO be made clear that I felt nothing but love from the fans of Quebec City. The city so deserves another NHL franchise. Quebec is a hockey mecca, and the fans were supportive of me, as most home crowds were. Quebec City is a sophisticated hockey town, and there was a backlash after my demotion. The fans had disapproved of my unjust reassignment at training camp, and the entire city was abuzz with excitement when I finally arrived. But even that put extra pressure on me. I did not do enough in those six games to maintain the fans' support.

I remember one particular play where I was racing through the neutral zone with the puck. The Sher-Wood hockey stick representative had brought me a new bundle of sticks that day and I put them into play immediately. As I attacked the offensive zone, I attempted to pass to the other winger in a fairly routine play, but the rocker on my new stick blade was a little off and the pass was errant. You could hear a thundering groan from the packed le Colisée fans as they wanted so badly for me to do well.

The fact that they were so receptive is not surprising. I was not the first Black player to skate in le Colisée. In fact, if ever a Black Hockey Hall of Fame were built, it should be erected in Quebec City, a virtual underground railway for Black hockey players. This walled fortress of a city on the banks of the St. Lawrence River welcomed many of the founding brothers: Herb Carnegie, Quebec Aces; Willie O'Ree, Quebec Aces; Stan Maxwell, Quebec Aces; Bernie Saunders, Quebec Nordiques; Val James, Quebec Remparts; Tony McKegney, Quebec Nordiques; Reggie Savage, Quebec Nordiques. Claude Vilgrain grew up there. Anson Carter was drafted by Quebec, and I apologize if there is anyone I missed.

Heck, even Jackie Robinson passed through *la belle province*.

LET ME DIGRESS for just a moment. I learned a lot from my experiences with various coaches and later gave back and coached youth players on a high level. I coached the West Michigan Warriors AAA team in Michigan, and later the New Jersey Rockets AAA in New Jersey. In my coaching I tried to borrow from Sherry Bassin's approach, where I coached individuals, not teams. Using my own sons as an example, Jonathan and I had a system down pat. When we were outside the rink, I was Dad, but when we were in the arena, I was Coach. I was probably tougher on him than other players, but he was able to absorb it as solid direction from his coach. Shawn had immense talent, but he couldn't isolate the two. Any time I attempted to give him direction on the ice, his eyes widened as he seemed horrified that the other players were seeing me addressing him. So, I always had the other coach, Jim Dyer, address Shawn. I often whispered in Jim's ear to tell him what I wanted Shawn to do. As a coach, I tried to adapt to the needs of each individual player.

I am proud to say that several of my former players achieved college scholarships, and two made it to the NHL. Because of their age, I worked hard on the fundamentals at the expense of other things because I knew they needed a solid foundation. This used to drive the parents nuts because they wanted me to work on things like the power play so we could win games. Well, we won our share of games because these players became so sound on the fundamentals.

I adopted the Sherry Bassin style of coaching, and "sideboards" was my favourite drill. I yelled and screamed and put on a show, trying to push the players, and the parents preferred to sit in the bleachers to watch the show. One practice, we were in a different rink and it was freezing, so the parents were watching from the snack bar. This was one of those sessions when I punished the players for some bad behaviour after a loss. I was in the midst of a rant, which was really a disguise for giving them a rest period, when Matt Greene skated over to the team bench and puked his guts out. Out of the corner of my eye, I could see his mother, Darcy, darting for the door to access the ice surface. My heart stopped as I feared I was about to be under another heavy attack from a parent. But upon reaching the glass, she leaned over and told me to tell Matt to get his ass off the bench as she wanted him to fight through the pain with his teammates. What a great family. There is nearly a direct correlation between parents and their child.

Scott Parse was a hockey prodigy. He was a year younger than the rest of the players and had a physical disadvantage. Whenever we did sideboards, Scott would line up on the goal line, using the corner of the rink to decrease the distance that he had to skate. He probably thought he was pulling one over on me, but I allowed it because he was underaged. Scott had press box vision and could see the ice as well as the best players in the game. Both he and Matt Greene played on the L.A. Kings. Matt went on to win two Stanley Cups, while Scott's career was cut short because of an injury. That was disappointing because I believe Scott would have been a star.

Can you imagine? I'm home on the couch, watching the Kings as they finally clinched their first Stanley Cup championship. Matt played a big part in the winning drive. When the final buzzer sounded, my heart swelled with happiness for the two. The NHL tradition is for the team captain to hoist the Cup first and then pass it, player by player, until each participant has hoisted the Cup and taken a victory lap. Dustin Brown began the celebration, followed by Willie Mitchell, Simon Gagné, Anze Kopitar, and then Matt Greene got his turn. While flashing the patented grin I recognized from his childhood, Greene hoisted the Stanley Cup over his head.

As he did, I heard Mike "Doc" Emrick, the Hall of Fame broadcaster, spin yet another yarn from his mental encyclopedia of hockey memories. Only this one made me tingle: "Matt Greene, who was coached by Bernie Saunders five years in youth hockey, the old pro, how proud he must be."

Yes, Doc, this old pro was proud. Thanks for noticing.

Doc recently retired and wrote his own book, *Off Mike*. He was the best-prepared man in the business.

As for me, getting back to 1980, I had to prepare my psyche for a return to the minors.

CHAPTER 39

Kunta Kinte

Following the gut punch in Quebec, it was back to Halifax. I am not into sloganeering, but I am a person who tries to control what I can control and not sweat the things that I can't. Returning to the minors was a nightmare for me because it meant I'd be back on the fourth line. I wouldn't be able to score my way back to the NHL. My fate was not within my control.

Playing in the minors was hell. It had been hell for me in Cincinnati and in Syracuse, and all over again now that I was back with the Voyageurs. And as disgruntled as we Nordiques prospects were, exiled to Montreal's top farm club, the Canadiens' prospects were just as unhappy with their parent team. Experienced players like Dan Métivier, Dave Gorman and Reg Thomas, bright prospects like Guy Carbonneau, Dan Daoust, Rick Wamsley and Craig Laughlin, even coach Bert Templeton, impatiently waiting for an NHL job . . . we all felt like refugees trying to find a home.

Not even a guy like Carbonneau, a top prospect and a future Hockey Hall of Famer, could be totally secure about his future. And you could see why: Métivier—coming off his second 30-goal season, in which he was named an AHL all-star—had had a great training camp in Montreal, but he was still in Halifax. I knew Carbonneau would make it, as he had an explosive offensive rookie season one year after he dominated offensively in the Quebec Major Junior Hockey League. We sat beside each other in the dressing room and always clowned around. Guy was shy about speaking English, but we forged a fun relationship. One day after my call-up, Guy asked me what it was like to play in the NHL. At the time, I was the veteran because I had had two stints in the big league.

I laughed and told him he was going to be a star one day soon. As a joke, I asked him to autograph his Voyageurs marketing photo, and I hung it over my stall. I still have that today.

"Someday, when I have a son, I'm going to have him get your autograph," I teased Guy, having no idea that, seven years later, I would bring my six-year-old son, Jonathan, to a Habs game at Chicago Stadium so that he could meet Montreal's future Selke Trophy–winning centre, who eventually won two Stanley Cups with Montreal and a third with the Dallas Stars. Guy, gracious as ever and one of the NHL's true class acts, kibitzed with Jonathan and gave my wide-eyed son an autographed stick.

As impressed as Jonathan was to be in the Canadiens' dressing room, he was infatuated with goalies, as most kids are that age. Guy observed Jonathan staring at Patrick Roy, so he barked something in French and Patrick dropped everything and started playing with Jonathan. Hockey players are just the best.

. . .

THE 1980–81 VEES were a great team on paper. But with prospects from two different organizations, Montreal and Quebec, the potential would never be put into practice. Michael Farber of the Montreal Gazette was embedded in our travelling party during one road trip, and he examined the issue.

> *How do the boys divide themselves? As 19 Canadians and two Americans? Twenty whites and one black? Seventeen players who are owned by the Canadiens, three who belong to the Nordiques? Seventeen anglophones and four francophones? Three college graduates and 18 products of the Canadian junior system? One coach and 21 players? Too many small forwards and not enough defencemen?*

To me, it felt like 20 against one that season. I had never felt so frustrated and alone. Not only was I returned from the NHL, but I was relegated to the fourth line, and because we had a small team, my role changed. I was called upon to fight more than I ever had. And the racist attacks persisted, following me at every stop around the league. I quickly learned it was easier to deal with the racial hatred when I could shut them up with a big goal. As a fourth-liner, the filth wore me down.

At home, my race neither helped nor hurt me. Bill Riley had been captain of the Vees the season before, so the Halifax fans did not consider me unique. The media barely covered the team, so my presence on the Halifax bench was a non-factor. But just as I wondered how teammates would have treated me if I were a foe, I always wondered how each city in which I played would have treated me as the enemy.

Consider Val James. As bad as my experience was playing in Rochester, Val ended up playing four seasons for the

Amerks and became a fan favourite. He scored the Calder Cup–winning goal in 1983, when Rochester won the title under coach Mike Keenan. In James's autobiography, *Black Ice*, Rochester Americans broadcaster Tom George comments, "The Americans were rock stars in Rochester in those days. And none was more popular than Val. It was a lovefest between Val and the fans." Hello. This is the same town that brought everything but tiki torches whenever I visited. Tell me that doesn't screw with your head.

I never had to speculate about my reception from rival spectators. Some nights could be just brutal. After travelling with the team and witnessing the cruelty himself, Farber asked me to gauge the level of brutality I had just endured in a game in New Haven.

"Mild-to-average," says Bernie Saunders, when asked to rate the level of the night's verbal abuse.

Being called "Kunta Kinte," "suction lips," "N-word," is Saunders' idea of mild-to-average. Saunders, if you haven't guessed, is black, something the gentlefolk of New Haven— and most other cities around the league—never fail to remind him of.

"If I let it get to me, the crap from both the fans and the other teams, I'd live in the penalty box or be suspended all the time for going up in the stands," says Saunders.

Farber also wanted to know if the cruelty was getting to me, and whether I had a support system to help manage the stress.

Fact is, it has gotten to him.

Taunts get through.

*After leading the CHL in scoring last season, he has but
12 goals this season, which he attributes, in part, to the taunts.
"Last year, I'd pop in a few goals to shut people up. Now, well,
the goals aren't going in."*

When we were kids growing up and dreaming of playing
in the NHL, John would often provide a play-by-play commentary as we played sock hockey on our knees in the family
room. When someone would score, he would offer his best
imitation of Danny Gallivan's "He shoots . . . he *SCORES*!!!"
Following that refrain, the crowd always went crazy in support of the hockey hero.

That was the dream of hockey. Nowhere in my imagination did I ever account for the nightmare I would experience
playing the game.

I HAD NEVER even heard the name Brian Johnson until
he showed up in an Adirondack Red Wings uniform that
Saturday afternoon in Glens Falls, New York. I am sure he had
never heard of Bernie Saunders, either. Johnson played for the
Red Wings. Like me, he is Black. That's where the similarity
ended. By now, the age of the Black player had dawned, so I
wasn't shocked to see a Black on the opposing team. However,
it became crystal clear early in the contest that Brian wasn't
there to play hockey.

He was there to fight.

When the game began, he began chirping, trash-talking
and generally disrespecting our team. One of the many things
I love about the sport is that it's a game of honour: yes, the

officials patrol the ice, but in situations like this, there exists a system of self-policing. There was just no way we were going to allow Johnson to act out. One of our resident tough guys had to respond. Let's call him Player X.

Player X knew his way around a fight and quickly challenged Johnson. The two squared off, but the scuffle escalated and a few players on both teams became involved. At one point, Johnson raised his hand and pointed a finger skyward as if he had won his bout, creating an even bigger scene. Eventually, the benches emptied.

With a few minutes left in the period, the officials did the right thing and sent both teams off the ice to allow heads to cool and to restore the peace. We were in our dressing room, calming down, but Player X was still enraged by Johnson's ridiculous behaviour. From across the room, Player X shouted several epithets and concluded with "that f*cking [N-word]."

Upon hearing the N-bomb, I pounced from my stall and darted across the room, determined to challenge my own teammate! A few other players jumped up, intercepted me and quickly ushered me towards the door. They sat me down in an area outside our dressing room. I was fuming.

I broke down and cried. I'm talking body-shaking, snot-nosed bawling while wearing my macho hockey armour. I had lapsed to the point where I didn't care who saw me. I just couldn't take it anymore.

The game I loved was causing me so much pain. My sanctuary, hockey, was turning into a garbage dump. Templeton, my unsophisticated, pugnacious coach, tried to console me but only made matters worse. "[Player X] didn't mean *you* were a [N-word]," he said to me. "Just Brian Johnson."

It's amazing my head didn't explode.

But as I stated at the outset, I wasn't mad at Player X or Coach Templeton specifically. I was angry because this thing just would not go away. It kept rearing its ugly head, and the dressing room was where it was most unwanted.

It wasn't Johnson's fault, either. He was an average scorer and pugilist in the QMJHL, but he was clearly in the pros to fight. Player X was a tough guy, too, and did his job because Johnson needed to be dealt with.

My problem now was that nearly every encounter was reduced to race. I was hearing the racial abuse in nearly every road game, and now that it had crept into my locker room, it was more than I could take.

THE WARM GREETING in Winnipeg, drowned out by the insults in Chicago throughout my NHL debut. My teammate who thought nothing of spitting out the N-word during a day off in L.A. "Black is beautiful" from one of my advocates in Syracuse. Racial obscenity spewing from the rafters nearly every road game. And now another racial incident, right in my own locker room.

It felt worse than 20 against one. It felt like me against the world. If I had been an opponent, any one of my current teammates could be the player launching the same racist epithets towards me. I'd always considered that, but Player X brought it to light. That's exactly what I conveyed to Michael Farber:

Have you ever, he is asked, discussed race with your teammates?
"No," says Saunders. "I'm afraid if I were in another uniform, they might go out and do something very racial too."

That answer was as candid as anything I had ever said in an interview. I was at the lowest point in my career. I had always loved the comfort of my teammates. I had always regarded the dressing room as a spiritual home of sorts.

It now felt like there was no place where I could take shelter.

CHAPTER 40

Sticks and Stones

THERE IS ANOTHER angle to the Brian Johnson incident that I need to unpack. As soon as I saw his unruly behaviour on the ice, I wanted to crawl into a hole and hide. My Black brothers know exactly what I am talking about. I knew that his showing off and drawing attention to himself meant that many others would judge me in the same vein. It's another one-sided dynamic of my race.

Y'all think we all look alike and assume we all act alike. But this stereotype mysteriously fails to work in reverse. Why aren't we perceived as being like Barack Obama?

Brian Johnson had NHL dreams, just like me. Although I did not agree with his style of play, who am I to judge? He had every right to take that avenue, just as any white player has the right to fight his way into the league. The issue I had is that I knew I would be typecast in the same negative light. His bad behaviour automatically projected not only on me but on my entire race.

That doesn't happen to white players. Mario Lemieux was never judged based on Jeremy Roenick's antics.

I spent a career trying to conform and not draw attention. In slave terms, that's called a "house [N-word]." Brian brandished his fists and worked the hard labour like a slave out in the fields. In the end, I played 10 NHL games and he played three, so who am I to criticize? Johnson fought his way through the Quebec Major Junior Hockey League, so I can't imagine the abuse he faced trying to realize his dream.

I ain't mad at you, brother. I'm proud and honoured to have you as my hockey soulmate.

If you analyze the evolution of the Black man in the game, there was a parade of Black players who followed the same path. Val James and Brian Johnson started the battle, but Claude Vilgrain, Steve Fletcher, and Graeme Townshend quickly followed.

The complication with a player of colour struggling to fight his way into the NHL is that it is like shaking a hornet's nest with your bare hands. Google the CBS News *Sunday Morning* segment on Val James, and you will see what I mean. When a Black man shows up on the ice in the Salem–Roanoke County Civic Center as a villain prepared to kick the crap out of the local team's white boys, there is going to be some bigotry. Don't think that I am condoning xenophobia. There is no place or excuse for racism in any form, or in any situation.

But I was always careful not to rattle the hornet's nest.

For those who theorized that the racial vitriol aimed at a Black player who conformed and just played the game would not be as intense, I am living proof of the opposite. There were many nights when the hatred that rained down on me was just as intense as the hatred Val James received in West Virginia.

SOMETIMES, YOU HAVE to do what Murph did in Belleville and strip away your clothing and bare your soul to the world.

It's time I attempt to describe what the N-word means to me.

After all, it is "only" a word. Yeah, right. Just like a swastika is "only" a symbol. That's the closest parallel I can come up with. Apologies to those who just had a visceral reaction to the mention of that disgraceful mark.

The Black experience is very difficult to describe. Contrary to popular belief, Blacks are not monolithic. The N-word elicits a different meaning and different reactions from every individual. I don't dare assume that Willie O'Ree or Jarome Iginla reacted the same way as I did when they endured the filth. Early in his career, Tony McKegney shook off his experiences as no big deal, but later swung his stick at Joe Kocur's head in an NHL game like an angry Black man after Kocur called him the N-word.

As you have seen and read, I cannot even write the N-word on a page. The word is dehumanizing. It evokes a guttural reaction in my body, a raw pain. It is visceral. When I hear the word, I literally feel aching within my body . . . a deep inner pain. If we have a soul, this must be its location, because I feel it there. I suffer a quick stinging sensation and it vibrates within.

What it means to me is that no matter what I do in my life, how tirelessly I educate myself, how hard I work, how well I live with integrity, and how significantly I contribute to society, certain people will always view me as inferior simply because of my skin colour.

It is absurd.

Every white person, especially the naysayers who immediately brush this stuff off, should do what John Howard Griffin did for six weeks in writing *Black Like Me*: darken your skin for even a day. Live in my shoes for 24 hours.

People of colour are exposed to this stuff all the time. I am

65 years old and have become the sole caregiver for my girl-friend, Pam, who suffered a stroke in 2016 and remains phys-ically and mentally disabled. She lives with me, and I assist her with all of her basic daily activities.

Pam is white. With her mental limitations, she has a habit of staring. We were out for a walk and I was helping her navigate the sidewalk when she peered at a passerby. The man took it as a pass, so he smiled and winked.

I observed the exchange and gazed back at him with disgust as I continued to assist Pam. He returned the stare and blurted, "What are you looking at, [N-word]?"

It sent shivers up my spine. He was clearly a low-life, and I knew I should not have gotten upset. But I can't control what's in my gut.

But we are all different. My sons grew up in a different time. They are comfortable uttering the word in a Black-on-Black setting. When I asked them about their viewpoint for the best convention to follow in this book, they were comfortable with it. But for me, even when I hear my sons use the word, it shakes my inner core.

Let me do some Black-man-splaining. If you are white and ask me when it is appropriate to use the word, I offer a one-word response: never. Not singing along to a rap jam, not when engaged in a serious conversation on the subject, not when you are in an all-white setting, miles away from the nearest Black person. Am I clear on this point? Never!

There is a famous *Star Trek* episode that I love because it symbolically mocked the absurdity of race. The starship *Enterprise* has been assigned to help decontaminate the atmosphere on the planet Ariannus, which is heavily polluted. A weird force is sensed, and a disabled craft is taken aboard.

There is a strange alien aboard this craft who identifies himself as Lokai, a political refugee from the planet Cheron.

Lokai's skin is half black and half white, vertically split down the centre of his body. Later, a second alien is beamed aboard. He is in pursuit of Lokai. His name is Bele and his appearance is similar to Lokai's, except that his black and white halves are the mirror image of Lokai's—a difference that seemed irrelevant to the crew of the *Enterprise*. But in their world, the difference was significant. They hated each other. The episode concludes with the two attempting to kill each other.

That's how I see the world. Bigotry is a stupid social construct. As I gaze out into the world, I don't see my skin colour. I am a human being, period. That's what my childhood in Canada taught me. I see you as a human being, the same way I see myself.

It doesn't matter what you believe in, what your religion is, how you think we were created: we all likely came from the same form. We are all brothers and sisters.

I believe that explains why our instinct is to help each other in times of peril. The idea came through so compellingly in the car accident scene in the movie *Crash*.

Matt Dillon's character, Sergeant John Ryan, had groped Christine, played by Thandie Newton, in an earlier scene during a traffic stop. Officer Ryan was white, and Christine was Black. Christine was incensed at the personal intrusion from a white person of authority.

Later in the film, Christine is in a horrific automobile accident. She's trapped in her overturned vehicle, which is seconds from bursting into flames. Guess who shows up? Sergeant Ryan. In one of the most compelling scenes I can remember, Ryan risks his life to save Christine from the burning flames.

It took a life-or-death situation for Sergeant Ryan to view Christine as a human being.

The *Star Trek* episode ridiculed the senselessness of prejudice, while the accident scene in *Crash* depicted true human nature. Some prejudice is fear-based. If green, one-eyed aliens invaded Earth, we would all band together to fight them, strengthened by our similarities, not our differences. Although, sadly, I also know that, shortly after the aliens were defeated, prejudice would bubble back up to the surface in some. Ask Isaac Woodard.

And it's not just the overt attacks that impact the Black experience. While I was teaching hockey school in Kalamazoo, I was talking to a young camp participant off the ice. His father saw us, marched over and interrupted us by pronouncing, "I don't care who he is, son. Listen to this guy because he knows what he's talking about."

Those are the sorts of dog-whistle remarks people of colour hear all the time . . . far more often than we hear the blatant comments like the N-word. I was supposed to be honoured that this man was granting me permission to teach his son how to play hockey, despite my Blackness?

Scotty, beam me up!

CHAPTER 41

Can You See the Light?

Not long after we were married, I told my wife that I couldn't wait to introduce her to my buddy Terry Johnson, who was on loan to Hershey. TJ was my best friend from the Syracuse year, and I couldn't wait to see him. We played the Hershey Bears at home and made plans to meet for dinner after the game.

Hockey players understand that off-ice friendships melt away once you hop over the boards. The battles with John when we were kids are nothing compared to brothers dropping their gloves in the NHL. Early in the game, I gave TJ a relatively innocuous bodycheck after he passed the puck to his defensive partner. When I turned to join the play, I felt my head being pummelled by haymakers. TJ was giving me an odd greeting. He jumped me and was beating the crap out of me before I even realized I was in a fight. I don't think I got a glove off.

What the hell happened? I didn't run him from behind or do anything dirty. The incident had me fuming the entire game. When it ended, I contemplated cancelling dinner, but decided to go through with it for only one reason: I wanted an explanation.

When TJ arrived at the restaurant, he was embarrassed, and he wore that Big Bird grin. He started explaining before our butts even hit the chairs. He revealed that his coach, Bryan Murray, was not happy with his play. Murray insisted before the game that TJ be more aggressive. Murray told him in no uncertain terms that if he didn't fight the next person who checked him, he was gone.

As fate would have it, I happened to be that next player! We still laugh when we remember what happened before dinner that night against Hershey.

THE SEASON TOOK its mental toll, but it was also wearing me down physically. As arduous as an 80-game schedule is, I always had an extra burden to bear. There were games in which I knew the unnecessary shots at me were inspired by some locker-room bounty. Bowling Green had been particularly aggressive when I played for Western Michigan. In the AHL, I always received a special reception when we visited Maine.

There is a play in hockey that all wingers despise. In the defensive zone, if your defenceman is under heavy pressure, he will wind the puck around the boards. When he does, the winger is expected to corral the pass at the faceoff-circle hash marks, scrape it off the boards and onto his stick, and either clear the zone or execute a breakout pass to the circling centre. It is a choreographed play that happens so often in a game that I practised it as diligently as my Guy Lafleur slapper. I took pride in executing that play while under heavy pressure, because it's the subtle plays that make a complete hockey player.

The difficulty is that if the opposing team's defenceman anticipates the wraparound, he can come crashing down the boards and demolish the defenceless winger. In most other situations, you can evade a check by redirecting your body, but in this situation, you must stay home to make sure the puck is cleared.

One game in Maine, I happened to face at least five instances where the defenceman flew down the boards to annihilate me. The crowd jumped to its feet each time, yelling things like "Kill the [N-word]!"

A coward would have bailed out of the play, but I stayed home each time, cleared the puck and took the beating. The focal point of that game became abusing me rather than the outcome. Every time I touched the puck, there grew a sense of anticipation in the air. I don't use this term lightly, but getting crucified in front of that angry mob felt like hockey's version of a public whipping.

In other games, it was an individual player who took it upon himself to show his prejudice—sometimes with a verbal attack, sometimes with a challenge that would escalate into a fight. One night at the Halifax Metro Centre, it started at a routine faceoff at the beginning of a period, when I lined up against the visiting team's resident goon.

Although I will never forget this guy's name, I will refrain from sharing it with you. No words were spoken, but clearly, I was being singled out for some "unknown" reason. Hmmm. This guy was the type that any opponent would fear because he was more than a little bit off mentally. He always skated with a crazed look in his eyes. These are the guys who got your attention because you never knew what they were going to do.

When opposing wingers line up, they typically cross sticks. It's standard protocol. Sometimes the two players will jostle for position, each trying to place his stick on top of his opponent's just as the puck is dropped, in order to gain a quick advantage should the puck squirt his way. When I lined up next to the crazy-eyed foe, I began with my stick atop his.

He didn't say a word; he just slowly and methodically slid his stick out from mine, like a knight pulling his sword from a scabbard. It was clear he meant business. I had no reason to fight him, so I let the situation go. It wasn't worth the effort for a neutral-zone faceoff.

As soon as the linesman dropped the puck, the player took his undefended stick and pile-drove it into my eye like a pitchfork. Because his stick was lying atop mine, I had no way to protect myself. It was a brutal attack. This guy didn't want to fight me; he wanted to *hurt* me. I dropped to the ice like a rock. In my mind, this was a hate crime, and the assault was so forceful, my eye socket swelled instantly, blowing up like a balloon.

I was quickly ushered into the medical room, blood painting my white Voyageurs jersey red. The immediate concern of the training staff was that the eye had taken such a direct hit, they feared I might have lost the use of it. Panicked, they administered a "high-tech" procedure whereby the doctor fished around the bloody mess with his surgically gloved fingers while shining a flashlight into the debris.

He kept asking me, "Can you see the light? Can you see the light?"

Following a suspenseful few minutes that felt like hours, I finally caught a glimpse of the light. The relieved doctor determined that the eye was intact, so the next step was to treat the wound. He scheduled an appointment with the ophthalmologist the next day. I missed several games and wore a Plexiglas face shield when I returned.

The scar protrudes from my eyebrow to this day, and it reminds me every time I shave that I was inches from another eerie connection to Willie O'Ree.

Joe Kowal was our most consistent tough guy in Halifax, and I believe he took care of that repulsive goon that night in my defence. The irony is that it wouldn't have surprised me if it was Player X who jumped to my defence. The guys always had my back—that was never an issue. The problem was that I always lived on the edge. I couldn't trust what the same teammate would do if he were lining up on the opposite team.

Kowal is a great example. A whole backstory existed between Joe, my brother, John, and me. Joe lived near us in Ajax, and he and John had several fights during summer games that included Joe crossing the line with his sports intimidation and hyperbole. They despised one another on the ice. During one contentious game, they weren't satisfied with their on-ice dispute, so they took the battle to the streets afterwards. Everyone thought they were literally going to kill one another, as both were uncontrolled hotheads.

But in Halifax that night, Kowal imitated Sergeant John Ryan in that dramatic scene from *Crash*. Shifting roles from my brother's racial assailant to my protector, he fought the unhinged opponent while I was being treated by our medical staff.

Off the ice, Joe was a great guy. I trained with him in the summer, which included boxing training in an actual ring at the Ajax Community Centre. I wanted to improve my fighting technique, and what better way than boxing? Joe was a logical sparring partner because he stood 6-foot-5, and in hockey that automatically brands you as a fighter.

There was another fighting incident late in the regular season that affected me in a profound way. I didn't know it at the time, but it became clear as I thought back to this season that it was the beginning of the end of my NHL hockey dream.

I was depressed with the way the season had evolved. Although we were in third place and certain to qualify for the Calder Cup playoffs, the year was an utter waste. The Nordiques had responded to Bergeron's bombastic style and were winning. They were not going to be calling me up again. And the mountain of racial crap I had endured this season had me wondering about my chosen profession.

This was supposed to be my breakout season, but now my career was deteriorating.

During a late-season game in the Metro Centre, a melee broke out. Not a bench clearer, but a "line brawl"—one of those fights where all five skaters from each team square off. I was on the bench, watching the proceedings, when one of the visitors' combatants decked our guy, leaving him sprawled on the ice.

This guy wanted another dance partner, so he skated over to our bench and called me out. Why me? Let's just say I stood out. Now, I never minded spontaneous combat on the ice, and my penalty minutes had doubled in 1980–81 because, as a fourth-line winger, I needed to play a protector role.

But this challenge was just stupid.

Getting called out so overtly is a question of honour. The unwritten rule is unequivocal, but I hesitated. Something came over me at that moment on the bench. The notion of accepting this challenge seemed senseless all of a sudden. Why should I fight this idiot? I was big and strong and feared no one, but why do it?

As I wavered, Templeton screamed at me to get my ass out there. And all this was happening while four other fights continued on the ice. It was an afternoon game, and the Metro Centre had glass windows where the walls met the ceiling, so the daylight was shining through. I remember gazing up at that light and wanting so badly to be outside, basking in its warmth.

By now, my challenger had grown impatient. He came right up to the bench, leaned in and began tugging at me. Eventually, I was drawn to the ice and we fought. But even the fight was different.

In most of my fights, I drifted into a trance that allowed my instincts to rule. The best way to fight is to drop all form of logical thought along with your gloves, engage fully in the battle and reflect logically later.

Throughout this entire bout, however, I thought like a civilian. I held my own and threw a few haymakers, but it was an embarrassing moment, the first time I ever hesitated. I just wasn't into it. I felt disgraced for having behaved that way in front of my teammates and couldn't look them in the eye in the dressing room. I'd violated hockey's code of honour and lost face.

I was beginning to see the light.

CHAPTER 42

Broken-Winged Bird

Dreams
Hold fast to dreams
For if dreams die
Life is a broken-winged bird
That cannot fly.
Hold fast to dreams
For when dreams go
Life is a barren field
Frozen with snow.
—LANGSTON HUGHES

A s I think back, I wonder if that is when I knew I was done.

I still had another year on my contract, but I felt lost in a foreign land. Hockey's greatest currency is pride, and I was losing mine.

I feel ineptly unqualified to explain my state of mind at this point in my career. The experience was incredibly difficult for me to process. Imagine being a musician and working your entire life to perfect your craft. Then, you finally make it to

Carnegie Hall and play beautiful music, yet everybody boos and rejects you. People mock you by making monkey sounds and scratching their armpits. Each incident just wore on me like a snowball rolling down a mountain. I felt so intensely connected to hockey while, at the same time, feeling brutally out of place.

The Voyageurs ended up third in the Northern Division, but we were knocked out of the Calder Cup playoffs in the first round, and that was that. Many of the talented Montreal players eventually graduated to the mother ship: Carbonneau, Daoust, Laughlin and Wamsley. But there is no question in my mind this season of exile in the Canadiens' system had a domino effect on my career. Had I not been relegated to minimal fourth-line playing time, I likely would have been a top AHL scorer. That would have positioned me better for another shot with the Nordiques, or at least attracted the attention of other NHL clubs who might've traded for me. The same thing happened to my linemate, Rollie Cloutier. And we were the lucky ones. Our left wing from the prior season, Louis Sleigher, had been rewarded with a demotion to the EHL. It was a mess.

As the season ended, it was the last I saw of Cloutier and Reg Thomas.

With my career circling the toilet and one year left on my three-year contract with Quebec, my plan was to give myself one more season to become an established NHLer. I wanted to pour everything I had into 1981–82. I refused to become a minor-league "lifer," which made this a make-or-break season.

With a firm deadline in mind, I knew changes were necessary and I wanted a clean slate. I phoned my agent, Art Kaminsky, to tell him he was fired. With all the high-profile

NHLers sitting in his in-basket, Kaminsky had limited time to work for me. I wanted someone representing me who could focus on my needs.

I expected Art to send me a final bill and to never hear from him again. I never could've anticipated what happened next. He pleaded with me to keep him. He had a reputation for being a smooth talker, and he promised that if I stayed with his agency, he would make me a top priority that summer.

Art pledged to get me moved out of Quebec City.

This is a win-win situation, I told myself. I would retain one of the best agents in the business and leap to the top of his to-do list. It didn't take long for me to agree, excited about the prospects of starting over with a new team.

I kept in close contact with Art throughout the summer. He told me he had three teams lined up to acquire my services. My excitement grew every time the phone rang. But May turned to June, and then June to July. The summer drifted by, and nothing happened.

With training camp approaching, Kaminsky and I had a heart-to-heart and he indicated that the Nordiques would not trade me. I was in disbelief. To this day, I don't understand what happened. Were these other teams not offering enough in trade? Were the Nordiques asking too much for me? The problem with having an agent representing you is that you are not in the room or on the phone when the key conversations are taking place.

And it was my life they were talking about!

Kaminsky and I were forced to conclude that if the Nordiques were unwilling to let me go, it could only mean they had plans for me. Accordingly, I attended my third Nordiques training camp, optimistic that I would get a fair shot. And since I had complete confidence in what I could control—my performance in camp and the NHL exhibition season—I expected this to be my breakout year.

But I've always been able to sense a vibe. Intuition seldom fails me. And when I checked into Quebec's training camp in September 1981, I sensed that my star had dimmed.

The Nordiques had signed Peter and Anton's older brother, Marian. A third Stastny forward on the roster pushed me farther down the depth chart. And because my production had dropped in Nova Scotia, my worst nightmare had turned into reality: there was no longer a buzz in Quebec City about Bernie Saunders, the mystery Black prospect.

Reporters strolling around the locker room weren't stopping at my stall. Nobody cared to hear the valid reasons for my decline in offensive production. Suffice it to say, I don't recall much about my third NHL training camp. My emotions blocked it all out. I didn't play an NHL exhibition game, got cut relatively early and was quickly dispatched to the Fredericton Express.

Yes, Fredericton, New Brunswick.

The Nordiques had been trying to launch a farm team in the Maritimes for two years. Having failed to operate an AHL team in 1980–81 after their Saint John bid fell through, they set their sights 70 miles north. Ironically, Willie O'Ree was born in Fredericton, and an arena there is named in his honour.

My body reported to Fredericton, but my heart got lost somewhere in baggage claim. It didn't make sense to me to be demoted so quickly. It was just so puzzling. Why wouldn't they trade me if this was the plan? I wasn't 100 percent certain what to do, but I knew I needed to talk to management myself, not through my agent. I didn't trust anyone at this point.

The truth is, I didn't take this reassignment well and I started behaving badly. I partied each of the first few nights with John Wensink, a colourful former Boston Bruin who had played the previous season with the Nordiques and was nearing the end of his career. He was trying to hang on in the NHL, too, so we spent the first few days of our life in Fredericton drowning our sorrows. He contemplated retirement instead of playing for the Express, but before the season began, he got his release from Quebec and signed with the Colorado Rockies.

I wasn't so lucky.

The Nordiques installed my old coach, Demers, as the first general manager and head coach of the Express. Because they anticipated the inevitable growing pains of a first-year franchise in an informed hockey town like Fredericton, Jacques tried everything to generate excitement. He called a bunch of his old WHA buddies in an attempt to lure a "big name" onto the roster, but one by one, players declined. In addition, he had five local players trying out for the team. How ridiculous is that? Prospects like Terry Johnson and me are a stride away from the NHL, and Demers was insulting us by relying on gimmicks to fill the seats rather than adding legitimate talent to bolster the roster.

To launch the new operation and start on the right foot in this new city, the Nordiques planned an exhibition game pitting the Express against the parent club. Quebec rolled into town, packed 3,300 fans into the Aitken University Centre and patted themselves on the backs as marketing geniuses.

The local paper listed me as the only right wing with pro experience, and Demers placed me on a line with two locals: Wayne Hallihan and Jean Belliveau. As you can see from the spelling, this was not Gentleman Jean of the Montreal Canadiens—that was the Herb Carnegie story. This was some local guy signed by the franchise in an attempt to stimulate some fan interest.

I was livid! I thought playing fourth-line minutes in Halifax was embarrassing. Now I'm playing with locals in Fredericton against the club that was rejecting me?

TJ and I played particularly chippy games in this gala. I played well but committed two penalties after I took unnecessary shots at Quebec's stars. Marian Stastny wasn't in the lineup, but Peter and Anton were. TJ took runs at them, too, and later told me Bergeron was furious. The Nordiques failed to pummel us, winning only by 5–3.

When the game ended, I was fuming, but I still voiced the politically correct sound bites to the *Daily Gleaner* immediately after the game. "Saunders said he enjoyed working on a line with Hallihan and Belliveau. 'They were nervous in the early going,' Saunders said, 'but they kept going up and down the ice and proved they could skate with the big boys.'"

The Nordiques brass was embarrassed that the score was so close. Bergeron tried to make nice:

"The young kids on the Express really gave a 150 percent effort out there, they really wanted to prove something," he said, "while the players on the Nordiques had trouble getting motivated for the game and were trying to play fancy instead of working hard."

And Michel also threw what I interpreted as a postgame bone:

"After this weekend I'll be making a few more decisions,"
Michel said. "And I might be recalling a couple of players from
the Express if they prove they deserve another look. But right
now it is hard to say which players."

Cryptic, but I took it as a way to motivate a sullen me. I
wanted answers. Still dripping wet in my uniform, I pulled
Filion aside and demanded an immediate meeting. This time,
I would not allow him to sneak out the back door or hide
behind a speakerphone.

We found a small janitorial closet, just him and me.
Nobody else would have fit in the tiny room stinking of Diet
Coke and vomit. A mop standing in a bucket of dirty water
was the only witness to the exchange.

Filion was impeccably dressed in a suit tailored perfectly
for his overweight frame. He was dressed more appropriately
for the theatre than this forum. His suit provided a stark contrast to this undignified scene, and the irony was comical.

The ghosts inside me screamed, "Is this it? I had worked so
hard for so long, and this is my final stand?"

It was so repugnant it was perfect.

Using a tone of bold confidence, given the gravity of the
situation, I asked Filion what the Nordiques had planned for
me. You could tell he wanted out of that room more than I.
His response still echoes in my mind. Maurice suggested that
I might play 10–15 NHL games that season, but he offered no
guarantee, while mainly saying that he wanted me to "tutor"
the Nordiques' young kids in Fredericton.

Translation? Since most of the other players in the organization had played in the EHL the previous season, they needed
a "veteran" like me with AHL experience to take the lead in

Fredericton's inaugural season. He probably knew he needed to offer me a carrot, and that's why he threw out the possibility of a cup of coffee in the NHL.

The word *tutor* cut the deepest. Here I stood, at age 25, with only two seasons of professional experience, needing to help this inept organization out of this rabbit hole. They didn't have enough prospects to field a competent team in Fredericton and generate local support. They probably hoped for another Bernie Saunders Fan Club.

It was more than I could take. I was losing faith in humanity.

My strategy for this meeting was to react based on wherever the conversation flowed. If Filion started talking about Quebec, I would see where that led. If it strayed in a different direction, then I planned on asking to be traded. I didn't anticipate Maurice essentially asking me to prove myself yet again in the minors.

He wanted an indentured servant. I was shocked, insulted, disappointed, relieved, mad, happy . . . and those were my reactions the first two seconds. Instead of negotiating for more time with the big club or asking to be traded, I demanded a buyout. It was the only way out of that room with dignity. I wanted out of this smelly room, I wanted out of this rancid organization, I wanted out of this nauseating game. I was done.

As difficult as it was to hear, I appreciated Filion's honesty. In a situation where most lie or prevaricate, his message was unequivocal. It served his purpose for me to play that year in Fredericton, and I don't believe there was a doubt in his mind that I wouldn't stay.

The next day, I sat in Demers's office. As polished as Filion was, Demers always looked dishevelled. He tried to talk me out of leaving, emphasizing that I was making a life-altering mistake. He reminded me of how hard I had worked and how much I had sacrificed to reach this level.

Jacques was kind, and he said all the right things. He assured me I was an NHLer, and reminded me that *he* was an NHLer. He promised we would get back to the NHL together. Jacques asked me to be one of the Express's captains and promised we would fight through this thing together. I appreciated his support and vote of confidence.

But I was done. For me, it wasn't another year of dues-paying in the minors; it was another season where I would be subjected to bigotry and hatred. I called J.P. LeBlanc, the newly appointed coach of the Kalamazoo Wings, and asked if he wanted a broken-down right winger.

The irony is that playing the season in Fredericton could have been the best thing for my career. I stood to take a regular shift, play the power play, kill penalties and, if they wanted, sell popcorn between periods. It could have been a banner season where I could've run up my stats and landed a new contract with a new team.

Quitting is not in my DNA, and I have never felt that I quit. For most my life, I would have given my left eye for an NHL contract, but now I felt very differently. The NHL just wasn't the league I had dreamed of as a kid. When you play hockey, it feels like you have crossed an energy field that transports you into a new dimension. Games provided me a freedom that I am challenged to describe. But the game itself rejected me and left a scar that will never heal. I loved playing hockey, but I hated the game.

I walked away with a year left on my contract.

The next day, Friday, September 25, 1981, the Express were hosting my former team, the Voyageurs. Team administrators were hoping this would develop into a regional rivalry, and they were eager to highlight me as an ex-Vee.

Steve Gilliland of the *Daily Gleaner* interviewed me for a feature article to tee things up. My decision had not been announced yet, so I had to agree to the interview and go through the motions. We discussed my status with the Nords, sitting on the bench the previous year in Halifax, and the youth on Fredericton's roster.

> *Saunders says he has no hard feelings towards the Vees, even though he is considered a goal scorer but was used in a defensive role with the Vees.*
>
> *Saunders likes what he has seen of the Express this week. "Things are going pretty good in camp, we have a lot of young players and they have a lot of enthusiasm, which is good."*

Shortly after the article hit the newsstands, my decision was announced, and I left town before the game. A much different article appeared the next day, highlighting a picture of me in my Express uniform, sulking in the dressing room, clutching one of my sticks. The headline in the *Daily Gleaner* on September 28, 1981, read, "Saunders Decides to Quit Express."

I made it sound as if it was all about money and the exchange rate. I have never believed in burning a bridge, so I felt I had to be coy with my rationale. But really, money had nothing to do with it.

> *Saunders has a business degree from Western Michigan University and has a couple of job offers to consider. "Kalamazoo has an IHL team and I may play some for them, but other than*

that my pro career is done. It was a tough decision to make and I hope it's the right one," he concluded.

"(Losing Saunders) is a big loss," Demers said. "But we've talked about it the last three or four days and I appreciate him making the decision now rather than at mid-season."

Jacques and I had been discussing my future daily. It was only appropriate that the last quote in my professional hockey saga came from him, in the birthplace of Willie O'Ree.

I was letting go of my dream . . .

CHAPTER 43

Inflamed Dreams

We all reach forks in the road, knowing the direction we take will have a profound effect on the rest of our lives. It's human nature to wonder what would have happened had we gone left instead of right. Let me tell you what happened in Fredericton without me.

The inaugural season was a disaster, exactly as predicted. The Nordiques didn't have their act together in Syracuse, and they didn't have their act together in Quebec City. Why should the Express have been any different? Demers did his best, but given a patchwork crop of mediocre prospects, they never could find a competent roster. They really did need me to help tutor their kids.

The team burned through an astounding 56 players who officially played at least one AHL game for the club . . . and more than 60 wore the powder blue of the Fredericton Express if you include the handful of locals invited to skate in the exhibition games, or veterans like Wensink and me, who knew what was coming and fled.

The season was a debacle. Demers literally apologized to the fans for the team's embarrassing play following an early-season 10–1 drubbing. The Express finished 20–55–5, dead last in the AHL's Northern Division. They missed the playoffs by 33 points and finished 62 points behind the first-place New Brunswick Hawks, who played their games in Moncton, 110 miles and a world of talent away from Aitken Centre.

But here's the kicker, something I understood at the time: the veterans on the Express got the ice time to shine. Richard David led the Express in scoring with 51 goals and 32 assists. Louis Sleigher was second, with 32 goals and 34 assists. I had outscored both when we played in Syracuse two seasons earlier, and both endured a season of exile in the EHL when I was sent to Nova Scotia. The two leveraged the opportunity to play major minutes, and both rose from the futility in Fredericton to reach the NHL: Sleigher in Quebec and Boston, David in Quebec.

I considered that, but I had hit my Herb Carnegie moment feeling I had already proven myself. Not only had I been a top scorer in the AHL, but I also performed well in my two brief NHL stints. And now they were asking me to prove myself yet again, a season after they pasted me to the bench by exiling me to Nova Scotia.

Most important, I was drained from the racial acrimony. I just did not want to subject myself to another season of hatred game after game and night after night.

I wasn't willing to leave a pound of my flesh in Fredericton.

Jacques Demers chose a different direction for his journey. Having already coached in the WHA and NHL, Demers accepted the job of managing this terrible bunch. He could have walked away with his dignity, and few would have faulted him. But he stuck it out, and he willed 20 victories out of that roster in what knowledgeable minds would rate as a masterful bit of coaching. He ended up revitalizing his coaching career.

He coached another season in Fredericton and then was hired by the St. Louis Blues in 1983–84. And Demers, being the loyal guy he was, remained true to his word. His NHL teams those first few years in St. Louis were sprinkled with players he had instructed with the Express: Basil McRae, Terry Johnson, Lee Norwood and Dave Pichette. I know Bernie Saunders would have been a fifth, because that's what he promised me.

It's always fun to look back. But I have no regrets.

Not only did Demers win a Stanley Cup in 1993, but he won it with Montreal, his beloved hometown team. With a team that included Guy Carbonneau, the blue-chip prospect I'd played with 12 years earlier. I grinned from ear to ear the night Demers hoisted the Cup over his head, knowing much of Jacques's backstory, all the way back to Coca-Cola delivery trucks and Junior B. Later, I had Jacques sign a picture of the moment. I have it to this day.

WITH MY CELEBRITY status in Kalamazoo, I knew that if I moved back, I could leverage the Bernie Saunders brand and get a real job in the business world. My first step was to call J.P. LeBlanc.

The year before, J.P. had been the player/coach of the AHL's Adirondack Red Wings, so he was familiar with my résumé. Jeep, who was a WHA and NHL journeyman, packed a physique that said he could still play, but now he was emerging as a coaching prospect in the Detroit Red Wings organization.

Jeep was excited with my decision, but a little surprised to see his AHL rival for two seasons joining him in his office, having dropped out of the northern sky. His first question was what I expected to produce that season.

"Fifty goals, fifty assists" was my sincere answer.

Jeep smiled, and I signed a one-year contract with the Wings.

In choosing the IHL, I was conceding that my dream of playing hockey in the NHL was over. It was a solemn time. I felt a need to do something for Bernie Saunders to recognize the importance of this occasion, something to soothe the pain. I decided to adopt a very personal scoring celebration as a silent protest. Eschewing the time-honoured tradition of raising my stick when I scored, I opted to raise my stickless right hand in the form of a fist. The Black Power salute. Tommie Smith and John Carlos would have been proud.

I used that defiant pose throughout my final season in the IHL. It helped me get through the only season I would ever play without NHL dreams hovering in the background. Ironically, the gesture flew under the radar. I, of course, preferred it that way since I never wanted to draw undue attention or disrespect the game. It was a private protest targeted at a game that seemed so unfair. A very personal "FU" that felt good when it began to rain in opposing rinks.

Several game stories that captured a photo of my stickless post-goal pose failed to make mention of its significance. I guess with my hands encased in bulky hockey gloves, nobody understood what I was doing.

My goal was to go out with a bang, but unfortunately, early in the season I aggravated my groin injury, conjuring bad memories of that innovative stretching program in Quebec.

Since I knew this was my last season, there was no way I would sit out for a long time to allow the injury to properly heal. K-Wings trainer Terry Roof and I became best friends because Roofer had to work his magic daily to prepare me for games and practices. Although I was gimpy all year and played a chunk of the season injured, Roofer's brilliance enabled me to play 70 of the schedule's 80 games.

Roofer put most MDs to shame. Before he'd let me on the ice, he would heat my groin and then wrap an Ace bandage around my thigh so tightly, I could barely limp out of the trainer's room. The idea was to prevent my muscle from pulling farther away from the bone. The bandage essentially served as my groin.

Long story short, I played the season on one wheel. My numbers reflected the injury, but I still managed to score 38 goals and 37 assists in 70 games. But there was a silver lining to the season. My focus shifted to my phenomenally talented linemate, Brent "B.J." Jarrett.

He was only 5-foot-9 and 160 pounds, but Brent was quick, slippery and an amazing stickhandler with exceptional vision. Like Rollie Cloutier, he had a knack for finding the open man in tight traffic. It was easy to adapt my style to his prodigious talent. The secret to playing with a player like that is to expect the unexpected, get open despite circumstances telling you otherwise. B.J. led the IHL in scoring with 122 points, won the scoring title and won the James Gatschene Memorial Trophy as the IHL's most valuable player. Our line was the top line in the league.

For the first time since my freshman year at WMU, I played the off wing for the K-Wings. Neil Meadmore or Mike Corrigan cruised our right side. Both were big, bruising power forwards who could crash the net while also offering a measure of protection. Mike Brown, my suitemate at WMU, was also on the team, and his presence added a dose of physical security. Playing the opposite side provides distinct disadvantages in the defensive zone, but I was adept enough to overcome them at this level. I don't think I could have played the off wing in the NHL.

Offensively, though, being a right-handed shot on the left wing enabled me to have some fun in the offensive zone. As had occurred throughout my career, I kept scoring. I scored some clutch goals, and I was targeted because of my race. As the *Kalamazoo Gazette* reported,

SAUNDERS' OVERTIME GOAL BAILS OUT WINGS

Bernie Saunders, who has been a target for physical intimidation ever since he came into the International Hockey League, exacted a measure of revenge here Sunday afternoon. Saunders, the former WMU MVP, scored three minutes, 44 seconds into sudden death overtime to give the Kalamazoo Wings a bruising 5–4 victory.

The catcalls from the stands continued, but it became tolerable again since I was filling the enemy nets with pucks. A place like Toledo, Ohio, was particularly onerous. In the tiny Toledo rink, the visiting team literally had to walk through the crowd to access the ice surface. Suffice it to say, it was a difficult walk for me.

Although I still heard the racial crap throughout the IHL, interestingly, the volume seemed to be turned down a notch. I don't know if it was real or my imagination because it was my swan song and I knew I was done. But the IHL trail had already been blazed.

When I was in college, the K-Wings played against the Grand Rapids Owls, who had two brothers on their team: Mark Izzard and Henry Taylor. Taylor could flat-out play. Bill Riley played in Dayton in 1974. A decade earlier, Alton White played in the league for Fort Wayne and Columbus.

Playing with Jarrett made the year for me, as the theme became his pursuit of the scoring championship. B.J. summarized the year nicely in an article in the *Kalamazoo Gazette*:

> *Bernie really helped me out a lot, coming down from the pro ranks and all. He's a smart hockey player. And he's deceiving— quicker than most people realize. First he's there and then he's gone. We got it worked out so we knew where each other was going to be at all times. Too bad he's retiring.*

The scoring-title chase provided a measure of motivation, but for me, there was no looking back.

I remember playing one game in particular, in Muskegon, Michigan, against the Mohawks. One of the Mohawks was Jeff Carlson, who played one of the notorious Hanson brothers from the movie *Slap Shot*. The Hanson brothers were actually based on Jeff and his brothers, Jack and Steve, who rampaged through the old Eastern Hockey League in Johnstown, Pennsylvania.

When I depict the IHL as *Slap Shot* hockey, I am being literal and figurative. Carlson and I got into a fight, which was fine, but when we collapsed to the ice, he reached around the linesman who was attempting to separate us, and he tried to gouge my eye out. That was the "I," a league full of infamous combatants and staged fights.

It was all further confirmation that it was time to get on

with my life, not that I doubted the decision. An eye simply was not worth it anymore. I would have given one earlier in my career, like Willie O'Ree, but heavens no, not now. Not against the Muskegon Mohawks.

When the season ended, LeBlanc approached and asked me to promise to tell him the truth. He wanted to know if I was genuinely injured the entire season.

There are hockey players known for "pulling the chute"— rink speak for malingering. I had ample reason to set it on cruise control, but no, I would never do that. I wanted to break the tape at the finish line the same way I had conducted my career. The injury just prevented me from going out with a bang.

Even if I had led the league in scoring and another NHL team wanted to throw me a life vest, there was no turning back. The homecoming to Kalamazoo was a means to an end. And the plan worked perfectly, as I negotiated a job with the local pharmaceutical company and started work there on the Monday after my last game.

The postscript to that season still brings a smile. At the year-end awards ceremony, Jarrett carted off most of the trophies, but they felt Bernie Saunders deserved some form of recognition. Consequently, they presented me with the MIP award.

Think about that: in my final season, I won the most improved player award. It seemed fitting, given my passion for development.

SEPARATION FROM THE game wasn't going to be easy, as I was leaving a piece of me behind. Hockey had always been my frame of reference. I knew that in order to turn the page,

I needed to do something significant to properly recognize the grief.

A few weeks after my final game for the K-Wings, I drove to the bar for a few drinks with friends. We spent a couple of hours reminiscing, and from there moved to a familiar bridge on the WMU campus, near the dorms where I lived in my freshman season. The bridge was within a few strides of the Boomba Bernie incident, and within earshot of where John had been cussed out by those angry coeds. Bob Wagner of the *Kalamazoo Gazette*, who had done several feature articles on me, even reported on the ceremony.

Skates in River, Hockey Career Ends

Saunders came to Kalamazoo fully intending to finish his career here before entering the business world. He followed his game plan. "I was kinda disappointed this year. I thought I could score 50 goals and well over 100 points, but it turned out I had injury after injury."

Standing together on the bridge, my friends and I soaked my skates in lighter fluid and ignited them with a match. As the flames began to char the boots, I held them for one final time before letting go.

We stood there silently as my hockey life, and a part of me, made ripples in the water and sank to the bottom of the pond.

I had made my peace.

CHAPTER 44

Waiting on the World to Change

I'm not a world-changer. I've never been big on heroes, probably because I've gotten close to many people others consider idols, and I've seen how enormously flawed they are.

If you pressed me to name my one hero, it would be Martin Luther King Jr. He changed the world. I so admire his impact, wishing I could do that. But it's not me.

The world does change for those who have the patience to wait. An incident with my son 25 years ago injected me with a dose of optimism. Ironically, it was one of the worst days of my life. But metaphorically speaking, it was one of the best. Life works that way.

I never wanted my boys to play hockey, but from the crib, Jonathan was smitten with the game when I first began to coach. When he was 12, I was coaching his Kalamazoo travel team. We were in Pittsburgh when an ugly altercation erupted, with Jonathan smack dab in the middle.

From the time he could hear, I prepared him on how to react to the inevitable. Not to drop the gloves, like I did when I was young, and to remember that he was playing a team sport.

The team needed to be the priority. I promised to buy him a tennis racquet if he wanted to be an individual.

I taught Jonathan that reacting to the N-word on the ice was selfish. It gave the opposing team an advantage because it would remove one of our more valuable players—our captain—from the ice. Jonathan obeyed the first few times he heard the filth. He was an incredibly coachable kid.

But when a Pittsburgh player dropped the N-bomb that day, Jonathan lost it. I watched in horror as my enraged son dropped his gloves and attacked the offender. These kids weighed no more than 100 pounds, so when the linesman grabbed Jonathan from behind by the top of his shoulder pad, Jonathan's lower body flung forward. The referee saw Jonathan's skate fly outward and called a match penalty, ruling that Jonathan had tried to kick his foe.

This meant Jonathan was suspended indefinitely. The penalty required a meeting with the league authorities to determine the length of the automatic suspension. It's hockey's version of a major felony.

I was livid. This may have been the angriest I have ever been in my life. But my anger was indistinct. I was mad at Jonathan for disobeying my instruction, mad at the other kid for the racial affront, mad at the referee for blowing the call, mad at myself for allowing this to happen to my child, mad at the game for causing me so much pain and mad at the world for its cruelty.

This was one of the few times Jonathan disobeyed my direction. But he needed a chance to deal with a life I couldn't shelter him from. At this moment, he was feeling that guttural pain that I had experienced my entire career, the same pain that forced me out of a game I loved.

And one more thing: sometimes the high road sucks. Jonathan wanted to kick some Pittsburgh ass.

I made it a practice to never swear in front of my kids. Telling a child not to do something while doing that very thing yourself is ludicrous. Even as a hockey coach—they pass out F-bombs like friction tape—I never swore in front of my players. But at this instant, I had a meltdown.

I waited until the period ended and every player was in the locker room before I shut the door and dropped an F-bomb on Jonathan to open my rant. He had done exactly what I had taught him not to do, and the consequences were exactly as I had described—even worse. He would miss multiple games pending review by the league authorities.

When I finished my tirade, I rushed out of the room, found an empty closet and bawled. The pain of seeing my son suffer the way I had suffered was excruciating. I hated hockey and was incensed at myself for failing to protect my son.

I expected a painful review the next day before the board, culminating with my son being subjected to a heavy suspension. But a remarkable thing happened. We received a call from the player on the Pittsburgh team who was involved in the altercation. He called to apologize. The apology was on behalf of himself, his family and his team. Jonathan also received subsequent letters of apology from many of the team's family members.

Apparently, the families were appalled when they learned the incident was racially motivated. The committee ruled in Jonathan's favour, and he was not suspended any further. I never saw it coming. It was one of the most moving moments in my life. My heart grew three sizes that day.

As I contemplated this transformative moment, I began to

see a world changing before my eyes. It was not moving at the pace I wanted, but change *was* happening.

When I consider Willie O'Ree's experiences playing for the Boston Bruins the year after I was born, I couldn't fathom the social injustice he had faced. And before him, hockey players in the Coloured Hockey League had no opportunity at all. Then there were my own experiences.

Now, my son was receiving an outpouring of support in the wake of the kind of incident that had happened to me on countless occasions. It provided me with a new sense of hope.

Prejudice is still a major problem in the world, but over the course of three generations, I witnessed an arc of gradual improvement. It's why, at one point, I believed that future generations would be born into a very different world. Hope was on the horizon.

But today, sadly, I have a renewed sense of skepticism.

With a predictable trajectory, forecast experts can normally take a trend line—in this case, plotting when social injustice will dissolve—and calculate the date when the curve will reach bottom. Sadly, social science doesn't follow a predictable path. Along with this superficial steady progress, America in 2008 elected its first Black president, Barack Obama.

These promising and progressive events have awoken the beast. We are now facing an age where white supremacy is trying to counter progressive social improvements. In the U.S., there remains a healthy minority that embraces white dominant values and seems to be willing to do anything to protect them. So much for trends. The recent counteroffensive against social progress has only served to widen the racial divide. The curve has been flattened.

In a perverse way, the present generation of Blacks are

worse off than their predecessors because racism is less overt. Far better to call me the N-word to my face than do it behind my back . . . or mistreat me in the workplace or everywhere else whites dominate.

Census projections suggest that in 2042, whites will no longer be the majority race in America. That prediction has stoked fears in many. The next 20 years will be an interesting period.

There could be a day of reckoning coming. As John Mayer sang, "I just keep waiting on the world to change."

CHAPTER 45

The Other Side of the Coin

Imagine watching a NASCAR race at Daytona International Speedway. The cars whizzing by at breakneck speed are all white, with large blue numbers on each hood. Except for one car, which is painted black with white numbers.

What do you think would happen?

You'd find yourself watching that black car, whether you wanted to or not. When it did well, you would notice. When it fared poorly, you would notice. Some would despise the car for its nonconformity, while others would love it because it was unique.

I'm guilty of this myself. I've been to basketball games where there were nine Blacks and one white on the court. The visual anomaly is impossible to ignore.

As the great philosopher Tupac suggested, "All eyez on me!"

When I was the black car, I like to think I drove a hard and honest race, but without frills. With so many eyes riveted on me, I didn't dare do anything flashy, because I believed it would only cause ire.

I also believed the black car represented all the black cars to follow, which meant the person driving the black car carried a sense of responsibility. A social *noblesse oblige*. Jarome Iginla drove the black car elegantly and superbly and became the darling of Calgary. That is the safe thing to do.

When I saw P.K. Subban early in his career, driving more flamboyantly in Montreal, a city steeped in hockey tradition, I worried. Several years before he died in 2016, my brother, John, did an ESPN interview with P.K. and Willie O'Ree and told me what a great kid P.K. is. Can you imagine the sense of pride John and I felt watching this young Black star play for the same team we worshipped as kids?

But I told John I was worried about P.K. because of the attention he called to himself. With such a flashy style, the black car had better win, lest it be rejected. That's why I barely raised my stick when I scored. Jaromir Jagr could do whatever he wanted to do when he scored, but P.K. couldn't. The black car has too many critical eyes cast its way.

P.K. has immense talent on the ice. Off the ice, the man reached into his pocket in 2015 and committed $10 million to the Montreal Children's Hospital. And still, as I was afraid they would, they ran him out of town. Hockey is a conformist league, and P.K. seemed oblivious to conformity. The brother showed up at the Bell Centre and acted like, well, himself. The man is Black. Acting like himself means he acted Black. That is a daring act. Most of us speak in a "white voice" throughout the day, conforming to white social expectations, and hide any of the tropes of a Black male until we get home. Not P.K.

As a millennial, he is emblematic of a new generation and shrugs off the criticism. But I had hoped he would have learned to play rhythm guitar in Nashville. He didn't, and now he is in New Jersey. *Sports Illustrated* had him listed as the "most hated" player in hockey. That's what happens when you drive a flamboyant black car. Tony McKegney wasn't even flamboyant. He played for eight NHL teams in 13 NHL seasons. Anytime his scoring stalled, he was told to pack his bags. Other players were given more leeway.

I purposely didn't want to overload this book with stories focused on racial inequities. I'm providing a taste, but there were many other stories I could have included. In many situations, people tend to focus on the negative and neglect the positive. I don't want to make that mistake. It's a theme of this book (and of my life). Instead of allowing negativity to suck the lifeblood out of you, why not counterbalance the story with the wellspring of good feelings that I experienced as well. There is a counterbalancing response when you are behind the wheel of that black car. In most cities where I played, I became the "fan favourite." Often, I drew more positive attention from the home crowd than any white counterpart. I believe it was due to two reasons: yes, because of my, let's say, "uniqueness," but also because I had a go-for-broke style, which many loved and appreciated. Fans respected the fact I was going to play the game hard and attempt to earn every cent of their entertainment dollar. Many articles refer to these two attributes.

As an example, read the feature story that ran in the *Syracuse Herald-American* on April 6, 1980:

SAUNDERS HAS BIG-TIME ICE APPEAL

Bernie Saunders has major league personality, one which local hockey fans can rally around. Ever since his arrival in the Salt City last December, Saunders has emerged as the most visible and exciting Syracuse Firebird. He plays both ends of the ice with vigor, buzzing around the net offensively and pestering his opponents in the defensive end. It's not often that a coach will put a rookie on the ice in short-handed situations, but Syracuse coach Duane Rupp has enough confidence in Saunders' defensive abilities to pair him with Roland Cloutier on the Birds top penalty-killing unit.

Wherever I voyaged in my career, it was the same. As I expressed earlier, while at Western Michigan University, I became the fan favourite and the darling of Kalamazoo. Here is a sampling as reported from the Kalamazoo papers following my sophomore year.

SAUNDERS' HUSTLE LEADS SKATERS, 42 POINTS ON SEASON

Saunders is one of the leaders of the team, and the crowd favorite. "My main success is that I hustle all of the time, and people like that. I try and lead my teammates by example. I'm not the rah-rah type."

Saunders has come a long way from the little boy who cried when he couldn't play hockey with his brother. He is a leading scorer, leader on the team and the crowd favorite.

I received an inordinate amount of positive attention in junior hockey and earlier in my career. It is easy to point out the social injustice, but I also want to point out the beauty. Although my time in Syracuse was abbreviated—only half a season—the Syracuse University College of Law went as far as to create a Bernie Saunders Fan Club! A large contingent of law students attended games, bringing banners, and they would jump to their feet seemingly every time I touched the puck.

My productivity helped, but there lacked a Gordie Brooks Fan Club, as an example. Gordie, an AHL all-star-calibre player, led the team in scoring and had a dynamic style of his own. Yet, it was I who became the fan favourite. In Quebec City, the fans embraced me immediately and there was an outcry of support during the Bernie Saunders Controversy and my inequitable demotion. I offered an interesting mix: a solid scorer, a Charlie Hustle attitude, and I was Black. It drew a lot of positive attention my way—that odd Black player buzzing around the rink.

There are two sides to every story, and the favourable response warmed my heart throughout my career—it counterbalanced the bigotry. For all the racism, I received amazingly welcoming support from a great many. Most important to me, it provided documented evidence that the world is inching forward. No way Herb Carnegie or Willie O'Ree would have been recipients of such warmth.

CHAPTER 46

Your Brother . . .

Back in the days when ESPN still had NHL broadcast rights, John evolved as one of hockey's leading advocates in the U.S., and he and I would laugh about the times his network received comments from baffled viewers questioning the presence of a Black sportscaster covering hockey on television. Of course, there were no objections to his assignments to cover basketball!

What those uninformed viewers didn't understand is that hockey was in John's DNA. Basketball? . . . Well, let's just say it was more of an acquired taste. John had to work harder at the other sports because they were not as prominent in Canada. The stereotyping is understandable but ironic, given John's upbringing.

John's hockey-playing career was cut short, but he still managed to make an impact on the game. He blazed the trail for Black hockey broadcasters. I smile every time I see Kevin Weekes and Anson Carter on the air. And I was proud to learn that the expansion Seattle Kraken hired Everett Fitzhugh as their radio play-by-play broadcaster, hockey's first. When John passed away, the NHL performed a touching tribute in his honour, which I attended. I could feel John smiling down from heaven.

John loved all his sports assignments, but his time working with Barry Melrose, Steve Levy and the rest of the hockey crew was extra special. Barry and Steve did a piece at John's memorial, held on the ESPN campus, that makes me chuckle whenever I think about it.

When John was working on *The Sports Reporters*, it became a standing joke whenever he closed the program with a "parting shot" spotlighting hockey. His fellow panelists— Mike Lupica, Mitch Albom and Bob Ryan—would roll their eyes in unison. "Here goes Saunders again." For a time, other than Melrose and his cameo appearances, no one other than John was talking about hockey nationally on TV in the States.

John told me an interesting story one day. He and a producer ran into Michel Bergeron at a major hockey event. John, in rare big brother form, felt compelled to introduce himself. John approached Michel and, in his inimitable friendly style, said, "Hey, Michel. You know my brother."

Bergeron had no idea who John was talking about.

John explained that his younger brother is Bernie Saunders, who played for him in Quebec. Bergeron's eyes lit up.

"Your brother was the best player in our training camp one year and we cut him," said Michel, who proceeded to laugh.

John and his producer didn't find it so funny. They exited in disbelief.

Who knows what Bergeron actually said that day. He probably blurted out something stupid in one of those socially awkward moments we all would love to do over, if we only could.

The bottom line is, I don't blame anyone else for my career. I take full responsibility for my life and my actions. I only scored one NHL point for him in six NHL games, and I blame nobody but myself.

NEIL SMITH LIKES to tell me the story about Tom McVie when he was coaching in Maine. McVie was one of those classic hockey guys. Whenever a player got sent down to the minors, Tom would sit the guy down in his office and ask, in his characteristically gravelly voice, "OK, let's get this off the table right now. Tell me who fucked you."

Players seldom take responsibility for their careers; it is easier to place the blame on someone else. I understand that, and I understand that I don't hold a patent on minor-league misery. The truth of the matter is, a lot of stars have to align in order for someone to get to play at hockey's highest level.

So, it's time for you to ask me the Question: Why did my hockey career end?

The simple answer is me. I take full responsibility. And I had to take responsibility when it ended, because if I didn't, it would have been difficult to transition to a new life. When you turn the page, you have to release it from your grip.

I seized the power in the situation and refused to be the victim.

I had a year left on my contract, but I demanded a buyout. I have consistently said the colour of my skin was a part of the reason I did not make it, but I never said it was the *only* reason. The steady stream of injustice at every turn wore me down. The ignorance and insensitivity in my own dressing room, ignorance that was more punishing than the abuse from my opponents or the fans, wore me down. The incompetence and injustice of the Quebec Nordiques wore me down. Sprinkle in some bad timing and good, old-fashioned bad luck.

I could have spent a lifetime mourning my bad luck about the Stastny brothers defecting right into my path. But what about me stealing a roster spot on the Pickering Panthers from Birdhead? Life can be like those Russian nesting dolls. Most people remember when they get gobbled up, but forget when it happens in reverse.

I know the impulse of the sports world will be to debate whether Bernie Saunders should have played in the NHL and how well I would have done. Those discussions are silly because we will never know. The real intent of this book is to illustrate the rejection of my race.

Was I shut out? Like Herb Carnegie, there was a pathway for me to reach the NHL had I been willing to prove myself anew in the minor leagues. But in the 40 years since my skates sank to the bottom of a tiny pond on the campus of Western Michigan University in Kalamazoo, Michigan, I have developed a clear picture of the ultimate reason I failed to have an NHL career.

My middle-child ethic developed in me a sense that I am responsible for any outcomes in my life, good or bad. As much as I love my parents, I learned early that I could not always rely upon them. As much as I love my brother, I never relied on him or anyone else to make a decision for me. I made my own decisions because I knew that it was I who would suffer the consequences.

It wasn't easy for me to disclose such personal parts of my life in print. But the day after I was released from my holding cell after the Boomba Bernie incident, I sat quietly in my dorm room. I was crushed, but not for the reasons I would have predicted.

I thought it would be because I'd let my family down, as I'd enjoyed an opportunity to be the first in my family to gain a college education. I thought it might be because I let my hockey team down. But none of those things dominated my thinking. I was crushed because I felt I'd let myself down. I was mad at myself.

To me, personal responsibility is the only answer. Many people adore Barack Obama, but when he suggested that Blacks needed to take personal responsibility and "stop watching too much television," he was heavily criticized. Jesse Jackson accused him of "talking down to Blacks."

I look at it in reverse. If you disagree with this ethic of personal responsibility, it means you think people should be taken care of by others. That, of course, is nonsense.

I recognize, support and agree with the notion that life is not fair for Blacks. It is so infuriating to me that the symbol of white entitlement complains about a rigged system. Yes, the system is rigged. But it is rigged dramatically in the white man's favour. But you can fight or capitulate.

I fought the hockey forces by seizing power and charting a new course. I battled forces in business for 40 years and allowed myself to retire early. And I am exhausted. But I still don't believe there is any alternative other than to fight.

Personal responsibility extends way beyond holding oneself accountable for life's outcomes. It is what made me work harder than my competition in hockey and in business. Personal responsibility should include taking ownership of your thoughts and actions. When my mother stole portions of my NHL signing bonus, I decided I was going to love her and embrace her for all the positive things she provided in my life. But I also promised myself I would never do something of that nature to my own child.

Plus, there is another side to the ethic that Barack Obama mentioned, but not many listened. The headline blared "Barack Obama Talks Down to Blacks," but if you listen to his entire speech, he also recommended, at the same time, that we work hard to change the system, "to demand more from Washington."

It is a push/pull philosophy. Take personal responsibility while actively working to change the system. The day in that stinking closet with Maurice Filion was one of the most liberating of my life. Thanks to my father, I held a card most players were never dealt in that era. In this case, I didn't like the system, so I chose to leave it and transfer to another profession.

There was no doubt in my mind I would have played in the NHL if I had stuck to it, but at a certain point, it no longer became worth it. The irony is, I believe hockey needed me more than I needed it. The sport still struggles with racism. The effort to combat it is so fragmented, the game sometimes feels like it's going in the wrong direction on the issue.

With my star power, I believe I could have been a great ambassador as a player. I had the perfect professional profile to contribute to the effort while I was a professional: Black, played in the league, lived in Canada and the U.S., college-educated, successful career with a Fortune 500 company, a marketing professional. I was hiding in plain sight.

In this binary system, I have always tried to take personal responsibility and try never to let myself down. However, regretfully, I have never tried to "change the system." That is a big part of the reason why I decided to come forward with my story. This shit has to stop. K'Andre Miller shouldn't be going through the same abuse that I endured in the '70s. P.K. Subban shouldn't be one of the most hated players in the sport. Black men should not be lying on the ground with a police officer's knee on their neck while white men can storm the Capitol and interrupt Congress. It wasn't easy for me to exhume such intimate details of my life and share them with the world. But it was time for me to take that step.

Discrimination is an invisible force, a headwind gusting into the path of every person of colour. My hope is that this book helps calm the storm for all my Black brothers in the game. All those years ago, I thought I was working hard in school to maintain my eligibility to play hockey. But it was working hard at hockey that prepared me for the reality of life.

Although I don't expect to ever return to hockey, I am not mad at hockey. I am indebted to hockey for the man it helped me become. But if hockey wants to become more inclusive and diverse, then I believe the players are going to have to work to become more accepting of our cultural differences.

Our differences should be a blessing and not a curse . . .

—Bernie Saunders, May 25, 2021
—BLM
—RIP GF

Acknowledgements

Family is the glue that binds our society. As such, I'd like to thank my grandparents; my parents; my siblings, John and Gail; and my three remarkable sons, Jonathan, Shawn and Andrew. The true measure of a man is his legacy, and although I was never a world-changer, my three sons sure are making a positive dent. Jonathan traded in the get-rich-quick allure of Wall Street for a socially responsible venture that betters the lives of Kenyans by improving the yields of their crops. It's a game-changer. Shawn, my middle child, followed in my footsteps and became a health-care expert who works with medical professionals to improve the lives of patients every day. He also holds patents. Andrew, the baby, deviated from hockey after being dragged to practices and games, and I love him for that. He started out in criminal justice as a police officer and now is a sought-after leader in education—both amazingly noble professions. Andrew also runs a start-up venture designed to address policing controversies head-on through reformed recruitment and training. My impact multiplies every day through my three incredible sons. Thanks also to Blair and Merary and the family future spanning Micah, Summer and beyond, and to Wanda, Aleah and Jenna, and Auntie Yve, Loretta, Nicholas and Jordyn, and Paul and the Hughes crew: Stephanie, Chris, Courtney, Sammy and Josh, and all others who share my bloodline.

But because we are all family, I also thank everyone who has walked this Earth. We are all one, and I embrace our common humanity.

Thanks also to the Bad Boys Club. We all skate towards a colour-blind society on the same line. So, to the players of the Coloured Hockey League, from James Robinson Johnston to Herb Carnegie and Willie O'Ree, to Mike Marson, Bill Riley and Tony McKegney, and from Grant Fuhr to Kevin Weekes and Malcolm Subban, all the way to the emerging generation of K'Andre Miller and Quinton Byfield: Keep up the fight, my brothers. They'll get it someday.

Thanks to Pam for your bravery, love and companionship.

Thanks to Barry for helping to turn my thoughts and words into my story.

Thank you, Neil, for being my surrogate brother, and Margaret, for being you.

Thanks to Gary Murphy for being the type of person we should all strive to be.

Thanks to Sherry Bassin for coaching people, not players.

Thanks, Erin.

Thanks to Richard Curtis for insisting that I tell the story. Thanks to Patrick Crean for believing in my story and spearheading the project.

We'd also like to thank the many people and places whose kind thoughts and deeds helped make this project a reality: John Bacon, the *Binghamton Press and Sun-Bulletin*, the Birmingham (Alabama) Public Library, Mike Brown,

ACKNOWLEDGEMENTS

Leonard Davis, Matt Dietz, Steve Doherty, Chuck Durocher, Folio Literary Management, Michael Gold and Jeff Scott at the NHL, Michel Goulet, Robin Hook, Keith Horn, George Jepson, Terry Johnson, Alan Jones, Julia at the Halifax (Nova Scotia) Public Libraries, Nicolas Labbé, Gerry Magee, Jean Martineau, Tom McCarthy, Natalie Meditsky, Reggie Moore, NewspaperArchive, Newspapers.com, John Peterson, Lynn Ross, Frank Sheffield, Louis Sleigher, Miranda Snyder, Paul Stewart, Bill Sturtevant, D.A. Thomas, Reg Thomas, John Winchell and Art Wurfel.

The Blacklist

One of my great disappointments is the lack of a comprehensive and complete record of Black hockey history. It's one thing to acknowledge our historical role in the sport (from Coloured Hockey League players to Quinton Byfield and beyond), but quite another to tell our story accurately. You have to know where you've been in order to chart where you are going.

I want history to better understand the roles Alton White and Mike Marson and Tony McKegney played in Black hockey history. As one who played in the early 1980s, I would argue that I know Black hockey history better than most . . . because I lived it. I endured it. Sadly, I don't believe hockey historians appreciate the impact of the 16-year drought.

It was historic when Willie O'Ree was recalled by the visiting Boston Bruins and broke the colour barrier in 1958. But hockey's colour barrier had to be breached twice. The handful of Black players like me, who were arriving in the mid- to late '70s, were landing on the beaches of Normandy.

When Marson arrived, it was as if Willie hadn't happened. Marson was an original member of the expansion

Washington Capitals when they joined the NHL for the 1974–75 season.

Marson had enormous talent, and his career could have been so much more. The man had the weight of the world on his shoulders: taken by the Caps in the second round of the 1974 NHL draft and on the roster for their inaugural game at the age of 19. The brother showed up in Washington, DC, with a 10-inch Black Power Afro and Fu Manchu beard. During his four seasons in Washington, he married a white woman.

Can you imagine the difficulties he faced? His career ended way too early, when he was 25, and he has drifted away from hockey's consciousness. Hockey history fails to properly recognize his significance. I think about what could have been.

And what about Bill Riley, who took a circuitous route to the NHL? Riley was first brought to Washington on December 26, 1974. His NHL debut was the only game he played that season, against the Philadelphia Flyers, and that date marked the first time two Blacks were in the same NHL lineup.

All the incoming fire directed at Marson, the first Black NHLer in 16 years, was absorbed by Riley as well. The man was right there on the front lines with Marson in 1976–77 and 1977–78. He was tough as nails and could play. He eventually retreated to the Maritimes and was inducted into the Nova Scotia Sport Hall of Fame in 1998. Brother, please take a bow.

Another player hiding in plain sight is McKegney, the NHL's first Black star. McKegney scored 320 NHL goals in 912 NHL games from 1978 through 1991, yet was traded seven times in 13 seasons. Twice to Quebec. McKegney was the perfect man for the job as he shrugged off a lot of the noise and let his scoring do the talking. He had the decency, when he was traded to

Detroit in December 1989, to reach out and shake the hand of new teammate Joey Kocur, even though Kocur had dropped an N-bomb that prompted an enraged McKegney to swing his stick at Kocur's head.

Does anybody appreciate the amount of grace that takes?

But the story that distresses me the most is Alton White's. White is the second Black to play major professional hockey. Yes, even before Marson. But White has been forgotten because he played in the WHA, an original New York Raider, in 1972–73. This brother toiled in the IHL and the AHL before playing two WHA seasons with the Raiders and Los Angeles Sharks.

In fact, he played for the North American Hockey League's Syracuse Blazers in 1974–75, blazing the trail in that New York town before I arrived. I can't imagine what this brother went through, yet he is seldom mentioned.

Where are the hockey historians?

You can find on the internet, and in books written over the years, numerous accounts of the trail-blazing Blacks. But some omit a player; others inaccurately list the order of Blacks in hockey. Each time a researcher explores Black hockey history, these published works regurgitate the inaccurate information, and the lie perpetuates.

What follows is an attempt to list the first 20 brothers to play in the NHL, along with the date of each player's first game.

The risk in creating such a record is leaving someone out or making an error. As a result, I create this list as a working document. If I have missed any of my brothers, please call that to my attention and we will correct the record. The goal is that none of my brave brothers is lost to history.

THE FIRST 20 BLACKS TO PLAY IN THE NHL, WITH DATE AND PLACE OF DEBUT

1. Willie O'Ree, Boston: January 18, 1958, at Montreal

The NHL's Jackie Robinson. Lost sight in his right eye early in his career, kept it a secret to enhance his chances of making it to the NHL, and broke the league's colour barrier. Played two games for the Boston Bruins in 1957–58, and 43 more in 1960–61. Scored 4 goals and 10 assists. Played 1,247 professional games and scored 450 pro goals. At the age of 85, he is the NHL's director of youth development and ambassador for NHL Diversity, a post he has held since January 1998.

* Alton White, New York Raiders: October 12, 1972, vs. Winnipeg

True, he didn't play in the NHL, but I will not omit him from this list. The World Hockey Association's Jackie Robinson. More than 14 years after O'Ree, White became the second Black to play major professional hockey, and the only Black to play in the seven-year history of the WHA. Scored 21 goals in 1972–73 for the Raiders and Los Angeles Sharks. Toiled for seven seasons in the IHL and AHL before he got his major-league shot, to bridge the gap between O'Ree and the crop of young Blacks who would soon follow.

2. Mike Marson, Washington: October 9, 1974, at New York Rangers

Broke the 16-year NHL drought after O'Ree. A second-round pick, 19th overall, in the 1974 NHL Amateur Draft. Selected as a 19-year-old, he was the first teenaged Black to play in the NHL, and he was an original Washington Capital who was in the lineup for the expansion franchise's inaugural game. Played parts of five NHL seasons and retired at the age of 25.

3. Bill Riley, Washington: December 26, 1974, vs. Philadelphia

Played one game with Washington in 1974–75 before joining the Capitals in 1976–77 for three seasons. When he
joined Marson in Washington against the Flyers the day after
Christmas 1974, the pair became the first Black NHL teammates. Captained the New Brunswick Hawks to the AHL's
Calder Cup championship in 1981–82.

4. Tony McKegney, Buffalo: October 12, 1978, vs. New York Islanders

The NHL's first Black star. Scored 320 NHL goals in 13 NHL
seasons. Scored the Buffalo Sabres' first goal of the 1978–79
season in his NHL debut. First Black to score 30 or more
goals in an NHL season (37 for Buffalo in 1980–81) and first
Black to score 40 goals in an NHL season (40 for St. Louis in
1987–88).

5. Bernie Saunders, Quebec: March 19, 1980, at Chicago

Younger brother of ESPN broadcaster John Saunders. Author
of *Shut Out*. Only played 10 NHL games for Quebec in 1979–
80 and 1980–81. Registered one assist. Hit a goalpost.

6. Ray Neufeld, Hartford: March 21, 1980, vs. Philadelphia

Scored 157 goals in 11 NHL seasons with Hartford, Winnipeg
and Boston between 1979 and 1990. Hard-nosed power forward who registered five 20-goal NHL seasons and four
seasons of 100 or more penalty minutes.

7. Grant Fuhr, Edmonton: October 14, 1981, vs. Winnipeg

The first Black goaltender to play in the NHL, the first Black
player to be elected to the Hockey Hall of Fame, and the first
Black player to have his name etched on the Stanley Cup. Won

four Cups with the Edmonton Oilers. Named one of the 100 greatest players in NHL history during the NHL's centennial season celebrations.

8. Val James, Buffalo: November 1, 1981, vs. Philadelphia

The first U.S.-born Black to play in the NHL. Born in Ocala, Florida, and raised in Hauppauge, New York, on Long Island. One of the most feared minor-league fighters in hockey history. Scored the 1983 Calder Cup–winning goal for the AHL's Rochester Americans. Played 11 NHL games for Buffalo (7 in 1981–82) and Toronto (4 in 1986–87).

9. Brian Johnson, Detroit: October 9, 1983, at Chicago

Rugged defenceman who played three NHL games for the Red Wings in 1983–84. Product of the QMJHL, where he scored more than 30 goals twice, while racking up significant penalty minutes.

10. Dirk Graham, Minnesota: February 15, 1984, at Toronto

First Black to be named an NHL team captain, by the Chicago Blackhawks in 1988–89. First Black to be hired as an NHL head coach, by the Blackhawks in 1998–99. Won the Selke Trophy as best defensive forward in 1990–91. Rugged two-way player who scored 219 goals and 270 assists in 772 NHL games over 12 seasons for the Minnesota North Stars and Chicago, with 919 PIM.

11. Darren Lowe, Pittsburgh: February 29, 1984, vs. Vancouver

Toronto-born right wing scored one goal and two assists in eight NHL games for the Pittsburgh Penguins in 1983–84. Member of the 1984 Canadian Olympic Team.

12. Eldon "Pokey" Reddick, Winnipeg: October 9, 1986, vs. Buffalo

Second Black goaltender in NHL history. Won his first two NHL starts. In his second game, his Winnipeg Jets defeated Grant Fuhr and the Edmonton Oilers, 5–3. It was the first game in NHL history featuring two Black goaltenders.

13. Claude Vilgrain, Vancouver: March 1, 1988, vs. Philadelphia

First Haitian to play in the NHL. Raised in Quebec City. Right wing played 89 games and scored 21 goals over parts of five seasons between 1987 and 1994 for Vancouver, New Jersey and Philadelphia.

14. Steven Fletcher, Montreal: April 22, 1988, at Boston

Career minor-leaguer known for his toughness. Remembered for NHL debut, a Stanley Cup playoff game at Boston in which he got into a fight. Played three NHL games for Winnipeg in 1988–89.

15. Paul Jerrard, Minnesota: October 28, 1988, at Detroit

Played five NHL games for the Minnesota North Stars in 1988–89. Product of the CCHA, where he played at Lake Superior State University. Long-time collegiate and minor-league assistant coach.

16. Mike McHugh, Minnesota: December 15, 1988, vs. Buffalo

Played 20 NHL games over four seasons between 1988 and 1992 for the Minnesota North Stars and San Jose Sharks. Scored one NHL goal, for San Jose in 1991–92. Former Hockey East and New England Player of the Year at Maine University.

17. Graeme Townshend, Boston: February 1, 1990, vs. Montreal

Jamaican-born right wing played 45 games over five NHL seasons between 1989 and 1994 for Boston, New York Islanders and Ottawa.

18. Reggie Savage, Washington: February 5, 1991, vs. Montreal

The Capitals' first-round pick in 1988. Scored five NHL goals in 34 games in parts of three seasons for Washington and Quebec. Centre who scored his first NHL goal at the Capital Centre on a penalty shot, November 19, 1992.

19. Dale Craigwell, San Jose: December 12, 1991, vs. Edmonton

Toronto-born centre. Scored 21 NHL goals in 98 games over three seasons for the Sharks. Craigwell was drafted by the Sharks in the 10th round. He was the 11th player ever drafted by the Sharks.

20. Darren Banks, Boston Bruins: October 8, 1992, vs. Hartford

Scored two goals in 20 NHL games for the Bruins. Played for Brock University in the CIAU. After four minor-league seasons, was signed as a free agent by Boston. Played in a variety of minor leagues, including Roller Hockey International, until 2005.

BLACK HOCKEY PLAYER COMMONALITIES

THIS IS A challenging issue, and if society struggles with solutions, it is naive to believe that hockey will crack the code. But for any problem, one should begin by studying history while also dissecting the subject at hand—in this case, what it is like being a minority playing a white man's sport. Here's a good place to start. I stumbled across these Black hockey player commonalities while doing research for this book. As hockey wrestles with the issue of diversity and inclusion, I hope some of these observations will make people think.

1. Many left hockey for good and rarely returned to the game because of the pain, exhibiting behaviours suggestive of post-traumatic stress disorder.
2. Many felt that the best way to combat racism was to beat the opposing team on the scoreboard (self-sacrifice).
3. Most minimized the impact of racism while playing and rarely discussed the issue with teammates or others.
4. Many felt lonely and isolated throughout their careers and suffered in silence.
5. Many felt duplicitous in their own locker room, and some had to swallow their pride and share a locker room with their assailant.
6. Many felt cheated and don't feel that they got a fair shot.
7. Many who did wear an NHL jersey were traded an inordinate number of times.
8. Most never had anyone to talk to, as there were no support networks (until recently).
9. Many players came from biracial families, and a few were adopted into white families.
10. Many had to learn how to relate to other Blacks.
11. Many had to walk on eggshells and had to "colour inside the lines" for their entire careers. (P.K. Subban let his personality shine, and he was dubbed the most hated player in hockey.)
12. Many claim they were the hardest workers.

13. Many became enforcers.
14. Most felt their love for the game was unrequited.
15. Many have been forgotten by hockey historians.
16. Many detested the special attention from opponents, fans and the media.
17. Many reported being "targeted" by the other team. (Mike Marson said teams would offer a bounty to the player who injured or cut him.)
18. Many hated being asked why a Black man would play hockey.

CREDITS

CREDITS

"Weinsink et Paddock au Repos" by Claude Allaire, *Le Journal de Quebec*, Mercredi Novembre 12, 1980. All rights reserved: *Le Journal de Québec*.

INDEX